C-447   CAREER EXAMINATION SERIES

This is your
PASSBOOK for...

Immigration Services Officer

Test Preparation Study Guide
Questions & Answers

NATIONAL LEARNING CORPORATION®

COPYRIGHT NOTICE

This book is SOLELY intended for, is sold ONLY to, and its use is RESTRICTED to individual, bona fide applicants or candidates who qualify by virtue of having seriously filed applications for appropriate license, certificate, professional and/or promotional advancement, higher school matriculation, scholarship, or other legitimate requirements of education and/or governmental authorities.

This book is NOT intended for use, class instruction, tutoring, training, duplication, copying, reprinting, excerption, or adaptation, etc., by:

1) Other publishers
2) Proprietors and/or Instructors of "Coaching" and/or Preparatory Courses
3) Personnel and/or Training Divisions of commercial, industrial, and governmental organizations
4) Schools, colleges, or universities and/or their departments and staffs, including teachers and other personnel
5) Testing Agencies or Bureaus
6) Study groups which seek by the purchase of a single volume to copy and/or duplicate and/or adapt this material for use by the group as a whole without having purchased individual volumes for each of the members of the group
7) Et al.

Such persons would be in violation of appropriate Federal and State statutes.

PROVISION OF LICENSING AGREEMENTS – Recognized educational, commercial, industrial, and governmental institutions and organizations, and others legitimately engaged in educational pursuits, including training, testing, and measurement activities, may address request for a licensing agreement to the copyright owners, who will determine whether, and under what conditions, including fees and charges, the materials in this book may be used them. In other words, a licensing facility exists for the legitimate use of the material in this book on other than an individual basis. However, it is asseverated and affirmed here that the material in this book CANNOT be used without the receipt of the express permission of such a licensing agreement from the Publishers. Inquiries re licensing should be addressed to the company, attention rights and permissions department.

All rights reserved, including the right of reproduction in whole or in part, in any form or by any means, electronic or mechanical, including photocopying, recording, or by any information storage and retrieval system, without permission in writing from the Publisher.

Copyright © 2024 by
National Learning Corporation

212 Michael Drive, Syosset, NY 11791
(516) 921-8888 • www.passbooks.com
E-mail: info@passbooks.com

PUBLISHED IN THE UNITED STATES OF AMERICA

PASSBOOK® SERIES

THE *PASSBOOK® SERIES* has been created to prepare applicants and candidates for the ultimate academic battlefield – the examination room.

At some time in our lives, each and every one of us may be required to take an examination – for validation, matriculation, admission, qualification, registration, certification, or licensure.

Based on the assumption that every applicant or candidate has met the basic formal educational standards, has taken the required number of courses, and read the necessary texts, the *PASSBOOK® SERIES* furnishes the one special preparation which may assure passing with confidence, instead of failing with insecurity. Examination questions – together with answers – are furnished as the basic vehicle for study so that the mysteries of the examination and its compounding difficulties may be eliminated or diminished by a sure method.

This book is meant to help you pass your examination provided that you qualify and are serious in your objective.

The entire field is reviewed through the huge store of content information which is succinctly presented through a provocative and challenging approach – the question-and-answer method.

A climate of success is established by furnishing the correct answers at the end of each test.

You soon learn to recognize types of questions, forms of questions, and patterns of questioning. You may even begin to anticipate expected outcomes.

You perceive that many questions are repeated or adapted so that you can gain acute insights, which may enable you to score many sure points.

You learn how to confront new questions, or types of questions, and to attack them confidently and work out the correct answers.

You note objectives and emphases, and recognize pitfalls and dangers, so that you may make positive educational adjustments.

Moreover, you are kept fully informed in relation to new concepts, methods, practices, and directions in the field.

You discover that you are actually taking the examination all the time: you are preparing for the examination by "taking" an examination, not by reading extraneous and/or supererogatory textbooks.

In short, this PASSBOOK®, used directedly, should be an important factor in helping you to pass your test.

IMMIGRATION SERVICES OFFICER

DUTIES:

Immigration Services Officers are agents of the USCIS. Job duties include researching and analyzing applications, petitions and supporting documentation; interviewing petitioners and applicants to assess credibility; and denying or granting petitions and applications. Immigration services officers may also interact with the media and community groups. At times, they work with other agencies and lawyers, and they might represent the Department of Homeland Security in court proceedings.

The purpose of this book is to help you prepare to take the Immigration Services Officer (ISO) Test. This book will familiarize you with the Logical Reasoning Test and the Writing Skills Test and will give you a chance to study some sample questions and explanations for the correct answers to each question. If you have not had much practice taking written, multiple-choice tests, you will have an opportunity to see what the tests look like and to practice taking questions similar to those on the tests.

This book is organized into three sections. The first section provides some tips for taking the test. The second section provides preparation material for the Logical Reasoning Test and includes a practice test with explanations for the answers to the practice test. The third section provides preparation material for the Writing Skills Test and includes a practice test with explanations for the answers to the practice test.

Preparation Manual for the
Immigration Services Officer Test Battery

CONTENTS

	Page
INTRODUCTION	1
SECTION I: TEST TAKING TIPS	2
SECTION II: PREPARING FOR THE LOGICAL REASONING TEST	3
INTRODUCTION	3
PREPARING FOR LOGICAL REASONING QUESTIONS	4
LOGICAL REASONING PRACTICE TEST	16
SECTION III: WRITING SKILLS TEST	25
PREPARING FOR THE WRITING SKILLS TEST	25
WRITING SKILLS PRACTICE TEST	36

Preparation Manual for the Immigration Services Officer Test Battery

INTRODUCTION

Purpose of the Manual

The purpose of this manual is to help you prepare to take the Immigration Services Officer (ISO) Test. This manual will familiarize you with the Logical Reasoning Test and the Writing Skills Test and will give you a chance to study some sample questions and explanations for the correct answers to each question. If you have not had much practice taking written, multiple-choice tests, you will have an opportunity to see what the tests look like and to practice taking questions similar to those on the tests.

Organization of the Manual

The manual is organized into three sections. The first section provides some tips for taking the test. The second section provides preparation material for the Logical Reasoning Test and includes a practice test with explanations for the answers to the practice test. The third section provides preparation material for the Writing Skills Test and includes a practice test with explanations for the answers to the practice test.

Section I: Test Taking Tips

1. You will do your best on the test if you stay calm and relaxed. Take a few deep, slow breaths to help you maintain your calm.

2. Pay careful attention to all directions before beginning.

3. Answer the easier questions first. Skip questions you find to be very difficult and come back to them later.

4. For each question, read the entire question and all response options carefully before deciding upon an answer.

5. If you do not know the answer to a question, eliminate the response options that you know to be incorrect or probably incorrect and then guess from the remaining response options.

6. Your score is based only on the number of questions you answer correctly. You are not penalized for answering questions incorrectly. Therefore, you should answer every question, even questions that you must guess.

7. If you finish before time is up, go back and check your answers.

8. Be sure that you mark your answer sheet correctly. If you have to change an answer, erase the first answer before marking the new answer. If you skip a question, be sure to answer the next question in the appropriate place on the answer sheet.

9. Ignore any patterns of A's, B's, C's, D's, or E's on your answer sheet. These correct answer positions are chosen randomly and there is no way to improve your chances by guessing based on an answer sheet pattern.

Section II: Preparing for the Logical Reasoning Test

INTRODUCTION

Purpose of this Section

The purpose of this section is to help you prepare to take the Logical Reasoning Test. The test described in this section evaluates how well applicants can read, understand, and apply critical thinking skills to factual situations. This test is designed to select trainees who will be able to handle complex reasoning and decision-making situations on the job.

This section of the manual will familiarize you with the test and the instructions and will give you a chance to study some sample questions and explanations for the correct answers to each question. You will have an opportunity to see what the test looks like and to practice taking questions similar to those on the test.

Educated Guessing

There is no penalty for guessing on this test; therefore, you should answer every question. If you guess blindly, you have one chance in five of getting the right answer. However, your chance of choosing the right answer just by guessing is greatly improved by using a little mental detective work to eliminate one or more response options that are probably or certainly wrong.

A poor guessing strategy is to try to determine the next answer based on its letter or on some pattern of letters among the answer choices. There may be several D's or A's or any other letter in a row, or there may not be. Trying to uncover some pattern in these letters and guessing based on that pattern is not an effective test-taking strategy.

PREPARING FOR LOGICAL REASONING QUESTIONS

Logical Reasoning

Reasoning is the single most important competency for successful performance on the job. Correct reasoning is useful for decision-making and problem solving, activities that prevail on the job. In this part, you will read some useful information about reasoning correctly.

The questions in this examination are designed to test your ability to understand complicated written material and to derive correct conclusions from it. The kind of reading that these questions ask you to do is different from ordinary reading in which you just follow the general meaning of a series of sentences to see what the writer thinks about a topic. It is the kind of reading you have to do with complex material when you intend to take some action or draw some conclusion based on that material.

The test asks you to make logical conclusions based on facts you are given in various paragraphs. These conclusions need to be based only on the facts in the paragraph. Therefore, answering requires careful reading and focused thought about what information is given and what information is not given.

The following information will give you some suggestions about how to approach the questions and some information about how you can develop your reasoning skills.

Reading the Paragraph

Every reading paragraph in the test is drawn from some kind of written material relating to ISO or Government work. There may be facts in a paragraph that do not actually apply to every part of the Federal Government or that may not always be true everywhere. In answering the questions, it is important that you **accept every fact in the paragraph as true**. Remember that you are not being judged on your knowledge of facts, but rather on your ability to read and reason on the basis of given facts.

Not all information is of the same type. There can be information about events or situations, and there can be information about individuals and groups (or categories). It is important to examine information in the paragraph closely to determine what kind of information it is. Is the information about two or more categories of things? Is the information about how two events or situations are linked together? It is also important to recognize whether the information is positive or negative. Usually, information is positive (for example, "these tire tracks are several days old"), but knowledge that something is not the case is also useful information (for example, "these tire tracks are not from a truck").

Reading the Lead-In or Basic Question

In this test, you will find a paragraph, followed by a lead-in phrase that asks you to complete a sentence by choosing one of several response options labeled from (A) to (E). The lead-in phrase may be either positive or negative:

"From the information given above, it can be validly concluded that"

or

"From the information given above, it CANNOT be validly concluded that"

It is important to focus on the lead-in phrase at the beginning of a question to determine whether it is positive or negative. Do not skim over the lead-in phrase.

Positive lead-in phrases are followed by four invalid conclusions and one valid conclusion. Your task is to find the valid one. Negative lead-in phrases, by contrast, are followed by four valid conclusions and only one invalid conclusion. The task in these questions is to determine what **cannot** be validly concluded based on the facts in the paragraph.

The lead-in phrase may also limit the possible answers in some way. For example, a lead-in phrase such as *"From the information given above, it can be validly concluded that, during the 1990's in California"* means that there might be different answers based on other times and places, but for the purpose of the test question, only conditions in California during the 1990's (as described in the paragraph) should be considered.

REASONING ABOUT GROUPS OR CATEGORIES

As was stated before, not all information is of the same type. There can be information about events or situations, and there can be information about individuals and groups (or categories). Next, we discuss how to deal with information about groups or categories.

"All" Statements

A statement about two groups that begins with the words "all" or "every" gives you some important information about how the two groups are related. The words "all" and "every" tell you that everything in the first group is also in the second group. For example, in the statement, "All the law enforcement officers on the case are Federal law enforcement officers," the first group, consisting of law enforcement officers on the case, is totally included in the second group, consisting of Federal law enforcement officers.

> "All" and "Every" are KEY WORDS that signify important information about how two groups are related.

The "all" statement does not provide sufficient information to determine whether or not all members of the second group are included in the first group. Suppose that a librarian told you "All the books on this set of shelves are about immigration." From this information, you might be tempted to conclude that all of the library's books on immigration (the second group) are on that set of shelves (the first group), but this conclusion is invalid. The books on those shelves might only be part of the entire group of books on immigration. The sentence does NOT provide information on whether or not other immigration books are placed elsewhere in the library. The following examples provide an "all" statement (all of Group A are Group B) followed by an invalid "all" statement (all of Group B are Group A). To develop a good grasp of this concept, try to create some examples of your own.

True:	All the people at my party speak Spanish.
Invalid Conclusion:	All the people who speak Spanish are at my party.
True:	All Supreme Court justices are lawyers.
Invalid Conclusion:	All lawyers are Supreme Court justices.
True:	All U.S. Presidents were elected officials.
Invalid Conclusion:	All officials who were elected are U.S. Presidents.
True:	Every ISO at CIS works for the U.S. Government.
Invalid Conclusion:	Everyone working for the U.S. Government is an ISO at CIS.
True:	Every U.S. Senator is a member of the U.S. Congress.
Invalid Conclusion:	Every member of the U.S. Congress is a U.S. Senator.

Every "all" statement provides sufficient information to determine that at least some members of the second group are included in the first group. Returning to our previous examples, we can validly conclude that "some Federal law enforcement officers are on the case" and that "some of the books about immigration are on this set of shelves." Developing numerous examples on your own of a true "all" statement (all of Group A are Group B) and a "some" statement (some of Group B are Group A) will help you to develop a mastery of this concept.

True:	All the people at my party speak Spanish.
Valid Conclusion:	Some people who speak Spanish are at my party.
True:	All Supreme Court justices are lawyers.
Valid Conclusion:	Some lawyers are Supreme Court justices.
True:	All U.S. Presidents were elected officials.
Valid Conclusion:	Some officials who were elected are U.S. Presidents.
True:	Every ISO at CIS works for the U.S. Government.
Valid Conclusion:	Some employees of the U.S. Government are ISOs at CIS.
True:	Every U.S. Senator is a member of the U.S. Congress.
Valid Conclusion:	Some members of the U.S. Congress are U.S. Senators.

Reasoning From "None" and "Not" Statements

Information that something is **NOT** true is useful information. For example, you may learn that one group of things is **NOT** part of another group of things. This is the same as saying that there is no overlap at all between the two groups of things. Here, you can draw conclusions about either group as it relates to the other since you can count on the fact that the two groups have no members in common. If you can say that none of the stolen cars recovered from the rail yards were cars stolen from Canada, you can **also** say that none of the cars stolen from Canada were recovered from the rail yards because you know that the first statement means that there is no overlap between the two groups. In the test, you will see phrases or terms such as "It is not the case that" or "Not all of" or words that begin with the prefix "non-." All of these are ways to say that a negative fact has been established.

> "No" and "not" are KEY WORDS that signify important information about how two groups are related.

Sometimes, our ordinary speech habits can cause us to jump to conclusions. Most people would not make a statement such as "Some of the pizza has no pepperoni" unless they are trying to suggest at the same time that some of the pizza **does** have pepperoni. By contrast, a detective might make a statement such as "some of the bloodstains were not human blood" simply because only part of the samples had come back from the laboratory. The detective is trying to suggest that <u>at least</u> some of the bloodstains were not human blood. The rest of the bloodstains might or might not be human blood.

As you work through the practice test, think about each negative phrase or term you find. Take care to assume only as much as is definitely indicated by the facts as given, and no more.

Reasoning About Parts of a Group

The term "some" refers to a part of a larger group. For example, in the statement "Some officers are taking specialized training," the term "some officers" refers to a portion of the group of all officers. You should note, however, that the fact that we know that "some officers are taking specialized training" implies nothing about the remaining portion of the set of officers: other officers may or may not be taking specialized training. Unless information is provided in the paragraph to the contrary, treat "some" as meaning "at least some."

Statements that refer to a portion of a set may contain other terms such as "most," "a few," or "almost all." Also, as discussed previously, they can be negative, as in "Many officers are not fluent in French." From this statement you may be tempted to infer that there are at least a few officers who <u>are</u> fluent in French, but that would be jumping to a conclusion. From this statement alone, you do not know about the entire group of officers and whether or not they are fluent in French. In these cases, you should remember that the term refers only to a part of the group and that from this partial information you cannot infer anything about the rest of the group. Unfortunately, neglecting this principle of sound reasoning can cause costly errors.

When you see a paragraph describing parts of a group, read the paragraph carefully to see if that description is based on knowledge of the entire group or only on knowledge of part of the group.

REASONING ABOUT "IF-THEN" STATEMENTS

As was said before, there can be information about events or situations, and there can be information about individuals and groups. Previously, we discussed how to deal with information about groups. Next, we discuss how to deal with information about the relationship between events or situations.

We are all familiar with the idea of a *cause and effect* in which one thing leads to another thing, which in turn leads to a third thing, and so on. For example, "if a financial institution suspects that a deposit of funds stems from criminal activity, the institution is required to report the deposit transaction to the authorities." In this example, a suspicious deposit is a cause and the institution reporting the deposit is the effect.

Cause and effect means that when the first thing happens, the later event MUST follow. For example, if First Salem Bank suspects that Mr. Tubill deposited funds stemming from criminal activity, First Salem Bank is required to report Mr. Tubill's deposit to the authorities.

The cause and effect relationship also informs you that if the effect never occurred, the cause MUST NOT have occurred. For example, if First Salem Bank is NOT required to report Mr. Tubill's deposit to the authorities, then First Salem Bank does NOT suspect that Mr. Tubill deposited funds stemming from criminal activity.

The wording we typically use to indicate this kind of cause and effect linkage between events includes the simple "if-then" sentence in which the first event is in a statement tagged by "if" and the second event is in a statement tagged by "then." The "if-then" statement can also be used to express relationships other than the cause and effect relationship. Permission is sometimes expressed using the "if-then" statement. For instance, if an individual wishes to open a checking account anonymously, the individual may not open the account. Obligation is also sometimes expressed using the "if-then" statement. For example, if an officer places an individual under arrest, the arrestee must be provided with Miranda warnings.

What cause and effect, permission, and obligation all have in common is that they relate one event or situation to another event or situation. In this relationship, two things are always true. First, whenever the first event or situation occurs, the second event or situation MUST occur. Second, whenever the second event or situation has not occurred, then the first event or situation MUST NOT have occurred.

It is important to realize that the relationship expressed by any "if-then" statement works in one direction only: the converse of the "if-then" statement is invalid. For example, you learn that "If the jet engines are reversed, then the speed of the plane will decrease very rapidly." This sentence does NOT mean that the only possible cause of the plane decreasing speed very rapidly is that the jet engines are reversed. Therefore, from this information you cannot validly infer the converse statement, "If the speed of the plane decreases very rapidly, then the jet engines have been reversed." There might be some other cause for the speed of the plane to decrease rapidly. The following examples start with a true "if-then" sentence, followed by an invalid "if-then" sentence with the relationship of the first and second statements conversed.

True:	If a person is an ISO at CIS, the person is an employee of the U.S. Government.
Invalid Conclusion:	If a person is an employee of the U.S. Government, the person is an ISO at CIS.
True:	If a criminal receives a pardon, the criminal will be released.
Invalid Conclusion:	If a criminal is released, the criminal has received a pardon.
True:	If a person is convicted of murder, that person is guilty of a felony.
Invalid Conclusion:	If a person is guilty of a felony, that person has been convicted of murder.
True:	If a person lives in Germany, the person lives in Europe.
Invalid Conclusion:	If a person lives in Europe, the person lives in Germany.
True:	If a car has no gas, the car will not run.
Invalid Conclusion:	If a car does not run, the car has no gas.

Whenever the second event or situation has not occurred, then the first event or situation MUST NOT have occurred. This means that you can validly converse the relationship of these two statements as long as the statements are negated (made opposite). For example, you learn that "If the jet engines are reversed (the first statement), the speed of the plane will decrease very rapidly (the second statement)." Given that the information is true, it cannot be the case that the jet engines are reversed but the speed of the plane does not decrease very rapidly. Therefore, you can validly infer that "If the speed of the plane does not decrease very rapidly (the negation or opposite of the second statement), then the jet engines have not been reversed" (the negation or opposite of the first statement). The following examples start with a true "if-then" sentence, followed by a true (or valid) "if-then" sentence with the relationship of the first and second statements conversed and the statements themselves made opposite (negated).

True:	If a person is an ISO at CIS, the person is an employee of the U.S. Government.
Therefore, True:	If a person is not an employee of the U.S. Government, the person is not an ISO at CIS.
True:	If a criminal receives a pardon, the criminal will be released.
Therefore, True:	If a criminal is not released, the criminal has not received a pardon.

True:	If a person is convicted of murder, that person is guilty of a felony.
Therefore, True:	If a person is not guilty of a felony, that person has not been convicted of murder.
True:	If a person lives in Germany, the person lives in Europe.
Therefore, True:	If a person does not live in Europe, the person does not live in Germany.
True:	If a car has no gas, the car will not run.
Therefore, True:	If a car runs, the car has gas.

> **When the effect in a cause and effect relationship has not happened, the cause must not have happened.**

As was said before, you can infer the opposite of the first statement from the opposite of the second statement. However, you cannot infer the opposite of the second statement from the opposite of the first statement. For example, you cannot validly infer that "If the jet engines are not reversed (the opposite of the first statement), then the speed of the plane does not decrease very rapidly" (the opposite of the second statement). The following examples start with a true "if-then" sentence followed by an invalid "if-then" sentence in which the first and second statements have been made opposite.

True:	If a person is an ISO at CIS, the person is an employee of the U.S. Government.
Invalid Conclusion:	If a person is not an ISO at CIS, the person is not an employee of the U.S. Government.
True:	If a criminal receives a pardon, the criminal will be released.
Invalid Conclusion:	If a criminal does not receive a pardon, the criminal will not be released.
True:	If a person is convicted of murder, that person is guilty of a felony.
Invalid Conclusion:	If a person is not convicted of murder, that person is not guilty of a felony.
True:	If a person lives in Germany, the person lives in Europe.
Invalid Conclusion:	If a person does not live in Germany, the person does not live in Europe.
True:	If a car has no gas, the car will not run.
Invalid Conclusion:	If a car has gas, the car will run.

A Few Final Cautions About Wording

There are test preparation classes that train people to take tests. In some of these classes, students are advised against choosing any answer in a reasoning test if it starts with the word "all" or the word "none." This is supposed to be useful advice because it is believed that most correct answers strike a balance between extremes and usually do not cover subjects that can be summarized in sentences beginning with "all" or "none." If you have heard this advice before, you should ignore it for this test. "All" statements and "none" statements occur in real-life situations and, consequently, you will be asked to work with them in this test in the reading paragraphs as well as in both correct and incorrect responses.

In general, you should pay attention to any words that provide information on groups or on linked events. This includes a wide range of negative words (such as "seldom" or "never" or "illegal" or "prohibited") and negative prefixes (such as "non-" "un-" or "dis-"). It also includes positive words (such as "all" or "some" or "most" or "always"). You should also watch for connectors such as "whenever" or "unless" or "except," since these words sometimes contain key information about relations among the facts given in the paragraph.

> **Look for KEY WORDS such as "all," "some," "none," and "if" and for negative prefixes such as "non-," "un-," or "dis-."**

English is a language that ordinarily uses single negatives. The word "not," by itself, does the job of making a formal English sentence into its opposite: "That bird is NOT an eagle." On this test, if you read a sentence such as "The cord is not wound," it means the cord is still unwound. When an English sentence has two negatives, the sentence has a positive meaning. For example, a sentence that reads "This application is NOT unworthy" means that the application IS worthy. The sentence "The bell did ring" could be stated, "It is NOT the case that the bell did NOT ring."

Finally, it is extremely important to pay close attention to the use of the word "ONLY." A sentence such as "The door will open IF AND ONLY IF both keys are used" is a very strong statement that means that there is just one way to open the door—with both keys. If the sentence just said, "The door will open if the key is used," there may be several other ways to open the door. But that is not the case when the expression "if and only if" is used.

DRAWING PROBABILISTIC CONCLUSIONS

Officers must make decisions and draw conclusions that have some probability of being true, but they are not definitely true. On the test, there are questions that ask you to apply this type of logic. In each of the questions of this type, you will be presented with a paragraph of information and five response options. Your task is to select the response option that can be validly concluded from the information given in the paragraph. Use **only** the information provided in the paragraph. Do not speculate or make assumptions that go beyond this information. Also, assume that all information given in the paragraph is true, even if it conflicts with some fact that is known to you. Keep in mind that each question has only **one** correct answer.

When you have information about a group, you can apply that information to an individual member of that group with a degree of certainty. In other words, you can establish the probability that the information you have about the group applies to a single member of the group. For example, if most felons are repeat offenders and K.B. is a felon, then you can conclude that K.B. is most likely a repeat offender.

In order to establish a numerical probability, you must have information about the entire group. Although it may not be immediately obvious, percentages provide information about an entire group. For example, if you know that 30% of all officers have led a fraud investigation, you know that **only** 30% of officers have led a fraud investigation. The percentage does not mean that at least 30% of officers have led a fraud investigation. Because only 30% percent have led such an investigation, you know that the remaining officers have **not** led a fraud investigation. Therefore, of all officers, 70% (100% - 30% = 70%) have not led a fraud investigation. The entire group of officers has been accounted for: 30% have led a fraud investigation and 70% have not.

Speaking more abstractly, we are dealing with statements about two groups in which a percentage is used to modify the first group. The percentage tells us that a portion of the first group is included in the second group, but the remainder of the first group is not included in the second group. Thus, the entire first group is accounted for. The following examples start with a true statement expressing something about a portion of a group using a percentage, followed by a true statement expressing the opposite about the remaining portion of the group.

True:	Of all Government employees, 5% work for the Department of Justice.
Therefore, True:	Of all Government employees, 95% do not work for the Department of Justice.
True:	Eighty-five percent of state criminals did not receive parole.
Therefore, True:	Fifteen percent of state criminals received parole.
True:	Of all the visa applications, 10% were denied.
Therefore, True:	Of all the visa applications, 90% were not denied.

To determine a probability, you apply the information about the group to an individual member of the group. For example, if you pick one of the officers at random, your chances of picking one who has led a fraud investigation is equal to the percentage of officers who have led such an investigation. Because 30% of all officers have led a fraud investigation, you can conclude that any particular officer has a 30% chance of having led such an investigation. Furthermore, if you pick one of the officers at random, your chances of picking one who has not led a fraud investigation is equal to the percentage of officers who have not led such an investigation. You can validly conclude that any particular officer has a 70% chance of not having led a fraud investigation because 70% of all officers have not led a fraud investigation. The following examples start with a true statement about a group, followed by two valid statements expressing probability about an individual member of the group.

> To determine a probability, you apply the information about the group to an individual member of the group.

True:	Of all Government employees, 5% work for the Department of Justice.
Therefore, True:	There is a 5% chance that a Government employee chosen at random works for the Department of Justice.
Therefore, True:	There is a 95% chance that a Government employee chosen at random does not work for the Department of Justice.
True:	Eighty-five percent of state criminals did not receive parole.
Therefore, True:	There is an 85% chance that a state criminal chosen at random did not receive parole.
Therefore, True:	There is a 15% chance that a state criminal chosen at random received parole.
True:	Of all the visa applications, 10% were denied.
Therefore, True:	There is a 10% chance that a visa application chosen at random was denied.
Therefore, True:	There is a 90% chance that a visa application chosen at random was not denied.

We looked at two types of valid conclusions. These valid conclusions were based on applying the given percentage to a member of the first group. Now, let us look at two types of invalid conclusions. These invalid conclusions are based on mistakenly applying the given percentage to a member of the second group.

Remember that a statement about two groups that begins with the word "all" gives you information about how the two groups are related. The word "all" tells you that everything in the first group is also in the second group. However, the "all" statement does not provide sufficient information to determine whether or not all members of the second group are included in the first group. Likewise, statements that use a percentage to describe the first group do not provide sufficient information to determine the portion of members of the second group that are included in the first group.

Having information about the entire first group in the statement is not the same as having information about the entire second group. For example, knowing that 60% of Adjudications Officers (AOs) have identified a fugitive (and, thus, that 40% of AOs have not identified a fugitive) is not the same as knowing that of everyone who has identified a fugitive, 60% are AOs. It may be the case that 60% of the people who have identified a fugitive are AOs, but it very well might not be the case. There is insufficient information about the entire set of people who have identified a fugitive to make exact percentage determinations about them.

In these statements that relate two groups using a percentage, the percentage given only applies to one group. In our example, the percentage applies to the first group, AOs, not to the second group (namely, those who have identified a fugitive). The following examples start with a true statement followed by two invalid statements where the percentage is incorrectly applied to the second group.

True:	Of all Government employees, 5% work for the Department of Justice.
Invalid Conclusion:	Of all employees of the Department of Justice, 5% work for the Government.
Invalid Conclusion:	Of all employees of the Department of Justice, 95% do not work for the Government.
True:	Eighty-five percent of state criminals did not receive parole.
Invalid Conclusion:	Eighty-five percent of those who received parole were not state criminals.
Invalid Conclusion:	Fifteen percent of those who received parole were state criminals.
True:	Of all the visa applications, 10% were denied.
Invalid Conclusion:	Of all the denied applications, 10% were visa applications.
Invalid Conclusion:	Of all the denied applications, 90% were not visa applications.

Because the percentage applies to the first group, not the second group, any statement of probability that is based on applying the percentage to the second group is invalid. For example, there is insufficient information about those who have identified a fugitive to determine the probability that a person who has identified a fugitive is an AO. Also, there is insufficient information to determine the probability that a person who has identified a fugitive is not an AO. The following examples start with a true statement followed by two invalid statements where a probability is determined based on the inappropriate application of the percentage to the second group.

True:	Of all Government employees, 5% work for the Department of Justice.
Invalid Conclusion:	An employee of the Department of Justice chosen at random has a 5% of working for the Government.
Invalid Conclusion:	An employee of the Department of Justice chosen at random has a 95% of not working for the Government.
True:	Eighty-five percent of state criminals did not receive parole.
Invalid Conclusion:	The chances are 85% that a person selected at random who received parole was not a state criminal.
Invalid Conclusion:	The chances are 15% that a person selected at random who received parole was a state criminal.
True:	Of all the visa applications, 10% were denied.
Invalid Conclusion:	The chances are 10% that a denied application chosen at random is a visa application.
Invalid Conclusion:	The chances are 90% that a denied application chosen at random is not a visa application.

REMEMBER THESE TIPS WHEN TAKING THE LOGICAL REASONING TEST

1. In questions with positive lead statements, always choose the only conclusion that can <u>definitely</u> be drawn from the information given in the paragraph.

2. Remember NOT to use any outside factual information to reach your conclusion.

3. Read the lead-in sentence and the paragraph very carefully. Also, read all the answer choices before you mark the one you think is correct.

4. Pay special attention whenever the question uses words such as "all," "some," or "none." Other terms such as "unless" or "except" or "only" are also important. These words help to define the facts from which you must draw conclusions.

5. Also pay special attention whenever you see a negative prefix such as "non-" or a negative verb such as "<u>dis</u>connect" or "<u>un</u>fasten." These may be crucial to understanding the basic facts in the paragraph.

6. Ignore any advice you may have received in the past about avoiding an answer that contains the word "all" or the word "none." These may be signs of an incorrect response in some tests, but not in this test. You will find these words in both right and wrong response options.

7. Take the sample test and study the explanation for each of the questions very carefully. This will help you fine-tune your reasoning on the actual test.

LOGICAL REASONING PRACTICE TEST

The practice test contains questions that are similar to, but not exactly the same as, the questions on the real test. The practice test is followed by detailed explanations of every practice test question. These explanations will give you information about what is correct about the correct response options and what is incorrect about the wrong response options. Understanding the reasons for the correct and incorrect response options should assist you in distinguishing between a right and wrong answer on the test.

PRACTICE TEST

*In questions 1 through 10, some questions will ask you to select the only answer that can be validly concluded from the paragraph. These questions include a paragraph followed by five response options. Preceding the five response options will be the phrase "From the information given above, it can be validly concluded that." In other questions you may be asked to select the only answer that **cannot** be validly concluded from the paragraph. These questions include a paragraph followed by five response options. Preceding the five response options will be the phrase "From the information given above, it CANNOT be validly concluded that."*

*You must use **only** the information provided in the paragraph, without using any outside information whatsoever.*

It is suggested that you take not more than 20 minutes to complete questions 1 through 10. The questions on this practice test will not be on the real test, but the real questions will be similar in form and difficulty to these. The explanations for the correct and incorrect responses are found after the sample questions.

1. Often, crimes are characterized as either *malum in se*—inherently evil—or *malum prohibitum*—criminal because they are declared as offenses by a legislature. Murder is an example of the former. Failing to file a tax return illustrates the latter. Some jurisdictions no longer distinguish between crimes *malum in se* and *malum prohibitum*, although many still do.

   From the information given above, it can be validly concluded that

   A) many jurisdictions no longer distinguish between crimes *malum in se* and *malum prohibitum*
   B) some jurisdictions still distinguish between crimes *malum in se* and *malum prohibitum*
   C) some crimes characterized as *malum in se* are not inherently evil
   D) some crimes characterized as *malum prohibitum* are not declared by a legislature to be an offense
   E) sometimes failing to file a tax return is characterized as *malum in se*

2. A trucking company can act as a *common carrier*—for hire to the general public at published rates. As a common carrier, it is liable for any cargo damage, unless the company can show that it was not negligent. If the company can demonstrate that it was not negligent, then it is not liable for cargo damage. In contrast, a *contract carrier* (a trucking company hired by a shipper under a specific contract) is only responsible for cargo damage as spelled out in the contract. A Claus Inc. tractor-trailer, acting under common carrier authority, was in a 5-vehicle accident that damaged its cargo. A Nichols Inc. tractor-trailer, acting under contract carrier authority, was involved in the same accident, and its cargo was also damaged.

   From the information given above, it can be validly concluded that, in reference to the accident,

   A) if Claus Inc. is liable, then it can show that it was not negligent
   B) if Claus Inc. cannot show that it was not negligent, then it is not liable
   C) if Claus Inc. can show that it was not negligent, then it is not liable
   D) if Nichols Inc. is liable, then it cannot show that it is negligent
   E) if Nichols Inc. can show that it is not negligent, then it is not liable

3. A rapidly changing technical environment in government is promoting greater reliance on electronic mail (e-mail) systems. As this usage grows, there are increasing chances of conflict between the users' expectations of privacy and public access rights. In some investigations, access to all e-mail, including those messages stored in archival files and messages outside the scope of the investigation, has been sought and granted. In spite of this, some people send messages through e-mail that would never be said face-to-face or written formally.

   From the information given above, it CANNOT be validly concluded that

   A) some e-mail messages that have been requested as part of investigations have contained messages that would never be said face-to-face
   B) some messages that people would never say face-to-face are sent in e-mail messages
   C) some e-mail messages have been requested as part of investigations
   D) e-mail messages have not been exempted from investigations
   E) some e-mail messages contain information that would be omitted from formal writing

4. Phyllis T. is a former Federal employee who was entitled to benefits under the Federal Employee Compensation Act because of a job-related, disabling injury. When an eligible Federal employee has such an injury, the benefit is determined by this test: If the beneficiary is married or has dependents, benefits are 3/4 of the person's salary at the time of the injury; otherwise, benefits are set at 2/3 of the salary. Phyllis T.'s benefits were 2/3 of her salary when she was injured.

   From the information given above, it can be validly concluded that, when Phyllis T. was injured, she

   A) was married but without dependents
   B) was not married and had no dependents
   C) was not married but had dependents
   D) was married and had dependents
   E) had never been married

5. Some 480,000 immigrants were living in a certain country in 1999. Although most of these immigrants were not employed in professional occupations, many of them were. For instance, many of them were engineers and many of them were nurses. Very few of these immigrants were librarians, another professional occupation.

   From the information given above, it can be validly concluded that, in 1999, in the country described above,

   A) most immigrants were either engineers or nurses
   B) it is not the case that some of the nurses were immigrants
   C) none of the engineers were immigrants
   D) most of those not employed in professional occupations were immigrants
   E) some of the engineers were immigrants

6. Police officers were led to believe that many weapons sold at a certain gun store were sold illegally. Upon investigating the lead, the officers learned that all of the weapons sold by the store that were made by Precision Arms were sold legally. Also, none of the illegally sold weapons were .45 caliber.

   From the information given above, it can be validly concluded that, concerning the weapons sold at the store,

   A) all of the .45 caliber weapons were made by Precision Arms
   B) none of the .45 caliber weapons were made by Precision Arms
   C) some of the weapons made by Precision Arms were .45 caliber weapons
   D) all of the .45 caliber weapons were sold legally
   E) some of the weapons made by Precision Arms were sold illegally

7. Impressions made by the ridges on the ends of the fingers and thumbs are useful means of identification, since no two persons have the same pattern of ridges. If finger patterns from fingerprints are not decipherable, then they cannot be classified by general shape and contour or by pattern type. If they cannot be classified by these characteristics, then it is impossible to identify the person to whom the fingerprints belong.

   From the information given above, it CANNOT be validly concluded that

   A) if it is possible to identify the person to whom fingerprints belong, then the fingerprints are decipherable
   B) if finger patterns from fingerprints are not decipherable, then it is impossible to identify the person to whom the fingerprints belong
   C) if fingerprints are decipherable, then it is impossible to identify the person to whom they belong
   D) if fingerprints can be classified by general shape and contour or by pattern type, then they are decipherable
   E) if it is possible to identify the person to whom fingerprints belong, then the fingerprints can be classified by general shape and contour or pattern type

8. Explosives are substances or devices capable of producing a volume of rapidly expanding gases that exert a sudden pressure on their surroundings. Chemical explosives are the most commonly used, although there are mechanical and nuclear explosives. All mechanical explosives are devices in which a physical reaction is produced, such as that caused by overloading a container with compressed air. While nuclear explosives are by far the most powerful, all nuclear explosives have been restricted to military weapons.

   From the information given above, it can be validly concluded that

   A) all explosives that have been restricted to military weapons are nuclear explosives
   B) no mechanical explosives are devices in which a physical reaction is produced, such as that caused by overloading a container with compressed air
   C) some nuclear explosives have not been restricted to military weapons
   D) all mechanical explosives have been restricted to military weapons
   E) some devices in which a physical reaction is produced, such as that caused by overloading a container with compressed air, are mechanical explosives

9. The alphanumeric coding of a fingerprint is a systematic description of the main patterns on the print. Within a certain metropolitan district, 90% of the population have fingerprints that can be alphanumerically coded.

   From the information given above, it can be validly concluded that the fingerprints of a person from this district, selected at random,

   A) can be alphanumerically coded, with a probability of 10%
   B) can be alphanumerically coded, with a probability of less than 90%
   C) cannot be alphanumerically coded, with a probability of 10%
   D) cannot be alphanumerically coded, with a probability of up to 90%
   E) may be coded alphanumerically, but the probability is unknown

10. The printed output of some computer-driven printers can be recognized by forensic analysts. The "Acme Model 200" printer was manufactured using two different inking mechanisms, one of which yields a "Type A" micropattern of ink spray around its characters. Of all Acme Model 200 printers, 70% produce this Type A micropattern, which is also characteristic of some models of other printers. Forensic analysts at a crime lab have been examining a kidnap ransom note which clearly exhibits the Type A micropattern.

    From the information given above, it can be validly concluded that this note

    A) was printed on an Acme Model 200 printer, with a probability of 70%
    B) was printed on an Acme Model 200 printer, with a probability of 30%
    C) was not printed on an Acme Model 200 printer, with a probability of 70%
    D) was not printed on an Acme Model 200 printer, with a probability of 30%
    E) may have been printed on an Acme Model 200 printer, but the probability cannot be estimated

ANALYSIS OF LOGICAL REASONING PRACTICE TEST QUESTIONS

1. Correct Answer: B) some jurisdictions still distinguish between crimes *malum in se* and *malum prohibitum*

This question is concerned with classification of crimes into sets—that is, with the classification of crimes as either *malum in se* or *malum prohibitum*. The last phrase in the last sentence tells us that many jurisdictions make the distinction between these two categories of crimes. Response B follows from that sentence, because if many jurisdictions make the distinction, some jurisdictions make the distinction. From the fact that many jurisdictions make the distinction, it cannot be inferred that many do not make the distinction. Therefore, Response A is incorrect.

Responses C, D, and E are based on erroneous definitions of the two classes of crimes. The paragraph tells us that all crimes characterized as *malum in se* are inherently evil. Response C is false because it cannot be the case that SOME crimes characterized as *malum in se* are NOT inherently evil. The paragraph also tells us that all crimes characterized as *malum prohibitum* are declared as offenses by a legislature. Response D is false because it cannot be the case that SOME crimes characterized as *malum prohibitum* are NOT declared by a legislature to be an offense. In the paragraph, we are told that filing a tax return late is *malum prohibitum*, rather than *malum in se*. Response E is incorrect because it cannot be the case that failing to file a tax return is *malum in se*.

2. Correct Answer: C) If Claus Inc. can show that it was not negligent, then it is not liable

The second sentence states the liability rule for common carriers: all common carriers are liable for cargo damage unless they can show that they are not negligent; if they can show that they are not negligent, then they are not liable for cargo damage. Claus Inc. is a common carrier, and accordingly this rule applies to it. From this rule it follows that if Claus Inc. can show it was not negligent, then it is not liable, Response C. Response A contradicts this rule by claiming that when Claus Inc. is liable it can show that it was not negligent. Response B contradicts this rule by claiming that Claus Inc. is not liable even when it cannot show that it is not negligent. Responses D and E concern Nichols Inc., a contract carrier. However, the terms of the Nichols Inc. contract were not disclosed in the paragraph, so neither response is supported.

3. Correct Answer: A) some e-mail messages that have been requested as part of investigations have contained messages that would never be said face-to-face

This is an example of a test question with a negative lead-in statement. It asks for the conclusion that is **NOT** supported by the paragraph. That means that four of the statements are valid conclusions from the paragraph while one is not. Response B (some messages that people would never say face-to-face are sent in e-mail messages) is a valid conclusion because it restates a fact given in the last sentence of the paragraph. Response E (some e-mail messages contain information that would be omitted from formal writing) is valid because it restates the other fact in the last sentence of the paragraph.

The next-to-last sentence in the paragraph is the source of both response C (some e-mail messages have been requested as part of investigations) and response D (e-mail messages have not been exempted from investigations). Both of these choices restate information in that sentence, based on the fact that access to e-mail messages was sought and granted. This leaves only the first option, response A (Some e-mail messages that have been requested as part of investigations have contained messages that would never be said face-to-face). This is the only choice that does **NOT** represent a valid conclusion, because even though we know from the paragraph that there is a group of e-mail messages that are requested in investigations and also that there is a group of messages that contain information that people would not say face-to-face, there is nothing that says that these groups overlap. We simply do not know.

4. Correct Answer: B) was not married and had no dependents

This question concerns an either/or situation. The paragraph states that benefits under the Federal Employees Compensation Act are awarded at one level (3/4 of salary) if a beneficiary is married or has dependents when injured and at another level (2/3 of salary) if this is not true.

Phyllis T. is eligible for benefits under the Act. The paragraph states that Phyllis T.'s benefit level was 2/3 of her salary. Given this benefit level, it is clear that Phyllis T. did not meet either of the conditions for the 3/4 level. Therefore, responses A, C, and D cannot be correct (A states that she was married, C states that she had dependents, and D states that she both was married and had dependents). Response E goes beyond the facts given because prior marriages are not listed as a factor relating to this benefit. The one correct conclusion is that Phyllis T. did not meet either requirement to qualify for the higher benefit level (3/4 of salary), so response B is the correct answer to the question.

5. Correct Answer: E) some of the engineers were immigrants

Response E is correct because it restates the third sentence in terms of the overlap between immigrants and engineers in the country described in the paragraph. Response A says that most immigrants are engineers or nurses, which are professional occupations. However, the second sentence says that most immigrants are not employed in professional occupations, so Response A is false. Response B is false because it denies that there is any overlap between immigrants and nurses, even though this overlap is clear from the third sentence of the paragraph. Response C is false because it denies the overlap between immigrants and engineers. Because the paragraph does not give complete information about the non-professionals (immigrant and non-immigrant) in the country described in the paragraph, Response D is invalid.

6. Correct Answer: D) all of the .45 caliber weapons were sold legally

The second and last sentences are the two main premises in the paragraph. These two sentences give information about three categories of weapons: weapons made by Precision Arms, weapons sold legally, and .45 caliber weapons.

The last sentence states that none of the illegally sold weapons were .45 caliber. This means that none of the .45 caliber weapons were sold illegally. Notice that this new statement is a double negative. In affirmative form the statement means that all of the .45 caliber weapons were sold legally, Choice D.

The information that all of the .45 caliber weapons were sold legally (last sentence), combined with the information that all of the weapons made by Precision Arms were sold legally (second sentence), allows us to draw no valid conclusions about the relationship between the .45 caliber weapons and the weapons made by Precision Arms. There is insufficient information about the entire group of weapons sold legally to know whether the group of .45 caliber weapons and the group of weapons made by Precision Arms overlapped entirely (Choice A), partially (Choice C), or not at all (Choice B).

Choice E contradicts the second sentence and is, therefore, invalid.

7. Correct Answer: C) if fingerprints are decipherable, then it is impossible to identify the person to whom they belong

This question asks for the response option that **cannot** be validly concluded from the information in the paragraph. The only response option that cannot be validly concluded is Response C, so the correct answer to question 7 is Response C. Response C is invalid because the paragraph does not provide enough information to conclude whether or not it would be possible to identify the person to whom the fingerprints belong from the mere fact that the fingerprints are decipherable.

Response A refers to a condition where it is possible to identify the person to whom fingerprints belong. Based on the final sentence in the paragraph, this condition of fingerprints means that the fingerprints could be classified by general shape and contour or by pattern type. Based on the second sentence, the ability to classify the fingerprints means that the fingerprints are decipherable.

Since Response B refers to a condition in which finger patterns from fingerprints are not decipherable, we know from the second sentence that, in that circumstance, they cannot be classified by general shape and contour or by pattern type. From the final sentence in the paragraph, we can infer that since they cannot be classified by these characteristics, then it is impossible to identify the person to whom the fingerprints belong.

According to the second sentence, fingerprints cannot be classified by general shape and contour or by pattern type when they are not decipherable. Therefore, if fingerprints can be classified by general shape and contour or by pattern type, then the fingerprints must be decipherable, Response D. According to the third sentence, it is impossible to identify the owner of a set of fingerprints when the fingerprints cannot be classified by general shape and contour or by pattern type. Therefore, if it is possible to identify the person to whom fingerprints belong, then the fingerprints must be able to be classified by general shape and contour or pattern type, Response E. Notice that Responses D and E are valid based on the same type of reasoning. The first and second statements of the second sentence were made opposite and reversed in Response D, and the first and second statements of the final sentence were made opposite and reversed in Response E.

8. **Correct Answer: E) some devices in which a physical reaction is produced, such as that caused by overloading a container with compressed air, are mechanical explosives**

The correct answer is E. The third sentence states the overlap between all mechanical explosives and devices in which a physical reaction is produced, such as that caused by overloading a container with compressed air. From this, we can safely conclude that some devices in which a physical reaction is produced, such as that caused by overloading a container with compressed air, are mechanical explosives.

Response A is incorrect because the paragraph does not provide sufficient information to validly conclude that all explosives which have been restricted to military weapons are nuclear weapons. It may be that some types of explosives other than nuclear weapons also have been restricted to military weapons.

Responses B and C are incorrect because they contradict the paragraph. Response B contradicts the third sentence, and Response C contradicts the last sentence.

Response D is incorrect because the paragraph provides no information about whether or not mechanical explosives are restricted to military weapons.

9. **Correct Answer: C)** the fingerprints of a person from this district, selected at random, cannot be alphanumerically coded, with a probability of 10%

We know from the second sentence that 90% of the people in this district have fingerprints that can be coded. Therefore, we know that 10% (100%-90%=10%) have fingerprints that cannot be coded. Given this information, the chance of selecting a person from this district with fingerprints that can be coded is 90% and the chance of selecting a person from this district with fingerprints that cannot be coded is 10%. Response A is incorrect because a probability of 10% is an underestimate of the probability that the fingerprints of a person from this district can be coded. Response B is incorrect because, like response A, it is an underestimate. Response D is incorrect because it is an overestimate of the probability that the fingerprints of a person from this district cannot be coded. Response E is incorrect because the probability that the fingerprints can be coded is known to be 90%.

10. **Correct Answer: E)** this note may have been printed on an Acme Model 200 printer, but the probability cannot be estimated

We know from the third sentence that the Type A micropattern exists in 70% of all Acme Model 200 printers and in some other models of printers. However, we know neither how many other models nor what percentage of other models produce the Type A micropattern. Hence, the probability that the note was printed on the Acme Model 200 printer cannot be determined. For that reason, responses A, B, C, and D are incorrect because the probability is based only on the characteristic of the one model printer that we know, the Acme Model 200, and not on all of the printer models that contain the Type A micropattern.

SECTION III: WRITING SKILLS TEST

This guide has been developed to help you prepare for the Writing Skills Test. This guide provides information that will refresh your knowledge of some basic rules of English grammar, syntax, usage, sentence and paragraph organization, and punctuation. Only a short summary of each topic is provided. For a more in-depth study, you may want to refer to English textbooks or writing handbooks. A reference list with some suggested readings is provided. Also, this guide presents a sample of the types of questions you can expect to find on the Writing Skills Test along with the correct answers and the rationale for them.

PREPARING FOR THE WRITING SKILLS TEST

Sentence Construction

- A sentence is a grammatically independent group of words that serves as a unit of expression.

- A sentence normally contains a stated *subject* (the noun(s) and/or pronoun(s) the sentence is about), and it must contain a *predicate* (the part that says something about or directs the subject) that consists of at least one word, a verb. Even the single-word command *Go!* is a sentence because it has an unstated but implied subject – whoever or whatever is being directed to go – and a verb.

Use of Phrases in Sentences

- A phrase is a group of related words lacking a subject and/or a predicate. A phrase can be used as a noun, adjective, adverb, or verb. On the basis of their form, phrases are classified as *prepositional, participial, gerund, infinitive,* and *verb* phrases.

Use of Clauses in Sentences

- Clauses are grammatical units containing a subject and a verb. They can be either dependent or independent. An independent clause expresses the main thought of the sentence and can stand alone as a sentence (**Example:** She laughed.). A dependent clause expresses an idea that is less important than the idea expressed in the main clause and cannot stand alone as a sentence (**Example:** As she was laughing…).

Restrictive and Nonrestrictive Phrases and Clauses

- A *restrictive* phrase or clause provides information that is necessary to specifically identify what is being described. A *nonrestrictive* phrase or clause provides information that is incidental to the meaning of the sentence.

- Generally speaking, restrictive phrases and clauses are <u>not</u> separated from the rest of the sentence by commas. Nonrestrictive phrases and clauses are separated from the rest of the sentence by commas.

Examples: The blue house that he built on a hill is quite large.
The blue house, which he built on a hill, is quite large.

The first sentence is written about a man who built several blue houses but only one on a hill. Therefore, the phrase *that he built on a hill* is essential for knowing which blue house is being referred to. The phrase is therefore restrictive and is not separated from the rest of the sentence by commas.

The second example is written about a man who built only one blue house, and it happens to be on a hill. Therefore, *which he built on a hill* is not essential for knowing which house is being referred to. The phrase is therefore nonrestrictive and is separated from the rest of the sentence by commas.

Examples: We should congratulate the student who won the prize.
Pat, who won the prize, deserves our congratulations.

In the first sentence the clause *who won the prize* is essential for indicating the person who should be congratulated. The clause is therefore restrictive and is not separated from the rest of the sentence by commas.

In the second sentence, the person to be congratulated is identified as Pat, and the clause *who won the prize* is not essential for identifying the person. The clause is therefore nonrestrictive and is separated from the rest of the sentence by commas.

Verb

Definition: A word or phrase used to assert an action or state of being.

Verb Voice

- The *voice* of a verb shows whether the subject performs an action (active voice) or receives it (passive voice).
  Example (active voice): The consultant wrote a proposal.
  Example (passive voice): The proposal was written by the consultant.

Verb Tense

- The tense of a verb shows the time of the action of the verb. There are an active and a passive form of all tenses in English. The six English verb tenses are:

Tense	Examples of Active Voice	Examples of Passive Voice
Present	she takes; she is taking	she is taken; she is being taken
Past	she took; she was taking	she was taken; she was being taken
Future	she will take; she will be taking	she will be taken
Present perfect	she has taken; she has been taking	she has been taken
Past perfect	she had taken; she had been taking	she had been taken
Future perfect	she will have taken; she will have been taking	she will have been taken

- The *present* tense represents action that is taking place now.
  Example: She *is attending* training today.

- The *past* tense represents action that took place in past time.
  Example: He *wrote* five letters yesterday.

- The *future* tense places action in future time.
  Example: She *will attend* the meeting later today.

- The *present perfect* tense represents action completed before the present time.
  Example: He *has taken* training.

- The *past perfect* tense represents action that occurs before another past action.
  Example: She counted the letters he *had written*.

- The *future perfect* tense represents action that will be completed before a specific time in the future.
  Example: By next week, he *will have completed* the analysis.

Verb Mood

- The *mood* of a verb shows whether an action is fact (indicative mood), something other than fact, such as a possibility, wish, or supposition (subjunctive mood), or a command (imperative mood).
  Example of indicative mood: They *are going* to the ball game.
  Example of subjunctive mood: I insist that he *go* to the ball game.
  Example of imperative mood: *Go* now!

- The subjunctive mood is also used to express a condition contrary to fact.
  Example: I wish I *were* president.

Other Rules Related to Verbs

- Transitive verbs require direct objects to complete their meaning.
  Example: The baseball player *signed the autographs*.

- Intransitive verbs do not require direct objects to complete their meaning.
  Example: The boat *has docked*.

- Linking verbs are not action verbs; rather, they express a state of being or existence. The various forms of the verb *to be* are primary linking verbs.

- Linking verbs never take objects but, instead, connect the subject to a word or idea in the predicate. **Examples:** It *was* he who bought the tickets. His proposal *is* unacceptable. Some dogs *are* excitable.

- The verb *to be* can also be used with another verb as a helping (auxiliary) verb to create a verb phrase. **Examples:** Flights *have been delayed*. The contract will *have to be reviewed*.

Infinitive

Definition: An infinitive is the form of a verb that expresses action or existence without reference to person, number, or tense. **Example:** *To run* is relaxing.

- A split infinitive has a word or several words between the *to* and the *verb* following it. Splitting an infinitive is generally considered incorrect, especially if more than one word intervenes between *to* and the verb. **Incorrect example:** You should try *to*, if you can, *attend* the briefing. **Correct usage:** You should try *to attend* the briefing, if you can.

- An infinitive may be used as the subject of a sentence. **Example:** *To become* champion has been her lifelong dream.

- An infinitive may be used as an adjectival modifier. **Example:** He had several papers *to review* during the trip.

Gerund

Definition: A gerund is the form of a verb ending in *ing* that is used as a noun. In fact, another name for a gerund is a verbal noun.

- A gerund may be used as the subject of a sentence. **Example:** *Drawing* was his favorite personal activity.

- A gerund may be used as the object of a sentence or a prepositional phrase.
  Example: She preferred *walking* over *bicycling*. *Walking* is the object of the verb *preferred* and *bicycling* is the object of the preposition *over*.

Participle

Definition: A participle is a form of the verb used as an adjective. Simple participle forms end in *ed* or *ing*. **Examples:** The candidate felt *betrayed*. The New Year's Eve party was *exciting*.

- When a participial phrase seems to modify a word that it cannot sensibly modify, then it is a dangling phrase. **Incorrect example:** Sailing on the open sea, many dolphins were spotted. (*Sailing* does not modify dolphins.) **Correct usage:** Sailing on the open sea, we spotted many dolphins.

Noun

Definition: A noun is a word that names a person, place, thing, quality, idea, or action.

- A common noun identifies one or more of a class of persons, places, things, qualities, ideas, or actions that are alike. **Examples:** The girl chained her *bicycle* to the *fence*.

- A proper noun identifies a particular person, place, thing, quality, idea, or action. (*Note*: Proper nouns must be capitalized.) **Examples:** *Joe Brown* drove his *Lincoln Towncar* to the *Kennedy Center*.

- A collective noun identifies a group of people or things that are related or acting as one. **Examples:** The *jury* arrives at the courthouse each day at nine in the morning. The *platoon* travels by night in order to avoid detection. Collective nouns are *single* in number; thus, they take a singular verb.

  ➢ If the individual members of the group are referred to, then the plural verb can be used. **Example:** A group of employees *are* sharing supplies with each other.

- The possessive of a singular noun is formed by adding an apostrophe and *s* to the noun. **Examples:** the boy's sweater; Alice's car

- The possessive of a plural noun ending in *s* is formed by adding an apostrophe only. **Examples:** officers' salaries; workers' union

Pronoun

Definition: A pronoun is a word that is used in place of a noun, most frequently to eliminate monotonous repetition of the noun. There are nine types of pronouns:

- Demonstrative pronouns point out a specific person or thing. **Examples:** this, that, these, those

- Indefinite pronouns refer to people or things generally rather than specifically. **Examples:** all, any, anybody, anyone, anything, both, each, either, everybody, everyone, everything, few, many, most, much, neither, no one, nobody, none, nothing, one, other, several, some, somebody, someone, something, such

- Verbs used with indefinite pronouns must agree with the pronoun in number. **Examples:** none *is*; much *is*; everyone *is*; many *are*

    ➢ *None* is generally used in a singular sense. If you think of *none* as *no one person or thing*, then it is easy to see that it is singular in meaning and takes a singular verb. However, when *none* is used in the sense of *not two* or *no amount*, then a plural verb is used. **Example:** None of the team members are in agreement.

- Interrogative pronouns are used to ask questions. **Examples:** who, what, which

- Relative pronouns relate a subordinate part of a sentence to the main clause. **Examples:** who, whoever, whom, whomever, whose, which, whichever, what, that

    ➢ *Who* and *whoever* are used as subjects in a sentence or phrase, while *whom* and *whomever* are used as objects in a sentence or phrase. **Examples:** *Who* will get the tickets? *Whoever* is going will buy the tickets. I need to give tickets to *whom*? The tickets will be given to *whomever* I see first.

- Personal pronouns refer to persons or things and change form in three different persons: first person (the person speaking), second person (the person spoken to), and third person (person or thing spoken about).

    ➢ First person pronouns: I, we (used as subject of sentences and clauses) me, us (used as objects of verbs and prepositions)

    ➢ Second person pronoun: you (used for singular and plural, for subjects and objects)

    ➢ Third person pronouns: he, she, it they (used as subject of sentences and clauses) him, her, it, them (used as objects of verbs and prepositions)

    Examples: Bill and *I* are going. She told Sally and *me*.

- Possessive pronouns determine ownership or possession without using an apostrophe followed by an *s*. **Examples:** my, mine, our, ours, yours, his, hers, its, their, theirs (*Note: it's* is not a personal pronoun; it is the contraction of *it is*.)

- Reflexive pronouns refer back to the pronoun used as the subject of the sentence. **Examples:** I burned *myself*. You are deceiving *yourself*.

- Intensive pronouns are used to emphasize the first pronoun. **Examples:** You *yourself* must register. I *myself* do not understand.

Adjective and Adverb

Definitions: An adjective is a word that modifies a noun. An adverb is a word that modifies a verb, an adjective, or another adverb.

- An adjective or an adverb should be placed so that there is no doubt as to which word it modifies. **Example:** The *angry* boy *quickly* threw the ball. *Angry* is an adjective modifying the noun *boy*. *Quickly* is an adverb modifying the verb *threw*.

- Adjectives and adverbs show degrees of quality or quantity by means of their positive, comparative, and superlative forms. The positive form expresses no comparison at all. The comparative form adds an *-er* to the positive form of the adjective or adverb or prefixes the positive form with the word *more* to express a greater degree or a comparison between two persons or things. The superlative form adds an *-est* to the positive form of the adjective or adverb or prefixes the positive form with the word *most* to express the greatest degree of quantity or quality among three or more persons or things.

    Examples:

Positive	Comparative	Superlative
short	shorter	shortest
beautiful	more beautiful	most beautiful
big	bigger	biggest
hard	harder	hardest

- Many adverbs have the characteristic *ly* ending. **Example:** quickly, slowly, angrily

Article

Definition: An article is a word that refers to a noun and gives definiteness or indefiniteness to the noun.

- The English articles are *a, an*, and *the*.

    - *A* and *an* are the indefinite articles. They are used for general nouns or when the audience does not know which thing you are referring to. *A* is used before words that begin with a consonant, and *an* is used before words that begin with a vowel.
      Examples: *An* attorney will meet you today. *A* file is missing from my desk.

    - *The* is the definite article. It is used when the audience knows which thing is being referred to. **Example:** *The* attorney that you met with last week has returned your call.

Preposition

Definition: A preposition is a word that connects a noun to some other word in the sentence. Prepositions usually establish a relationship of time or location. The use of a preposition automatically creates a prepositional phrase. **Examples:** *in* a month; *after* a year; *on* the table; *behind* the door

- There are over 40 prepositions in English, some of which are: *about, around, before, at, below, by, for, from, in, of, on, to, through, up, upon,* and *with*.

Conjunction

Definition: A conjunction (also known as a connective) is a word that joins together sentences, clauses, phrases, or words.

- Conjunctions that connect two or more parts of a sentence that are of equal rank (Example: two nouns or verbs or phrases, etc.) are called coordinating conjunctions. **Examples:** *and, but, or, nor, for,* and sometimes *yet*

- Subordinating conjunctions connect dependent (subordinate) clauses to independent (main) clauses. Subordinating conjunctions include *though, if, as, when, while, and since*.
  Example: *Since he took the course for his own advancement*, his employer wouldn't pay for it.

- Correlative conjunctions are pairs of words that connect sentence elements that are of equal rank. Correlative conjunctions must always appear together in the same sentence.
  Examples: *either-or, neither-nor, whether-or, both-and,* and *not only-but also*

  Examples used in sentences:
  Neither the manager *nor* the employee had a reasonable solution to the problem.
  Whether he stayed home *or* went to work depended on a change in his symptoms.
  Both the program office *and* the budget office agreed on the increase in funding for the new equipment.
  She was outstanding *not only* in her academic coursework *but also* in her fitness training.

- When two sentence elements are joined by a conjunction, they should have parallel structure.
  Correct example: She was outstanding not only *in her academic coursework* but also *in her fitness training*.
  Incorrect example: She was outstanding not only *in her academic coursework* but also *she excelled in fitness training*.

Avoiding Verb, Noun, and Pronoun Shifts

- Unnecessary shifts in person, number, tense, or voice confuse readers and seriously weaken communication. The examples below indicate these types of errors.

- A shift in person occurs when a writer shifts back and forth among the first, second, and third persons. **Incorrect example:** If *you* want to pass the physical, *a person* has to exercise daily.

- A shift in number occurs when a plural pronoun is used to refer back to a singular antecedent or vice versa. **Incorrect example:** *Anyone* who shops in that department store must seriously consider *their* budget.

- Unnecessary shifts in tense more commonly occur within a paragraph rather than within an individual sentence. **Incorrect example:** After the historian *spent* several hours describing the armies' strategies, he *gave* a horrifying account of the attack. He *points* out in great detail what *is* going on in the minds of each of the soldiers.

- A shift in voice occurs when a writer makes unnecessary shifts between the active and the passive voice. **Incorrect example:** *I wrote* the journal article; the *book chapter was* also *written* by me. (In this example, the first clause is active voice and the second shifts to passive voice.)

Sentence Organization within Paragraphs

- A paragraph presents a larger unit of thought than a sentence can contain.

A paragraph must meet certain requirements:

- A paragraph should have *unity,* that is, internal consistency. It should not digress from the dominant idea expressed in the topic sentence.

- A paragraph should have *completeness.* It should present enough detailed information about the topic sentence to answer any general questions the reader may have. More specific questions would require additional paragraphs with new topic sentences.

- A paragraph should have *coherence.* Sentences should flow into each other so that the reader experiences the paragraph as an integrated unit, not as a collection of separate sentences.

- A paragraph should have *order.* Like structure in a larger work, order in a paragraph grows partly out of the material and is partly imposed by the writer. Most paragraphs and essays follow one of the two patterns that follow.

    - *From the general to the particular:* This type of paragraph begins with a topic sentence that serves as an introductory summary of the topic. The remaining sentences explain or illustrate this statement, so that the idea becomes increasingly clear as the paragraph progresses. The topic sentence is usually at or near the beginning of the paragraph.

> *From the particular to the general:* This type of paragraph is the reverse of the previous pattern. It begins with a series of explanatory or illustrative statements that lead to a general statement or summary. The topic sentence is usually at or near the end of the paragraph.

A paragraph can be looked upon as a microcosm, an exact parallel in miniature of the entire work:

- It has a dominant idea, usually expressed in a topic sentence.

- The dominant idea is developed by examples, comparisons, explanations, or arguments to make the meaning of the topic sentence clear.

- There may be a concluding restatement of the topic idea.

Capitalization

Definition: Capitalization is the use of capital letters to place special emphasis on particular letters to set them off from lower-case letters.

- Sentences always begin with a capital letter.

- The first letter of a quotation is always capitalized.

- Proper nouns, that is, nouns that name particular persons, places, or things, must be capitalized. **Examples:** Appalachian Mountains, Mississippi River, Brooklyn Bridge

- Titles that precede a proper name are capitalized; those that follow a proper name are not. **Examples:** Chairperson John Smith and John Smith, the chairperson

Punctuation

Definition: Punctuation is the use of periods, commas, semicolons, colons, question marks, exclamation points, dashes, apostrophes, brackets, parentheses, slashes, and quotation marks to convey the pauses and gestures that we use in speech to clarify and emphasize meaning.

- Use a period to end a sentence. **Example:** She went to the beach.

- Use a period after abbreviations. **Examples:** Mr. Ms. U.S. Corp.

- Use a comma to separate independent clauses in a compound sentence.
  Example: Suzanne made a presentation at the conference, and then she spent the remainder of the day touring the city.

- Use a comma to separate an introductory phrase or clause from the main clause of a sentence. **Example:** After completing the work, the contractor left the site.

- Place a comma after every item in a series. **Example:** The new office is furnished with a desk, a computer, two chairs, and a supply cabinet.

- Two or more adjectives that modify the noun that they precede are separated by commas. **Example:** The cold, windy morning was not a good beginning for their vacation.

- Commas are used to set off the items in a date. **Example:** On Monday, August 17, 1998, he became the head of the office. Commas are not used when only the month and year are given. **Example:** August 2002

- A semicolon is used to separate elements in a series when some of the elements already contain commas. **Example:** Sally wishes us to attend the first, third, and fifth sessions on Wednesday; the second, fourth, and sixth sessions on Thursday; and the seventh only on Friday.

- A semicolon is used to join two closely related independent clauses that are not joined by a conjunction. **Example:** The project began slowly; thereafter, additional staff were assigned to it.

References

The Elements of Style. Strunk, Jr., W. & White, E.B. Needham Heights, MA: Allyn & Bacon, 2000. ISBN# 020530902X.

Better Sentence Writing in 30 Minutes a Day. Campbell, D. Franklin Lakes, NJ: The Career Press, Inc., 1995. ISBN# 1564142035.

Business English. Geffner, A. Hauppauge, N.Y.: Barron's Educational Services, Inc., 1998. ISBN# 0764102788.

Business Writing at Work. Davidson, E.J. Burr Ridge, IL: Irwin Mirror Press, 1994. ISBN# 0256142203.

Effective Business Writing. Piotrowski, M. New York, NY: HarperCollins, 1996. ISBN# 0062733818.

The Business Writer's Handbook. Brusaw, T., Alred, G. J. & Oliu, W.O. New York, NY: St. Martin's Press, 1993. ISBN# 0312198051.

The Classic Guide to Better Writing. Flesch, R. & Lass, A. H. New York, NY: Harper Collins, 1996. ISBN# 0062730487.

WRITING SKILLS PRACTICE TEST

For questions 1-2, select the one option that represents a change that should be made to correct the sentence. If no correction is necessary, choose option (E).

1. The U.S. Government will seek deportation of each of the defendants from the United States.

    (A) Change of each to each
    (B) Change of each to to each
    (C) Change defendants from to defendants per
    (D) Change defendants from to defendants of
    (E) No correction is necessary

2. Ms. Reece was a primary suspect, and the fraudulent visa documents were eventually traced back to she and Mr. Hanes.

    (A) Change she and Mr. Hanes to Mr. Hanes and she
    (B) Change she and Mr. Hanes to her and Mr. Hanes
    (C) Change she and Mr. Hanes to she and he
    (D) Change she and Mr. Hanes to her and he
    (E) No correction is necessary

For question 3, select the one word that completes the sentence correctly.

3. The suspect who confessed to taking the money explained that he was desperate and there was no _____ available.

    (A) substitute
    (B) alternate
    (C) decision
    (D) alternative
    (E) expedient

For question 4, select the correct spelling of the missing word.

4. Officials have received more than twenty reports of _____ Social Security Cards from those applying to work at restaurants and grocery stores since the beginning of September.

    (A) counterfit
    (B) counterfeit
    (C) counterfet
    (D) counterfete
    (E) counterfitt

For question 5, select the one option that is correctly punctuated.

5. (A) The documents were listed on the invoice as hospital records; however, the documents that I inspected were school records.
   (B) The documents were listed on the invoice as hospital records; however, the documents, that I inspected, were school records.
   (C) The documents were listed on the invoice as hospital records. However the documents that I inspected were school records.
   (D) The documents were listed on the invoice as hospital records. However, the documents, that I inspected, were school records.

For question 6, select the one sentence that uses the correct capitalization.

6. (A) Officer Taylor gave a briefing today to senator Barnes on the uses of the USA Patriot act.
   (B) Officer Taylor gave a briefing today to Senator Barnes on the uses of the USA Patriot act.
   (C) Officer Taylor gave a briefing today to Senator Barnes on the uses of the USA Patriot Act.
   (D) Officer Taylor gave a briefing today to senator Barnes on the uses of the USA Patriot act.

For question 7, select the correct sentence order to form a paragraph that is organized, clear, and coherent. If no correction is necessary, choose option (E).

7.
(1) Patient care incidental to teaching and/or research is permissible.
(2) Canadian-citizen foreign medical graduates coming to the United States under Schedule 2 of the Free Trade Agreement must be coming to engage in teaching and/or research.
(3) They may not come to engage in direct patient care.
(4) Patient care is incidental when it is casually incurred in conjunction with the physician's teaching or research.

A) 4 – 2 – 3 – 1
B) 3 – 1 – 4 – 2
C) 2 – 3 – 1 – 4
D) 2 – 1 – 4 – 3
E) no correction is necessary

For question 8, select the correct order of paragraphs to create a document that is organized, clear, and coherent. If no change to the paragraph order is necessary, choose option (E).

8.
(1) A non-U.S. citizen child "who was born out of wedlock and has not been legitimated is eligible for derivative citizenship when the [child's] mother becomes a naturalized citizen" of the United States, if the child meets all the other requirements for citizenship under sections 320 or 322 of the Immigration and Nationality Act, according to a memorandum dated Sept. 26, 2003, issued by William R. Yates, acting associate director of U.S. Citizenship and Immigration Services (CIS).

(2) Yates issued the memo to clarify how CIS officers are to interpret the definition of "child" in INA section 101(c)(1) when adjudicating applications for citizenship under INA sections 320 and 322. Under section 320, the non-U.S. citizen child of a U.S. citizen automatically derives U.S. citizenship from the parent if the child is residing in the United States and otherwise meets the requirements for citizenship; and section 322 provides that the non-citizen child of a U.S. citizen who regularly resides outside the United States may naturalize to U.S. citizenship via an application made by his or her U.S. citizen legal guardian or grandparent.

(3) This latest clarification was issued as a result of a request to the Justice Department's Office of Legal Counsel that it provide a legal opinion regarding whether a "non-legitimated" child may derive U.S. citizenship under the Child Citizenship Act. CIS, which took over the service functions of the INS when the latter was dissolved, received the legal opinion on July 24, 2003.

(4) According to the memo, the directions in it supercede previously issued policy clarifications "concerning children who are eligible for benefits under the Child Citizenship Act [of 2000] ... and is to be followed in all cases that are pending on [Sept. 26, 2003], as well as in cases filed on or after that date." (The Child Citizenship Act provides that certain foreign-born, non-U.S. citizen children may acquire U.S. citizenship automatically rather than having to apply for it via naturalization.) But even for cases that were adjudicated before Sept. 26, the new policy clarification is to be considered "a sufficient basis to grant an otherwise untimely motion to reopen or reconsider a previous decision, if the child is still otherwise eligible," according to the memo.

A) 1 – 4 – 2 – 3
B) 1 – 4 – 3 – 2
C) 1 – 2 – 4 – 3
D) 2 – 1 – 4 – 3
E) no correction is necessary

Answers to the Writing Skills Questions

1. **Correct Answer: E** No change to the sentence is necessary.

2. **Correct Answer: B** As the object of the preposition "to," the correct pronoun is "her."

3. **Correct Answer: D** "Alternative" means one of two possibilities and involves choice. In question three the suspect is claiming that no other choice was available.

4. **Correct Answer: B** The correct spelling is "counterfeit."

5. **Correct Answer: A** The correct answer is (A). The sentence offers correct punctuation.

6. **Correct Answer: C** The correct capitalization of the words "Officer Taylor, " "Senator Barnes," and "USA Patriot Act" are used in this sentence.

7. **Correct Answer: C** The most logical order of the passages is 2, 3, 1, 4. Sentence 3 uses the pronoun "they" which must refer to a group of people. The only sentence which contains a group of people is sentence 2; therefore, sentence 3 must follow and refer to sentence 2. Sentence 1, which states what type of patient care is permissible, logically follows from sentence 3, which states what kind of patient care is impermissible. Sentence 4 elaborates on the idea of incidental patient care first introduced in sentence 1; therefore, sentence 4 should follow sentence 1.

8. **Correct Answer: C** The most logical order of the passages is 1, 2, 4, 3. Paragraph 1 introduces the memo authored by William Yates concerning naturalization. Paragraph 2 refers to the memo and to Yates and, therefore, must follow paragraph 1. Paragraph 4 naturally follows paragraph 1 because paragraph 4 adds to the information presented in paragraph 1. Finally, paragraph 3 concludes the passage with information concerning the reason for Yates' memo.

HOW TO TAKE A TEST

I. YOU MUST PASS AN EXAMINATION

A. *WHAT EVERY CANDIDATE SHOULD KNOW*

Examination applicants often ask us for help in preparing for the written test. What can I study in advance? What kinds of questions will be asked? How will the test be given? How will the papers be graded?

As an applicant for a civil service examination, you may be wondering about some of these things. Our purpose here is to suggest effective methods of advance study and to describe civil service examinations.

Your chances for success on this examination can be increased if you know how to prepare. Those "pre-examination jitters" can be reduced if you know what to expect. You can even experience an adventure in good citizenship if you know why civil service exams are given.

B. *WHY ARE CIVIL SERVICE EXAMINATIONS GIVEN?*

Civil service examinations are important to you in two ways. As a citizen, you want public jobs filled by employees who know how to do their work. As a job seeker, you want a fair chance to compete for that job on an equal footing with other candidates. The best-known means of accomplishing this two-fold goal is the competitive examination.

Exams are widely publicized throughout the nation. They may be administered for jobs in federal, state, city, municipal, town or village governments or agencies.

Any citizen may apply, with some limitations, such as the age or residence of applicants. Your experience and education may be reviewed to see whether you meet the requirements for the particular examination. When these requirements exist, they are reasonable and applied consistently to all applicants. Thus, a competitive examination may cause you some uneasiness now, but it is your privilege and safeguard.

C. *HOW ARE CIVIL SERVICE EXAMS DEVELOPED?*

Examinations are carefully written by trained technicians who are specialists in the field known as "psychological measurement," in consultation with recognized authorities in the field of work that the test will cover. These experts recommend the subject matter areas or skills to be tested; only those knowledges or skills important to your success on the job are included. The most reliable books and source materials available are used as references. Together, the experts and technicians judge the difficulty level of the questions.

Test technicians know how to phrase questions so that the problem is clearly stated. Their ethics do not permit "trick" or "catch" questions. Questions may have been tried out on sample groups, or subjected to statistical analysis, to determine their usefulness.

Written tests are often used in combination with performance tests, ratings of training and experience, and oral interviews. All of these measures combine to form the best-known means of finding the right person for the right job.

II. HOW TO PASS THE WRITTEN TEST

A. NATURE OF THE EXAMINATION

To prepare intelligently for civil service examinations, you should know how they differ from school examinations you have taken. In school you were assigned certain definite pages to read or subjects to cover. The examination questions were quite detailed and usually emphasized memory. Civil service exams, on the other hand, try to discover your present ability to perform the duties of a position, plus your potentiality to learn these duties. In other words, a civil service exam attempts to predict how successful you will be. Questions cover such a broad area that they cannot be as minute and detailed as school exam questions.

In the public service similar kinds of work, or positions, are grouped together in one "class." This process is known as *position-classification*. All the positions in a class are paid according to the salary range for that class. One class title covers all of these positions, and they are all tested by the same examination.

B. FOUR BASIC STEPS

1) Study the announcement

How, then, can you know what subjects to study? Our best answer is: "Learn as much as possible about the class of positions for which you've applied." The exam will test the knowledge, skills and abilities needed to do the work.

Your most valuable source of information about the position you want is the official exam announcement. This announcement lists the training and experience qualifications. Check these standards and apply only if you come reasonably close to meeting them.

The brief description of the position in the examination announcement offers some clues to the subjects which will be tested. Think about the job itself. Review the duties in your mind. Can you perform them, or are there some in which you are rusty? Fill in the blank spots in your preparation.

Many jurisdictions preview the written test in the exam announcement by including a section called "Knowledge and Abilities Required," "Scope of the Examination," or some similar heading. Here you will find out specifically what fields will be tested.

2) Review your own background

Once you learn in general what the position is all about, and what you need to know to do the work, ask yourself which subjects you already know fairly well and which need improvement. You may wonder whether to concentrate on improving your strong areas or on building some background in your fields of weakness. When the announcement has specified "some knowledge" or "considerable knowledge," or has used adjectives like "beginning principles of..." or "advanced ... methods," you can get a clue as to the number and difficulty of questions to be asked in any given field. More questions, and hence broader coverage, would be included for those subjects which are more important in the work. Now weigh your strengths and weaknesses against the job requirements and prepare accordingly.

3) Determine the level of the position

Another way to tell how intensively you should prepare is to understand the level of the job for which you are applying. Is it the entering level? In other words, is this the position in which beginners in a field of work are hired? Or is it an intermediate or advanced level? Sometimes this is indicated by such words as "Junior" or "Senior" in the class title. Other jurisdictions use Roman numerals to designate the level – Clerk I, Clerk II, for example. The word "Supervisor" sometimes appears in the title. If the level is not indicated by the title, check the description of duties. Will you be working under very close supervision, or will you have responsibility for independent decisions in this work?

4) Choose appropriate study materials

Now that you know the subjects to be examined and the relative amount of each subject to be covered, you can choose suitable study materials. For beginning level jobs, or even advanced ones, if you have a pronounced weakness in some aspect of your training, read a modern, standard textbook in that field. Be sure it is up to date and has general coverage. Such books are normally available at your library, and the librarian will be glad to help you locate one. For entry-level positions, questions of appropriate difficulty are chosen – neither highly advanced questions, nor those too simple. Such questions require careful thought but not advanced training.

If the position for which you are applying is technical or advanced, you will read more advanced, specialized material. If you are already familiar with the basic principles of your field, elementary textbooks would waste your time. Concentrate on advanced textbooks and technical periodicals. Think through the concepts and review difficult problems in your field.

These are all general sources. You can get more ideas on your own initiative, following these leads. For example, training manuals and publications of the government agency which employs workers in your field can be useful, particularly for technical and professional positions. A letter or visit to the government department involved may result in more specific study suggestions, and certainly will provide you with a more definite idea of the exact nature of the position you are seeking.

III. KINDS OF TESTS

Tests are used for purposes other than measuring knowledge and ability to perform specified duties. For some positions, it is equally important to test ability to make adjustments to new situations or to profit from training. In others, basic mental abilities not dependent on information are essential. Questions which test these things may not appear as pertinent to the duties of the position as those which test for knowledge and information. Yet they are often highly important parts of a fair examination. For very general questions, it is almost impossible to help you direct your study efforts. What we can do is to point out some of the more common of these general abilities needed in public service positions and describe some typical questions.

1) General information

Broad, general information has been found useful for predicting job success in some kinds of work. This is tested in a variety of ways, from vocabulary lists to questions about current events. Basic background in some field of work, such as sociology or economics, may be sampled in a group of questions. Often these are principles which have become familiar to most persons through exposure rather than through formal training. It is difficult to advise you how to study for these questions; being alert to the world around you is our best suggestion.

2) Verbal ability

An example of an ability needed in many positions is verbal or language ability. Verbal ability is, in brief, the ability to use and understand words. Vocabulary and grammar tests are typical measures of this ability. Reading comprehension or paragraph interpretation questions are common in many kinds of civil service tests. You are given a paragraph of written material and asked to find its central meaning.

3) Numerical ability

Number skills can be tested by the familiar arithmetic problem, by checking paired lists of numbers to see which are alike and which are different, or by interpreting charts and graphs. In the latter test, a graph may be printed in the test booklet which you are asked to use as the basis for answering questions.

4) Observation

A popular test for law-enforcement positions is the observation test. A picture is shown to you for several minutes, then taken away. Questions about the picture test your ability to observe both details and larger elements.

5) Following directions

In many positions in the public service, the employee must be able to carry out written instructions dependably and accurately. You may be given a chart with several columns, each column listing a variety of information. The questions require you to carry out directions involving the information given in the chart.

6) Skills and aptitudes

Performance tests effectively measure some manual skills and aptitudes. When the skill is one in which you are trained, such as typing or shorthand, you can practice. These tests are often very much like those given in business school or high school courses. For many of the other skills and aptitudes, however, no short-time preparation can be made. Skills and abilities natural to you or that you have developed throughout your lifetime are being tested.

Many of the general questions just described provide all the data needed to answer the questions and ask you to use your reasoning ability to find the answers. Your best preparation for these tests, as well as for tests of facts and ideas, is to be at your physical and mental best. You, no doubt, have your own methods of getting into an exam-taking mood and keeping "in shape." The next section lists some ideas on this subject.

IV. KINDS OF QUESTIONS

Only rarely is the "essay" question, which you answer in narrative form, used in civil service tests. Civil service tests are usually of the short-answer type. Full instructions for answering these questions will be given to you at the examination. But in case this is your first experience with short-answer questions and separate answer sheets, here is what you need to know:

1) Multiple-choice Questions

Most popular of the short-answer questions is the "multiple choice" or "best answer" question. It can be used, for example, to test for factual knowledge, ability to solve problems or judgment in meeting situations found at work.

A multiple-choice question is normally one of three types—
- It can begin with an incomplete statement followed by several possible endings. You are to find the one ending which *best* completes the statement, although some of the others may not be entirely wrong.
- It can also be a complete statement in the form of a question which is answered by choosing one of the statements listed.

- It can be in the form of a problem – again you select the best answer.

Here is an example of a multiple-choice question with a discussion which should give you some clues as to the method for choosing the right answer:

When an employee has a complaint about his assignment, the action which will *best* help him overcome his difficulty is to
    A. discuss his difficulty with his coworkers
    B. take the problem to the head of the organization
    C. take the problem to the person who gave him the assignment
    D. say nothing to anyone about his complaint

In answering this question, you should study each of the choices to find which is best. Consider choice "A" – Certainly an employee may discuss his complaint with fellow employees, but no change or improvement can result, and the complaint remains unresolved. Choice "B" is a poor choice since the head of the organization probably does not know what assignment you have been given, and taking your problem to him is known as "going over the head" of the supervisor. The supervisor, or person who made the assignment, is the person who can clarify it or correct any injustice. Choice "C" is, therefore, correct. To say nothing, as in choice "D," is unwise. Supervisors have and interest in knowing the problems employees are facing, and the employee is seeking a solution to his problem.

2) True/False Questions

The "true/false" or "right/wrong" form of question is sometimes used. Here a complete statement is given. Your job is to decide whether the statement is right or wrong.

SAMPLE: A roaming cell-phone call to a nearby city costs less than a non-roaming call to a distant city.

This statement is wrong, or false, since roaming calls are more expensive.
This is not a complete list of all possible question forms, although most of the others are variations of these common types. You will always get complete directions for answering questions. Be sure you understand *how* to mark your answers – ask questions until you do.

V. RECORDING YOUR ANSWERS

Computer terminals are used more and more today for many different kinds of exams.
For an examination with very few applicants, you may be told to record your answers in the test booklet itself. Separate answer sheets are much more common. If this separate answer sheet is to be scored by machine – and this is often the case – it is highly important that you mark your answers correctly in order to get credit.
An electronic scoring machine is often used in civil service offices because of the speed with which papers can be scored. Machine-scored answer sheets must be marked with a pencil, which will be given to you. This pencil has a high graphite content which responds to the electronic scoring machine. As a matter of fact, stray dots may register as answers, so do not let your pencil rest on the answer sheet while you are pondering the correct answer. Also, if your pencil lead breaks or is otherwise defective, ask for another.

Since the answer sheet will be dropped in a slot in the scoring machine, be careful not to bend the corners or get the paper crumpled.

The answer sheet normally has five vertical columns of numbers, with 30 numbers to a column. These numbers correspond to the question numbers in your test booklet. After each number, going across the page are four or five pairs of dotted lines. These short dotted lines have small letters or numbers above them. The first two pairs may also have a "T" or "F" above the letters. This indicates that the first two pairs only are to be used if the questions are of the true-false type. If the questions are multiple choice, disregard the "T" and "F" and pay attention only to the small letters or numbers.

Answer your questions in the manner of the sample that follows:

32. The largest city in the United States is
    A. Washington, D.C.
    B. New York City
    C. Chicago
    D. Detroit
    E. San Francisco

1) Choose the answer you think is best. (New York City is the largest, so "B" is correct.)
2) Find the row of dotted lines numbered the same as the question you are answering. (Find row number 32)
3) Find the pair of dotted lines corresponding to the answer. (Find the pair of lines under the mark "B.")
4) Make a solid black mark between the dotted lines.

VI. BEFORE THE TEST

Common sense will help you find procedures to follow to get ready for an examination. Too many of us, however, overlook these sensible measures. Indeed, nervousness and fatigue have been found to be the most serious reasons why applicants fail to do their best on civil service tests. Here is a list of reminders:

- Begin your preparation early – Don't wait until the last minute to go scurrying around for books and materials or to find out what the position is all about.
- Prepare continuously – An hour a night for a week is better than an all-night cram session. This has been definitely established. What is more, a night a week for a month will return better dividends than crowding your study into a shorter period of time.
- Locate the place of the exam – You have been sent a notice telling you when and where to report for the examination. If the location is in a different town or otherwise unfamiliar to you, it would be well to inquire the best route and learn something about the building.
- Relax the night before the test – Allow your mind to rest. Do not study at all that night. Plan some mild recreation or diversion; then go to bed early and get a good night's sleep.
- Get up early enough to make a leisurely trip to the place for the test – This way unforeseen events, traffic snarls, unfamiliar buildings, etc. will not upset you.
- Dress comfortably – A written test is not a fashion show. You will be known by number and not by name, so wear something comfortable.

- Leave excess paraphernalia at home – Shopping bags and odd bundles will get in your way. You need bring only the items mentioned in the official notice you received; usually everything you need is provided. Do not bring reference books to the exam. They will only confuse those last minutes and be taken away from you when in the test room.
- Arrive somewhat ahead of time – If because of transportation schedules you must get there very early, bring a newspaper or magazine to take your mind off yourself while waiting.
- Locate the examination room – When you have found the proper room, you will be directed to the seat or part of the room where you will sit. Sometimes you are given a sheet of instructions to read while you are waiting. Do not fill out any forms until you are told to do so; just read them and be prepared.
- Relax and prepare to listen to the instructions
- If you have any physical problem that may keep you from doing your best, be sure to tell the test administrator. If you are sick or in poor health, you really cannot do your best on the exam. You can come back and take the test some other time.

VII. AT THE TEST

The day of the test is here and you have the test booklet in your hand. The temptation to get going is very strong. Caution! There is more to success than knowing the right answers. You must know how to identify your papers and understand variations in the type of short-answer question used in this particular examination. Follow these suggestions for maximum results from your efforts:

1) Cooperate with the monitor

The test administrator has a duty to create a situation in which you can be as much at ease as possible. He will give instructions, tell you when to begin, check to see that you are marking your answer sheet correctly, and so on. He is not there to guard you, although he will see that your competitors do not take unfair advantage. He wants to help you do your best.

2) Listen to all instructions

Don't jump the gun! Wait until you understand all directions. In most civil service tests you get more time than you need to answer the questions. So don't be in a hurry. Read each word of instructions until you clearly understand the meaning. Study the examples, listen to all announcements and follow directions. Ask questions if you do not understand what to do.

3) Identify your papers

Civil service exams are usually identified by number only. You will be assigned a number; you must not put your name on your test papers. Be sure to copy your number correctly. Since more than one exam may be given, copy your exact examination title.

4) Plan your time

Unless you are told that a test is a "speed" or "rate of work" test, speed itself is usually not important. Time enough to answer all the questions will be provided, but this does not mean that you have all day. An overall time limit has been set. Divide the total time (in minutes) by the number of questions to determine the approximate time you have for each question.

5) Do not linger over difficult questions

If you come across a difficult question, mark it with a paper clip (useful to have along) and come back to it when you have been through the booklet. One caution if you do this – be sure to skip a number on your answer sheet as well. Check often to be sure that you have not lost your place and that you are marking in the row numbered the same as the question you are answering.

6) Read the questions

Be sure you know what the question asks! Many capable people are unsuccessful because they failed to *read* the questions correctly.

7) Answer all questions

Unless you have been instructed that a penalty will be deducted for incorrect answers, it is better to guess than to omit a question.

8) Speed tests

It is often better NOT to guess on speed tests. It has been found that on timed tests people are tempted to spend the last few seconds before time is called in marking answers at random – without even reading them – in the hope of picking up a few extra points. To discourage this practice, the instructions may warn you that your score will be "corrected" for guessing. That is, a penalty will be applied. The incorrect answers will be deducted from the correct ones, or some other penalty formula will be used.

9) Review your answers

If you finish before time is called, go back to the questions you guessed or omitted to give them further thought. Review other answers if you have time.

10) Return your test materials

If you are ready to leave before others have finished or time is called, take ALL your materials to the monitor and leave quietly. Never take any test material with you. The monitor can discover whose papers are not complete, and taking a test booklet may be grounds for disqualification.

VIII. EXAMINATION TECHNIQUES

1) Read the general instructions carefully. These are usually printed on the first page of the exam booklet. As a rule, these instructions refer to the timing of the examination; the fact that you should not start work until the signal and must stop work at a signal, etc. If there are any *special* instructions, such as a choice of questions to be answered, make sure that you note this instruction carefully.

2) When you are ready to start work on the examination, that is as soon as the signal has been given, read the instructions to each question booklet, underline any key words or phrases, such as *least, best, outline, describe* and the like. In this way you will tend to answer as requested rather than discover on reviewing your paper that you *listed without describing*, that you selected the *worst* choice rather than the *best* choice, etc.

3) If the examination is of the objective or multiple-choice type – that is, each question will also give a series of possible answers: A, B, C or D, and you are called upon to select the best answer and write the letter next to that answer on your answer paper – it is advisable to start answering each question in turn. There may be anywhere from 50 to 100 such questions in the three or four hours allotted and you can see how much time would be taken if you read through all the questions before beginning to answer any. Furthermore, if you come across a question or group of questions which you know would be difficult to answer, it would undoubtedly affect your handling of all the other questions.

4) If the examination is of the essay type and contains but a few questions, it is a moot point as to whether you should read all the questions before starting to answer any one. Of course, if you are given a choice – say five out of seven and the like – then it is essential to read all the questions so you can eliminate the two that are most difficult. If, however, you are asked to answer all the questions, there may be danger in trying to answer the easiest one first because you may find that you will spend too much time on it. The best technique is to answer the first question, then proceed to the second, etc.

5) Time your answers. Before the exam begins, write down the time it started, then add the time allowed for the examination and write down the time it must be completed, then divide the time available somewhat as follows:
    - If 3-1/2 hours are allowed, that would be 210 minutes. If you have 80 objective-type questions, that would be an average of 2-1/2 minutes per question. Allow yourself no more than 2 minutes per question, or a total of 160 minutes, which will permit about 50 minutes to review.
    - If for the time allotment of 210 minutes there are 7 essay questions to answer, that would average about 30 minutes a question. Give yourself only 25 minutes per question so that you have about 35 minutes to review.

6) The most important instruction is to *read each question* and make sure you know what is wanted. The second most important instruction is to *time yourself properly* so that you answer every question. The third most important instruction is to *answer every question*. Guess if you have to but include something for each question. Remember that you will receive no credit for a blank and will probably receive some credit if you write something in answer to an essay question. If you guess a letter – say "B" for a multiple-choice question – you may have guessed right. If you leave a blank as an answer to a multiple-choice question, the examiners may respect your feelings but it will not add a point to your score. Some exams may penalize you for wrong answers, so in such cases *only*, you may not want to guess unless you have some basis for your answer.

7) Suggestions
    a. Objective-type questions
        1. Examine the question booklet for proper sequence of pages and questions
        2. Read all instructions carefully
        3. Skip any question which seems too difficult; return to it after all other questions have been answered
        4. Apportion your time properly; do not spend too much time on any single question or group of questions

5. Note and underline key words – *all, most, fewest, least, best, worst, same, opposite,* etc.
6. Pay particular attention to negatives
7. Note unusual option, e.g., unduly long, short, complex, different or similar in content to the body of the question
8. Observe the use of "hedging" words – *probably, may, most likely,* etc.
9. Make sure that your answer is put next to the same number as the question
10. Do not second-guess unless you have good reason to believe the second answer is definitely more correct
11. Cross out original answer if you decide another answer is more accurate; do not erase until you are ready to hand your paper in
12. Answer all questions; guess unless instructed otherwise
13. Leave time for review

   b. Essay questions
      1. Read each question carefully
      2. Determine exactly what is wanted. Underline key words or phrases.
      3. Decide on outline or paragraph answer
      4. Include many different points and elements unless asked to develop any one or two points or elements
      5. Show impartiality by giving pros and cons unless directed to select one side only
      6. Make and write down any assumptions you find necessary to answer the questions
      7. Watch your English, grammar, punctuation and choice of words
      8. Time your answers; don't crowd material

8) Answering the essay question

Most essay questions can be answered by framing the specific response around several key words or ideas. Here are a few such key words or ideas:

M's: manpower, materials, methods, money, management
P's: purpose, program, policy, plan, procedure, practice, problems, pitfalls, personnel, public relations

   a. Six basic steps in handling problems:
      1. Preliminary plan and background development
      2. Collect information, data and facts
      3. Analyze and interpret information, data and facts
      4. Analyze and develop solutions as well as make recommendations
      5. Prepare report and sell recommendations
      6. Install recommendations and follow up effectiveness

   b. Pitfalls to avoid
      1. *Taking things for granted* – A statement of the situation does not necessarily imply that each of the elements is necessarily true; for example, a complaint may be invalid and biased so that all that can be taken for granted is that a complaint has been registered

2. *Considering only one side of a situation* – Wherever possible, indicate several alternatives and then point out the reasons you selected the best one
3. *Failing to indicate follow up* – Whenever your answer indicates action on your part, make certain that you will take proper follow-up action to see how successful your recommendations, procedures or actions turn out to be
4. *Taking too long in answering any single question* – Remember to time your answers properly

IX. AFTER THE TEST

Scoring procedures differ in detail among civil service jurisdictions although the general principles are the same. Whether the papers are hand-scored or graded by machine we have described, they are nearly always graded by number. That is, the person who marks the paper knows only the number – never the name – of the applicant. Not until all the papers have been graded will they be matched with names. If other tests, such as training and experience or oral interview ratings have been given, scores will be combined. Different parts of the examination usually have different weights. For example, the written test might count 60 percent of the final grade, and a rating of training and experience 40 percent. In many jurisdictions, veterans will have a certain number of points added to their grades.

After the final grade has been determined, the names are placed in grade order and an eligible list is established. There are various methods for resolving ties between those who get the same final grade – probably the most common is to place first the name of the person whose application was received first. Job offers are made from the eligible list in the order the names appear on it. You will be notified of your grade and your rank as soon as all these computations have been made. This will be done as rapidly as possible.

People who are found to meet the requirements in the announcement are called "eligibles." Their names are put on a list of eligible candidates. An eligible's chances of getting a job depend on how high he stands on this list and how fast agencies are filling jobs from the list.

When a job is to be filled from a list of eligibles, the agency asks for the names of people on the list of eligibles for that job. When the civil service commission receives this request, it sends to the agency the names of the three people highest on this list. Or, if the job to be filled has specialized requirements, the office sends the agency the names of the top three persons who meet these requirements from the general list.

The appointing officer makes a choice from among the three people whose names were sent to him. If the selected person accepts the appointment, the names of the others are put back on the list to be considered for future openings.

That is the rule in hiring from all kinds of eligible lists, whether they are for typist, carpenter, chemist, or something else. For every vacancy, the appointing officer has his choice of any one of the top three eligibles on the list. This explains why the person whose name is on top of the list sometimes does not get an appointment when some of the persons lower on the list do. If the appointing officer chooses the second or third eligible, the No. 1 eligible does not get a job at once, but stays on the list until he is appointed or the list is terminated.

X. HOW TO PASS THE INTERVIEW TEST

The examination for which you applied requires an oral interview test. You have already taken the written test and you are now being called for the interview test – the final part of the formal examination.

You may think that it is not possible to prepare for an interview test and that there are no procedures to follow during an interview. Our purpose is to point out some things you can do in advance that will help you and some good rules to follow and pitfalls to avoid while you are being interviewed.

What is an interview supposed to test?

The written examination is designed to test the technical knowledge and competence of the candidate; the oral is designed to evaluate intangible qualities, not readily measured otherwise, and to establish a list showing the relative fitness of each candidate – as measured against his competitors – for the position sought. Scoring is not on the basis of "right" and "wrong," but on a sliding scale of values ranging from "not passable" to "outstanding." As a matter of fact, it is possible to achieve a relatively low score without a single "incorrect" answer because of evident weakness in the qualities being measured.

Occasionally, an examination may consist entirely of an oral test – either an individual or a group oral. In such cases, information is sought concerning the technical knowledges and abilities of the candidate, since there has been no written examination for this purpose. More commonly, however, an oral test is used to supplement a written examination.

Who conducts interviews?

The composition of oral boards varies among different jurisdictions. In nearly all, a representative of the personnel department serves as chairman. One of the members of the board may be a representative of the department in which the candidate would work. In some cases, "outside experts" are used, and, frequently, a businessman or some other representative of the general public is asked to serve. Labor and management or other special groups may be represented. The aim is to secure the services of experts in the appropriate field.

However the board is composed, it is a good idea (and not at all improper or unethical) to ascertain in advance of the interview who the members are and what groups they represent. When you are introduced to them, you will have some idea of their backgrounds and interests, and at least you will not stutter and stammer over their names.

What should be done before the interview?

While knowledge about the board members is useful and takes some of the surprise element out of the interview, there is other preparation which is more substantive. It *is* possible to prepare for an oral interview – in several ways:

1) Keep a copy of your application and review it carefully before the interview

This may be the only document before the oral board, and the starting point of the interview. Know what education and experience you have listed there, and the sequence and dates of all of it. Sometimes the board will ask you to review the highlights of your experience for them; you should not have to hem and haw doing it.

2) Study the class specification and the examination announcement

Usually, the oral board has one or both of these to guide them. The qualities, characteristics or knowledges required by the position sought are stated in these documents. They offer valuable clues as to the nature of the oral interview. For example, if the job involves supervisory responsibilities, the announcement will usually indicate that knowledge of modern supervisory methods and the qualifications of the candidate as a supervisor will be tested. If so, you can expect such questions, frequently in the form of a hypothetical situation which you are expected to solve. NEVER go into an oral without knowledge of the duties and responsibilities of the job you seek.

3) Think through each qualification required

Try to visualize the kind of questions you would ask if you were a board member. How well could you answer them? Try especially to appraise your own knowledge and background in each area, *measured against the job sought*, and identify any areas in which you are weak. Be critical and realistic – do not flatter yourself.

4) Do some general reading in areas in which you feel you may be weak

For example, if the job involves supervision and your past experience has NOT, some general reading in supervisory methods and practices, particularly in the field of human relations, might be useful. Do NOT study agency procedures or detailed manuals. The oral board will be testing your understanding and capacity, not your memory.

5) Get a good night's sleep and watch your general health and mental attitude

You will want a clear head at the interview. Take care of a cold or any other minor ailment, and of course, no hangovers.

What should be done on the day of the interview?

Now comes the day of the interview itself. Give yourself plenty of time to get there. Plan to arrive somewhat ahead of the scheduled time, particularly if your appointment is in the fore part of the day. If a previous candidate fails to appear, the board might be ready for you a bit early. By early afternoon an oral board is almost invariably behind schedule if there are many candidates, and you may have to wait. Take along a book or magazine to read, or your application to review, but leave any extraneous material in the waiting room when you go in for your interview. In any event, relax and compose yourself.

The matter of dress is important. The board is forming impressions about you – from your experience, your manners, your attitude, and your appearance. Give your personal appearance careful attention. Dress your best, but not your flashiest. Choose conservative, appropriate clothing, and be sure it is immaculate. This is a business interview, and your appearance should indicate that you regard it as such. Besides, being well groomed and properly dressed will help boost your confidence.

Sooner or later, someone will call your name and escort you into the interview room. *This is it.* From here on you are on your own. It is too late for any more preparation. But remember, you asked for this opportunity to prove your fitness, and you are here because your request was granted.

What happens when you go in?

The usual sequence of events will be as follows: The clerk (who is often the board stenographer) will introduce you to the chairman of the oral board, who will introduce you to the other members of the board. Acknowledge the introductions before you sit down. Do not be surprised if you find a microphone facing you or a stenotypist sitting by. Oral interviews are usually recorded in the event of an appeal or other review.

Usually the chairman of the board will open the interview by reviewing the highlights of your education and work experience from your application – primarily for the benefit of the other members of the board, as well as to get the material into the record. Do not interrupt or comment unless there is an error or significant misinterpretation; if that is the case, do not hesitate. But do not quibble about insignificant matters. Also, he will usually ask you some question about your education, experience or your present job – partly to get you to start talking and to establish the interviewing "rapport." He may start the actual questioning, or turn it over to one of the other members. Frequently, each member undertakes the questioning on a particular area, one in which he is perhaps most competent, so you can expect each member to participate in the examination. Because time is limited, you may also expect some rather abrupt switches in the direction the questioning takes, so do not be upset by it. Normally, a board member will not pursue a single line of questioning unless he discovers a particular strength or weakness.

After each member has participated, the chairman will usually ask whether any member has any further questions, then will ask you if you have anything you wish to add. Unless you are expecting this question, it may floor you. Worse, it may start you off on an extended, extemporaneous speech. The board is not usually seeking more information. The question is principally to offer you a last opportunity to present further qualifications or to indicate that you have nothing to add. So, if you feel that a significant qualification or characteristic has been overlooked, it is proper to point it out in a sentence or so. Do not compliment the board on the thoroughness of their examination – they have been sketchy, and you know it. If you wish, merely say, "No thank you, I have nothing further to add." This is a point where you can "talk yourself out" of a good impression or fail to present an important bit of information. Remember, *you close the interview yourself.*

The chairman will then say, "That is all, Mr. _____, thank you." Do not be startled; the interview is over, and quicker than you think. Thank him, gather your belongings and take your leave. Save your sigh of relief for the other side of the door.

How to put your best foot forward

Throughout this entire process, you may feel that the board individually and collectively is trying to pierce your defenses, seek out your hidden weaknesses and embarrass and confuse you. Actually, this is not true. They are obliged to make an appraisal of your qualifications for the job you are seeking, and they want to see you in your best light. Remember, they must interview all candidates and a non-cooperative candidate may become a failure in spite of their best efforts to bring out his qualifications. Here are 15 suggestions that will help you:

1) Be natural – Keep your attitude confident, not cocky

If you are not confident that you can do the job, do not expect the board to be. Do not apologize for your weaknesses, try to bring out your strong points. The board is interested in a positive, not negative, presentation. Cockiness will antagonize any board member and make him wonder if you are covering up a weakness by a false show of strength.

2) Get comfortable, but don't lounge or sprawl

Sit erectly but not stiffly. A careless posture may lead the board to conclude that you are careless in other things, or at least that you are not impressed by the importance of the occasion. Either conclusion is natural, even if incorrect. Do not fuss with your clothing, a pencil or an ashtray. Your hands may occasionally be useful to emphasize a point; do not let them become a point of distraction.

3) Do not wisecrack or make small talk

This is a serious situation, and your attitude should show that you consider it as such. Further, the time of the board is limited – they do not want to waste it, and neither should you.

4) Do not exaggerate your experience or abilities

In the first place, from information in the application or other interviews and sources, the board may know more about you than you think. Secondly, you probably will not get away with it. An experienced board is rather adept at spotting such a situation, so do not take the chance.

5) If you know a board member, do not make a point of it, yet do not hide it

Certainly you are not fooling him, and probably not the other members of the board. Do not try to take advantage of your acquaintanceship – it will probably do you little good.

6) Do not dominate the interview

Let the board do that. They will give you the clues – do not assume that you have to do all the talking. Realize that the board has a number of questions to ask you, and do not try to take up all the interview time by showing off your extensive knowledge of the answer to the first one.

7) Be attentive

You only have 20 minutes or so, and you should keep your attention at its sharpest throughout. When a member is addressing a problem or question to you, give him your undivided attention. Address your reply principally to him, but do not exclude the other board members.

8) Do not interrupt

A board member may be stating a problem for you to analyze. He will ask you a question when the time comes. Let him state the problem, and wait for the question.

9) Make sure you understand the question

Do not try to answer until you are sure what the question is. If it is not clear, restate it in your own words or ask the board member to clarify it for you. However, do not haggle about minor elements.

10) Reply promptly but not hastily

A common entry on oral board rating sheets is "candidate responded readily," or "candidate hesitated in replies." Respond as promptly and quickly as you can, but do not jump to a hasty, ill-considered answer.

11) Do not be peremptory in your answers

A brief answer is proper – but do not fire your answer back. That is a losing game from your point of view. The board member can probably ask questions much faster than you can answer them.

12) Do not try to create the answer you think the board member wants

He is interested in what kind of mind you have and how it works – not in playing games. Furthermore, he can usually spot this practice and will actually grade you down on it.

13) Do not switch sides in your reply merely to agree with a board member

Frequently, a member will take a contrary position merely to draw you out and to see if you are willing and able to defend your point of view. Do not start a debate, yet do not surrender a good position. If a position is worth taking, it is worth defending.

14) Do not be afraid to admit an error in judgment if you are shown to be wrong

The board knows that you are forced to reply without any opportunity for careful consideration. Your answer may be demonstrably wrong. If so, admit it and get on with the interview.

15) Do not dwell at length on your present job

The opening question may relate to your present assignment. Answer the question but do not go into an extended discussion. You are being examined for a *new* job, not your present one. As a matter of fact, try to phrase ALL your answers in terms of the job for which you are being examined.

Basis of Rating

Probably you will forget most of these "do's" and "don'ts" when you walk into the oral interview room. Even remembering them all will not ensure you a passing grade. Perhaps you did not have the qualifications in the first place. But remembering them will help you to put your best foot forward, without treading on the toes of the board members.

Rumor and popular opinion to the contrary notwithstanding, an oral board wants you to make the best appearance possible. They know you are under pressure – but they also want to see how you respond to it as a guide to what your reaction would be under the pressures of the job you seek. They will be influenced by the degree of poise you display, the personal traits you show and the manner in which you respond.

ABOUT THIS BOOK

This book contains tests divided into Examination Sections. Go through each test, answering every question in the margin. We have also attached a sample answer sheet at the back of the book that can be removed and used. At the end of each test look at the answer key and check your answers. On the ones you got wrong, look at the right answer choice and learn. Do not fill in the answers first. Do not memorize the questions and answers, but understand the answer and principles involved. On your test, the questions will likely be different from the samples. Questions are changed and new ones added. If you understand these past questions you should have success with any changes that arise. Tests may consist of several types of questions. We have additional books on each subject should more study be advisable or necessary for you. Finally, the more you study, the better prepared you will be. This book is intended to be the last thing you study before you walk into the examination room. Prior study of relevant texts is also recommended. NLC publishes some of these in our Fundamental Series. Knowledge and good sense are important factors in passing your exam. Good luck also helps. So now study this Passbook, absorb the material contained within and take that knowledge into the examination. Then do your best to pass that exam.

EXAMINATION SECTION

LOGICAL REASONING

The reasoning test assesses how well applicants can read, understand, and apply critical thinking skills to factual situations. Before entering your job, you will receive training that requires reading, understanding, and applying a wealth of detailed, written materials. Although some information must be memorized, much of the information you will use must be learned through independent reasoning. The test is, therefore, designed to select trainees who will be able to handle the academic workload and who will subsequently be able to handle complex reasoning and decision-making situations on the job.

The Logical Reasoning Questions

These sample questions are similar to the questions you will find in actual tests in terms of difficulty and format. Some of the questions in the test will be harder and some will be easier than those shown here.

Some of the questions in this manual deal with topics related to general government business. However, all of the questions in the actual test will deal with topics related to the work performed in entry-level positions. *You should remember, however, that knowledge of job-specific subject matter is **NOT** required to answer correctly the questions in this manual or the questions in the actual test.*

The kind of reading these questions require you to do is different from ordinary reading in which you just follow the general meaning of a series of sentences or paragraphs to see what the writer is saying about the topic. Instead, it is the kind of reading you must do with complex material when you intend to take some action or draw some conclusion based on that material.

This test asks you to make logical conclusions based on facts given in various paragraphs, and answering requires careful reading and focused thought about exactly what is given and what **is not** given. Therefore, you should read each question and the answer choices for each question very carefully before choosing your answer. The information below will give you some suggestions about how to approach this part of the test and some information about how you can improve your reasoning skills.

About the Questions

Reading the Paragraph (The Beginning of the Question)

There may be facts in the paragraph that may not always be true everywhere. However, it is important for testing purposes that you **accept** every fact in the paragraph as given or true. Also remember that, in this part of the test, you are not being judged on your knowledge of facts, but rather on your ability to read and reason on the basis of the facts presented to you.

Example of a Paragraph:

Law enforcement agencies use scientific techniques to identify suspects or to establish guilt. One obvious application of such techniques is the examination of a crime scene. Some substances found at a crime scene yield valuable clues under microscopic examination. Clothing fibers, dirt particles, and even pollen grains may reveal important information to the careful investigator. Nothing can be overlooked because all substances found at a crime scene are potential sources of evidence.

Reading the Question Lead-in

Each paragraph is followed by a lead-in statement that asks you to complete a sentence by choosing one of several phrases (possible answers) labeled (A) to (E). The lead-in sentence may be either positive or negative, as shown in the examples below:

From the information given above, it can be validly concluded that,
or
From the information given above, it CANNOT be validly concluded that,

It is important to focus on the lead-in statement because if you skim over it, you may miss a "**NOT**" and answer that question incorrectly. Positive lead-in statements are followed by four false conclusions (set of possible answers) and one correct conclusion (the correct answer). Your task is to find the correct one. Negative lead-in statements, by contrast, give you four correct conclusions and only one false conclusion; the task in these types of questions is to determine the one conclusion that **cannot** be supported by the facts in the paragraph (the false conclusion). If you do not pay close attention to negative lead-in questions, you could jump to the conclusion that the first correct option you read must be the right answer. The lead-in statement may also limit the possible answers in some way. For example, a lead-in statement such as

"from the information given above, it can be validly concluded that, during a crime scene investigation"

means that there might be different answers based on other times and places, but for the purpose of the test question, only conditions during a crime scene investigation (as described in the lead-in) should be considered.

The lead-in statement is followed by the set of conclusions or possible alternatives from which you will choose the correct answer. There are always five alternatives, which appear as follows:

A) all substances that yield valuable clues under microscopic examination are substances found at a crime scene
B) some potential sources of evidence are substances that yield valuable clues under microscopic examination
C) some substances found at a crime scene are not potential sources of evidence
D) no potential sources of evidence are substances found at a crime scene
E) some substances that yield valuable clues under microscopic examination are not substances found at a crime scene

Reasoning About Categories

Sometimes the information that you work with is based on your knowledge of how things can be categorized or grouped and combined with your knowledge of facts about those categories. You may have information about several categories that can be combined in various ways. You can also draw conclusions from facts that are not true and from facts about different events or indicators that are linked together. To understand these statements better, consider the following situation:

Think of a situation in which you are in charge of searching a vacant building for a missing child. The building has six floors. You have assigned one group to begin searching on the first floor of the building and then to move up to the next higher floor as they complete their search. A second group is sent to the top floor to begin searching there and then to move down as they complete searching. The first two floors of the building once contained a retail store and, therefore, broken glass shelves and metal hooks litter those floors. The next three floors once contained offices and, although they do not have any metal or broken glass on the floors, these floors do have plenty of leftover paper trash everywhere. The top floor used to be a penthouse apartment, and it is the only floor in the building that is still carpeted.

This situation gives you six floors that have in the past been used for three different purposes. There are two groups of searchers with two different search patterns. Within this situation, there are various categories into which information can be sorted. As the searchers report back to you on their progress, your level of certainty will depend on the completeness of the information you receive from them.

For example, if one group leader reports back "We've just finished searching a floor that is carpeted, and the child is not here," you **can** conclude that the child is not on the penthouse apartment level of the building. However, if the other group leader calls to say "We've just finished searching a floor with a lot of glass debris all over the place," you **cannot** conclude that the retail part of the building has been completely searched because the leader only told you about one floor while there were two floors in that category (two floors with glass all over the floor). However, if the leader told you "We've just finished searching two floors full of glass and metal hooks, and we're moving on to search the next floor up, where there seems to be a lot of paper all over," then you **could** conclude that the entire retail section had been searched because you have information that is complete about that category.

As you study the logical reasoning test questions, you must use the type of approach described above to reason about categories of information and draw conclusions through the process of elimination.

Statements Using the Quantifier "All"

One of the biggest mistakes people make when they jump to conclusions without basing them on all the facts is to misinterpret statements beginning with "all." A sentence that begins with the words "all" or "every" gives you information about how two different groups are linked. If a librarian told you "All the books on this set of shelves are about law enforcement," you might be tempted to conclude that all of the library's books on law enforcement were on that set of shelves, but you would be wrong. That sentence simply tells you that the books on those shelves are a subcategory of the category of books on law enforcement. That sentence does **not** tell you anything about where other law enforcement books are located in the library. Therefore, you do not have any information on the rest of that category.

It is easier to recognize the error in this kind of thinking if you consider two linked groups of things that are of very different sizes. Suppose a neighbor describes a children's birthday party at his house, saying "all the children at the party spoke Spanish fluently." It would **not** be correct to conclude that "all people who could speak Spanish fluently attended this birthday party." In this case, it is easy to recognize that "all the children at the party who spoke Spanish fluently" is really a subgroup of the category of "all people who could speak Spanish."

Reasoning From Disproved Facts ("NONE" and "NOT" Statements)

A lot of useful information can be gained when you learn that something is **NOT** true or when you know that one group of things is **NOT** part of a particular category. This is the same as saying that there is no overlap at all between two groups of things. Here, you can draw conclusions about either group as it relates to the other since you can count on the fact that the two groups have no members in common. If you can say "no reptiles are warm-blooded," you can also say "no warm-blooded creatures are reptiles" because you know that the first statement means that there is no overlap between the two categories. Many investigations hinge on negative facts. In the logical reasoning test part, you will see phrases such as "It is not the case that" or "Not all of the" or many words that begin with the prefix "non-." All of these are ways to say that a negative fact has been established.

Sometimes our ordinary speech habits get in the way. Most people would not make a statement such as "Some of the pizza has no pepperoni" unless they are trying to suggest at the same time that some of the pizza does have pepperoni. By contrast, a detective might make a statement such as "some of the bloodstains were not human blood" simply because only part of the samples had come back from the laboratory. The rest of the bloodstains might or might not be human.

As you work through the sample questions and practice test in this manual, think about each negative phrase or term you find. Take care to assume only as much as is definitely indicated by the facts as given, **AND NO MORE.**

LOGICAL REASONING
EVALUATING CONCLUSIONS IN LIGHT OF KNOWN FACTS

EXAMINATION SECTION
TEST 1

DIRECTIONS: For the following questions, select the letter before the statement below which BEST expresses the relationship between the facts and the conclusion. Mark your answer:
- A. The facts prove the conclusion; or
- B. The facts disprove the conclusion; or
- C. The facts neither prove nor disprove the conclusion.

PRINT THE LETTER OF THE CORRECT ANSWER IN THE SPACE AT THE RIGHT.

1. FACTS: Andy types half as fast as Bill. Bill types twice as slow as Charlie. Bill types 60 words a minute.

   CONCLUSION: Charlie types 30 words a minute.

2. FACTS: If Albert gets traded to the Cubs, Chris will have to be traded to the Padres. Albert will avoid being traded only if he hits a home run in his turn at bat.
   If Chris goes to the Padres, Dave will be traded to the Dodgers. Albert strikes out in this crucial at-bat.

   CONCLUSION: Dave gets traded to the Dodgers.

3. FACTS: All beads are forms of jewelry. All jewelry is expensive. Everyone loves expensive beads.

   CONCLUSION: All beads are expensive.

4. FACTS: No shrimp are mussels. Mussels are bivalves. All mussels have shells.

   CONCLUSION: Therefore, no shrimp have shells.

5. FACTS: On their latest diet, Abby, Bea, Celia, and Donna lost a combined total of 260 pounds. Abby lost twice as much as Celia. Celia lost half as much as the woman who lost the most. Donna lost 80 pounds.

   CONCLUSION: Abby lost 100 pounds; Bea, 30; Celia, 50; and Donna, 80.

6. FACTS: Ann's office is two floors above Brenda's.
   Brenda's office is one floor below the only woman in the building whose birthday is today. Sally's office is on the third floor. Ann's office is on the fourth floor.

   CONCLUSION: Today is Ann's birthday.

7. FACTS: Douglas Ave. is perpendicular to Bates St. Bates St. is parallel to Adams Ave. Douglas Ave. is parallel to Charles St. Evans Ave. is parallel to the streets that are perpendicular to Bates St.

   CONCLUSION: Evans Ave. is perpendicular to Douglas Ave.

8. FACTS: There's one out, and Bill is the runner on third base. If Arnie hits the ball hard, Bill will run, but so slowly that he will be out at home plate. The team captain, on second base, will not run unless Arnie hits the ball hard. The captain runs.

   CONCLUSION: Bill is safe.

9. FACTS: Some members of this genus are members of that species. All members of that species are butterflies. Some butterflies are different from others.

   CONCLUSION: Some members of this genus are butterflies.

10. FACTS: Some woodwinds are clarinets. Flutes are not clarinets. All clarinets are beautiful things.

    CONCLUSION: Therefore, all beautiful things are woodwinds.

11. FACTS: Using a grid exactly like the one below, Joe Genius filled in the numbers 1 through 9 in the boxes. Each horizontal, vertical, and diagonal row added up to 15. A different number went in each box.

    CONCLUSION: The number Joe put in the middle box was 6.

12. FACTS: Max, Nick, Pete, and Ollie all bought different colored suits: grey, green, blue, and brown, but not necessarily respectively. Max paid less for his green suit than Nick paid for his suit. Ollie paid twice what Pete paid. Pete paid the same as the man who bought the grey suit. Ollie bought the brown suit.

    CONCLUSION: Ollie paid the most.

13. FACTS: Four people (Alice, Bob, Carol, and Dave) are sitting at a square table, discussing their favorite sports. Bob sits directly across from the jogger. Carol sits to the right of the basketball player. Alice sits across from Dave. The golfer sits to the left of the tennis player. A man sits on Dave's right.

    CONCLUSION: Dave plays golf.

14. FACTS: An employer decided to offer a job to everyone who scored higher than 50 on an exam. Alice scored 20. Betty scored lower than Carol, but more than twice as high as Alice.

    CONCLUSION: Of the three women, only Carol was offered the job.

15. FACTS: If Camille's squirrel has rabies and the squirrel bites Casey's cat, the squirrel will have to be caught and the cat will get rabies. If the cat has had rabies shots within the last two years, the cat will not get rabies. Casey's cat did not get rabies.

    CONCLUSION: Casey's cat has had rabies shots within the last two years.

    15._____

16. FACTS: Sally will file a grievance only if Bill fires her. If Laura tells Frank the whole story, Frank will tell it to Bill. If Bill hears the whole story, he will not fire Sally. Laura tells Fred the whole story.

    CONCLUSION: Sally files a grievance.

    16._____

17. FACTS: If Alice leaves work early, Barb has to work late, and Barb wants to go to the game tonight. The singing of the National Anthem always precedes the game. Carl calls Alice and asks her out to dinner. Due to a thunderstorm, the singing of the National Anthem gets delayed. If Alice goes out to dinner with Carl, she will have to leave work early so she can go home and turn off her crockpot. Alice accepts Carl's invitation.

    CONCLUSION: Barb misses the first inning of the game.

    17._____

18. FACTS: Earl thinks of any whole number from 1 through 10. Because she is using the most efficient system, Eva absolutely guarantees Earl that she can correctly guess the number he's thinking of in five questions or less. Eva asks Earl a series of *yes/no* questions and guesses the number in five questions or less every time. Earl and Eva agree to play the game again in the exact same way, except that he will think of a whole number from 1 through 6.

    CONCLUSION: Using the same system, four is the absolute highest number of *yes/no* questions that Eva will need to ask in order to guess the number that Earl is thinking of this time.

    18._____

19. FACTS: Lois will cook dinner today only if Ted, Robbie, and Jennifer are all home by 6 P.M. Robbie will come home by 6 P.M. only if band practice ends early. If Ted plays Softball after work, he will take Jennifer with him, and they will not be home by 6 P.M. Band practice ends early today.

    CONCLUSION: Lois cooks dinner today.

    19._____

20. FACTS: Three card players each start with $10. Each round they play has two losers and one winner. The losers in each round have to give the winner $2 apiece. Chuck wins the first and third rounds; Bruce wins the second. At the end of the third round, Artie proposes that they change the rules so that the losers each have to give the winner half their accumulated money. They agree, play one more round, and Artie wins it.

    CONCLUSION: At the end of the fourth round, Chuck has less money than Artie.

    20._____

21. FACTS: No part-time workers at this plant get paid vacations. All cleaners at this plant are part-time workers. Joe gets a paid vacation.

    CONCLUSION: All cleaners at this plant get paid vacations.

    21._____

22. FACTS: If Myles breaks the lamp, Lucy will scream. If Tom finds Rachel spraying Windex into the cat's dish, he'll scream. If Geoffrey doesn't hear from the French soon, he'll scream. Tom screams.

    22._____

CONCLUSION: Myles broke the lamp.

23. FACTS: If Tina goes to the store, Ike will go with her. If Ike goes to the store, he will buy doughnuts. If Dick cleans the house, Sally will go to the store. If Sally goes to the store, Tina will go with her. Dick cleans the house.

    CONCLUSION: Ike buys doughnuts.

24. FACTS: If Joe passes the test, Jill won't apply for the job. If Jill applies for the job, she'll get it. If Jill doesn't apply for the job, Jeanne will be annoyed. Joe passes the test.

    CONCLUSION: Jeanne gets annoyed.

25. FACTS: Mary, Debbie, May, and Joan are the only people waiting for the photocopier to be fixed. When it's fixed, Debbie has to use it first because she's doing work for the boss. Joan has to use it right after the person who's been waiting the longest. The person who has the most work to copy gets to use the machine second. May has been waiting the longest. The person who has been waiting longest is not the person who has the most work to copy.

    CONCLUSION: Joan gets to use the photocopier third.

KEY (CORRECT ANSWERS)

1. B
2. A
3. A
4. C
5. C

6. B
7. B
8. B
9. A
10. C

11. B
12. A
13. A
14. C
15. C

16. C
17. C
18. A
19. C
20. A

21. B
22. C
23. A
24. A
25. B

SOLUTIONS

1. **CORRECT ANSWER: B**
This is an easy problem if you read it carefully. The third sentence says that Bill types 60 words a minute; the second sentence says that Bill types twice as slow as Charlie. If Bill types twice as slow as Charlie, then Charlie types twice as fast as Bill, or 2 x 60. This means that Charlie types 120 words a minute, not 30 words a minute. These two sentences alone are all you need to disprove the conclusion; the first sentence is just a decoy. If you had *fallen for it* and misread the paragraph, you would most likely have chosen A. You probably would have skimmed the second sentence and assumed that it said *twice as fast*, just because the first sentence said *half as fast*.

2. **CORRECT ANSWER: A**
This question may look more difficult than it is because the facts are thrown together haphazardly. Many of these logic questions present the *facts* in a very strange fashion. No one would ever talk like this in real life - at least not if they wanted to be understood. The point, of course, is to see how well you can sift through these things, avoid the pitfalls, and find the *truth* of the matter. If you approach a question carefully and attack it systematically, you will usually find that it is not really all that difficult. In this case, by studying the facts, you can see that Albert gets traded. He needs a home run to avoid being traded (sentence 2), but he strikes out in his at-bat (sentence 4). You can assume that this is the at-bat that determines his future because of the way the fourth sentence is worded. It uses the words, *this crucial at-bat.* Knowing the sad truth that he's been traded, you can then trace the chain of events: Chris goes to the Padres (sentence 1), which means that Dave goes to the Dodgers (sentence 3). So the conclusion is, indeed, proved by the facts given to us.

3. **CORRECT ANSWER: A**
This is a classic form of logic problem, and, like question 2, it doesn't correspond to reality. We all know perfectly well that some beads are cheap, but that has NO bearing on this problem. You often have to let go of your common sense and experience when doing problems like these. Just stick to the facts as they are stated in the problem. The first two sentences are given as facts, and they are enough to prove the conclusion that *all beads are expensive*. In any problem where you are told that a given fact is all-inclusive, such as that *all A are B,* you can just substitute A for B in any other factual sentence in the problem. What is true of B is true of A. Therefore, when you come across another all-inclusive *truth,* such as *all B are C,* you know that *all A are C* must be true too.
Here are two examples. Although only one corresponds to reality as we know it, they both follow the logic formula we've outlined above, and so both are *true* according to logic.

      All dogs (A) are mammals (B).
      All mammals (B) have backbones (C).
      All dogs (A) have backbones (C).

      All apples (A) are bananas (B).
      All bananas (B) have yellow skins (C).
      All apples (A) have yellow skins (C).

Note that this does not work in reverse. All bananas aren't necessarily apples, all things with yellow skins aren't necessarily bananas or apples, and all mammals aren't necessarily dogs. Don't worry if this is confusing to you. The key here is to know the formula and not think about it too much in terms of reality.

In this problem, the A is the beads, the B is the jewelry, and the C is expensive.

4. CORRECT ANSWER: C
This looks a lot like the previous question, but, in fact, the sentences show no relationship between shrimp and shells. You can eliminate the second sentence because it has nothing at all to do with the conclusion. Of the two remaining sentences, one says that mussels have shells, the other says that no shrimp are mussels. This doesn't tell us that no shrimp have shells because it is not really telling us anything about how these two animals compare with each other on this issue. It's as if we said, *all boys like sports* and *no boys are girls.* These statements don't tell us whether girls like sports. They tell us that boys and girls are different, but we don't know how different they are. Are they completely different, or do they have things in common? Is liking sports one of the ways they differ or one of the ways they are alike?

For this reason, there is also nothing in the question to show that shrimp do have shells. Here we have another case where common sense can get you into trouble. You may want to choose answer B, simply because you know that the conclusion is false. But you are not being asked whether the conclusion is true or false; you are being asked whether it is proved true or false by the facts as given. If sentence 3 had said, *only mussels have shells,* then the facts would prove the conclusion, even if that doesn't correspond to reality. But as it is, the facts neither prove nor disprove the conclusion.

5. CORRECT ANSWER: C
This is a tricky one. You may have added all the pounds in the conclusion, and been relieved to find that they totaled the 260 pounds mentioned in the first sentence. You would have been tricked into picking A because the numbers checked out. But it doesn't matter that the numbers match because the problem here is to decide whether the facts prove that those are the exact number of pounds each woman lost. And the facts show that, without knowing Bea's weight loss, we're sure of only one figure - Donna's 80-pound weight loss. This is shown below:

NAME	AMOUNT LOST
Abby	2 x Celia
Bea	?
Celia	1/2 of Abby
Donna	80

You may have tried to work the problem by assuming that Donna's 80 pounds was the highest amount lost because that clue is contained in the problem. If Donna's 80 pounds were the greatest weight loss, Celia would have lost 40 pounds because sentence 3 says that Celia lost half of the greatest amount lost. But this creates a problem because it would mean that Abby also lost 80. Sentence 2 says Abby lost twice what Celia lost. And Abby COULDN'T have lost 80 pounds because that would mean that two women (Abby and Donna) lost the most. This is impossible because sentence 3 says Celia lost half as much as the woman (not women) who lost the most. So the greatest amount lost must have been more than 80 pounds, and Abby must have been the one who lost it. All we know, then, is the following: Donna lost 80 pounds, the greatest amount lost was more than 80 pounds, Celia's amount was half the greatest amount, and Abby lost more than 80 pounds. As long as all these conditions are met, Bea's loss might be any amount that makes up the difference between 260 and the others' total weight loss. For example, the losses could have been:

Abby	84		Abby	90		Abby	94
Bea	54	OR	Bea	45	OR	Bea	39
Celia	42		Celia	45		Celia	47
Donna	80		Donna	80		Donna	80
	260			260			260

Or many other possible combinations. The facts simply don't give us enough information to either prove or disprove that the amounts given in the conclusion are the actual amounts each woman lost. That's why the correct answer is C.

6. **CORRECT ANSWER: B**
To see why B is the correct answer, it is helpful to draw a diagram of the floors. We know that Ann is on Four (sentence 4) and that Sally is on Three (sentence 3). If Ann is two floors above Brenda (sentence 1), Brenda must be on Two. Now we can draw:

```
Ann --------------(4)
Sally ------------(3)
Brenda -----------(2)
```

So, if Brenda is one floor below the birthday-girl (sentence 2), today must be Sally's birthday, not Ann's.

7. **CORRECT ANSWER: B**
Here, you need to know what <u>perpendicular</u> and <u>parallel</u> mean. If you do, a simple diagram should show you that the facts disprove the conclusion. Perpendicular streets are those at right angles to one another, like the two lines in a plus sign (+). Parallel streets are those that run in the same direction, never touching - like the two l's in the word <u>all</u>. The first three facts tell us that the streets look like this:

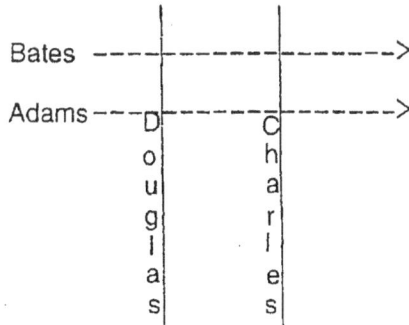

If Evans is parallel to the streets that are perpendicular to Bates (sentence 4), then Evans itself must be perpendicular to Bates. The completed diagram now looks like this:

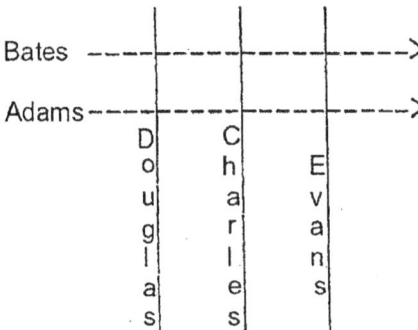

This diagram graphically shows that Evans is NOT perpendicular to Douglas, but parallel to it. The facts, then, disprove the conclusion.

8. CORRECT ANSWER: B
   If you start from the last fact given in this problem and work backwards, you will be able to find the cause of each event. This will enable you to either prove or disprove the conclusion. In this case, since the last fact says that the captain ran, that must have been because Arnie hit the ball hard (sentence 3). Even though Arnie hit the ball hard, Bill is out because Bill is so slow that he will be out at home plate (sentence 2). This disproves the conclusion, which says he is safe.

9. CORRECT ANSWER: A
   This is an easy problem if you translate the facts into a picture. First of all, ignore sentence 3, which has nothing to do with the problem. Now, draw a circle to represent all the members of this genus (sentence 1). Next, draw a smaller circle to represent the members of that species (sentence 1). You may know that a species is a subgroup of a genus, just as *semi-precious* is a subgroup of gems, or hardwoods is a subgroup of trees. For this reason, the *species* circle should be contained entirely within the *genus* circle. The problem doesn't tell you this about genus and species, but you don't need to know it to answer the question correctly. You could simply place the smaller circle partially in and partially out of the larger circle. No matter which way you portray the relationship, some members of the genus will belong to that species. You can see this in the diagrams below. Since all members of that species are butterflies (sentence 2), the *species* circle also represents butterflies.

Not <u>all</u> members of this genus are butterflies; this is demonstrated by the fact that there is plenty of room inside the *genus* circle for other, non-butterfly critters. But the picture clearly shows that <u>some</u> members of the genus are butterflies, as the conclusion states.

10. **CORRECT ANSWER: C**

The facts prove only that some woodwinds (those that are clarinets) are beautiful things; they do not prove that all beautiful things are woodwinds. If you draw circles to represent *beautiful things* and *clarinets,* the latter would have to be a smaller circle inside the former, since all clarinets are beautiful things (sentence 3).

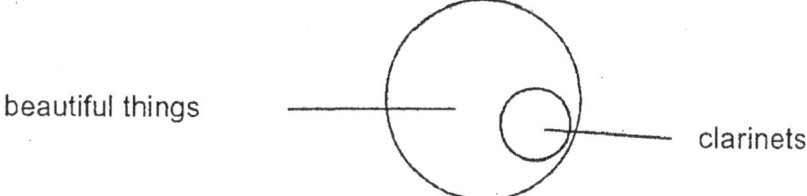

But where does the *woodwind* circle go? All the facts tell us is that some of its members are clarinets. We don't know whether it's bigger, smaller, or the same size as the circle of *beautiful things*. It could look like the following:

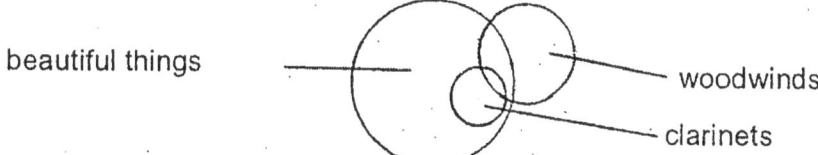

That way, there could be plenty of beautiful things that are not woodwinds, some beautiful things that are woodwinds and clarinets, and some woodwinds that are beautiful things but not clarinets. And the conclusion would be false.
OR, the *woodwinds* circle could be identical to the *beautiful things* circle:

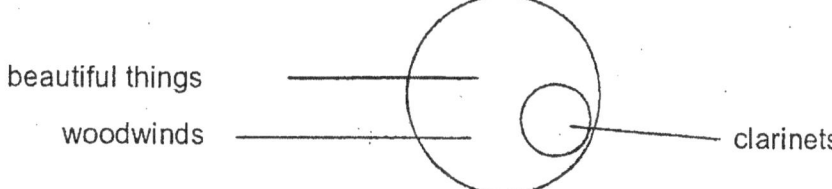

making the conclusion true.
You may have circled answer B, simply because the conclusion is obviously a false statement. But remember, the question is not whether the conclusion is true or false; it's whether it is proved or disproved by the facts given. In this case, it is neither proved nor disproved by the facts. Sentence 2, incidentally, is irrelevant, since the rest of the problem has nothing to do with flutes.

11. CORRECT ANSWER: B
    You could use a trial-and-error approach to this problem, but it would be very time-consuming. As you worked with this problem, you may have realized that, since the number in the middle box gets added to every other number, you can solve the problem more easily by putting 6 into the diagram and adding the larger numbers to it to see if it's workable. After placing 6 in the center, you can see there is nowhere to put 9. The horizontal, vertical, and diagonal rows must add up to 15, but wherever you try to put 9, you will have a row that adds up to more than 15. Since 9 + 6 = 15 and 0 is not one of the options, there is no number that can be put in the third box in the row.

    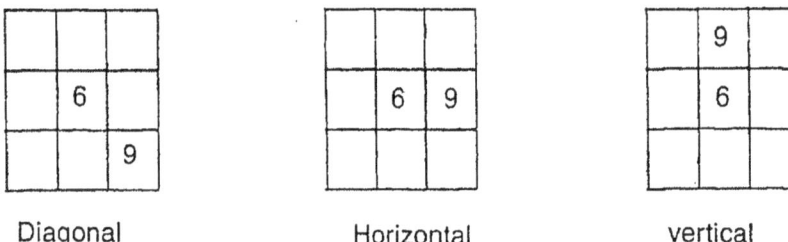

    Diagonal   Horizontal   vertical

    So, 6 cannot be the number in the middle box; it's too big. The facts disprove the conclusion.

12. CORRECT ANSWER: A
    The first sentence in this problem says that these men bought various colored suits, but not necessarily <u>respectively</u>. This means that the first man (Max) didn't necessarily buy the first color suit (grey), the second man (Nick) didn't necessarily buy the second color suit (green), and so on. <u>Respectively</u> means *in the same order.*
    At first glance, this problem looks impossible, but it can be simplified by drawing a chart to show what we *know* about each person:

NAME	PAID	FOR THIS COLOR SUIT
Max	less than Nick	green
Nick	same as Pete	grey (not green, brown or blue)
Pete	same as Nick	blue (not grey, green or brown)
Ollie	2x Nick; 2x Pete	brown

    Sentence 2 says Max's suit is green, and sentence 5 says Ollie's is brown, but how do we know Pete's is blue? Well, sentence 4 indicates that someone other than Pete bought the grey one. That means Nick got the grey one. Since the grey, green, and brown suits are all accounted for, the blue one must be Pete's.

    Now, all we need to know is who paid the most! Ollie paid twice what Pete paid (sentence 3). This means that he also paid twice what Nick paid because Pete paid the same as the man who bought the grey suit (sentence 4) - and Nick bought the grey suit. So the highest-payer can't be Nick or Pete; it must either be Ollie or Max. But sentence 2 says Max paid <u>less</u> than Nick. So the highest-payer must be Ollie, as proved by the facts given.

13. CORRECT ANSWER: A
    The man sitting on Dave's right (sentence 6) has to be Bob because he's the only other man in the group. Alice sits across from Dave (sentence 4). This means that Carol must be sitting across from Bob. From this information, you can draw a diagram of the table and the people seated at it:

    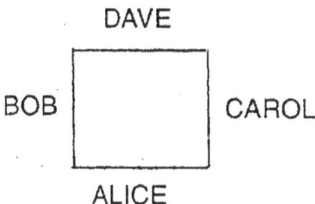

    Now all you need to know is whether Dave plays golf. It may help keep everything straight if you put the name of the sport next to the name of the proper person as you figure out each one. Here, we have abbreviated each sport using a lower-case initial (*j* for jogging, *g* for golf, and so on). Since Carol sits to the right of the basketball player (sentence 3), Alice must play basketball. (Remember, it's not Carol's right; it's the basketball player's right. This confuses some people.) Since Bob sits across from the jogger (sentence 2), Carol must jog. After adding this information, your diagram would look like this:

    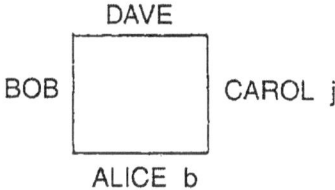

    At this point, all you need to know is: Does Bob golf and Dave play tennis, or is it the other way around? A quick trial-and-error produces the answer. Sentence 5 says the golfer sits to the left of the tennis player. If Dave played tennis, would this be true? No. So, it must be Bob who's the tennis player, and Dave who's the golfer. The conclusion is thus proved by the facts. If you have spatial problems, you might want to twist the diagram around to see this more clearly.

    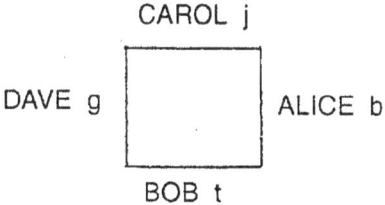

14. CORRECT ANSWER: C
    To visualize this problem it is helpful to draw a small chart, showing what we know about each woman's score.

NAME	SCORE
Carol	higher than Betty

Betty	higher than 40 (according to sentence 3 she scored more than twice as high as Alice
Alice	20

From this chart, we can see that Carol's score could have been <u>any</u> number higher than 41. It could have been 50, or 65, or 92–in which case she would have scored high enough to be hired. But it also could have been 42, or 43, or 47 – in which case she would not have scored high enough. So, we can't prove that Carol was offered the job, but we can't prove that she wasn't either. In addition, we can't prove that Carol was the only one who was offered the job. We know Alice didn't get an offer (with a score of 20), but we don't know about Betty. She could have gotten anything above 40. So, the facts here neither prove nor disprove the conclusion.

15. CORRECT ANSWER: C
    This is a sneaky little question. If you read it quickly, you might have thought it was easy. The cat didn't get rabies (sentence 3), so the cat had had its rabies shots within the last two years (sentence 2). But perhaps the cat didn't get rabies because the squirrel never bit it, or perhaps the squirrel never had rabies to begin with. The first sentence says, *If Camille's squirrel has rabies"* and *(if) the squirrel bites Casey's cat...the cat will get rabies.* (The second *if* is implied by the structure of the sentence.) Nothing in this paragraph ever tells us that the squirrel had rabies or that the squirrel bit the cat. As we said - sneaky. Since you don't know why the cat didn't get rabies, you can't prove that it was spared because it had had its shots, and you can't disprove it either. Therefore, C is the only possible answer.

16. CORRECT ANSWER: C
    This is another sneaky question. (The exams haven't used this kind of trick lately, but we wanted to give you practice – just in case.) If you didn't read the problem carefully, you might have chosen B. You would have thought that Laura told Frank (sentence 4), who told Bill (sentence 2), who chose not to fire Sally (sentence 3). Since Sally didn't get fired, she didn't file a grievance (sentence 1). The only problem is that Laura told <u>Fred</u>, not Frank, and we have no way of knowing how Fred fits into this crew. He could have told Frank, thereby setting in motion the cycle above and preventing Sally from getting fired. In that case, the conclusion would be false. Or he could have not told anyone, Sally would have gotten fired, she would have filed a grievance, and the conclusion would have been true. You just don't know, so C is the only option.

17. CORRECT ANSWER: C
    Obviously, if the *pre-game* song gets delayed, the game will also be delayed, but we don't know for how long. We also don't know how late Barb had to work. (We know that she <u>did</u> have to work late, because of sentences 1, 5, and 6.) For all we know, the game may have been delayed for an hour due to the storm, and Barb may have had to work only a half hour later than usual–thereby not missing any of the game at all. In questions of this type, it is always good to work backwards from the conclusion and try to see if there is a cause of that conclusion contained in the facts. In this case, although we can find a cause for Barb's having to work late (Alice's acceptance of Carl's invitation), we can find nothing that would <u>necessarily</u> cause Barb to miss the first inning of the game.

18. CORRECT ANSWER: A
The conclusion seems likely because it only takes Eva five tries to guess a number from 1 through 10. The most efficient way to guess is to eliminate half of all possible numbers with each guess. When the number is from 1 through 10, the first question should be, *Is the number you're thinking of 6 or more?* The answer to that question, whether it's yes or no, will eliminate five numbers - half of all the numbers Earl could possibly be thinking of. Let's say Earl said yes. The second question would be, *Is it 8 or more?* That answer will eliminate two or three of the five remaining possible numbers. No matter what range of numbers Earl wants to use, whether it be 1 through 50, 1 through 100, or whatever, Eva could use this method until she narrows the answers down to one possible number. (We can assume that she uses this method because sentence 2 says she is using the most efficient method.)

For the range 1 through 6, then, you can see that four is the highest number of guesses she will need using this system. The most she can be sure of eliminating with one guess is 3 numbers. *(Is the number you're thinking of 4 or more?)* At that point, she *may* need as many as three more guesses to eliminate the two remaining wrong numbers one by one and then to *guess* the right number. Since this is four guesses, the facts prove the conclusion.

19. CORRECT ANSWER: C
Here is a case in which it is clear that certain facts are missing. You know from sentences 4 and 2 that Robbie is home in time for Lois to make dinner, but what about Ted and Jennifer? Nowhere in the facts does it say whether or not Ted played softball after work. Since sentence 1 says Lois will cook only if all three are home by 6 P.M., we simply don't have enough information to either prove or disprove the conclusion.

20. CORRECT ANSWER: A
Unless you are excellent in math, just about the only way to figure this one out is to set up a grid showing the amount of money each player has after each round. After setting up such a grid, the answer can be found quite easily.

		ARTIE $10	BRUCE $10	CHUCK $10
AFTER ROUND	#1	$8	$8	$14
	#2	$6	$12	$12
	#3	$4	$10	$16
	#4	$17	$5	$8

Chuck won the first round (sentence 4). Since everyone started with $10 (sentence 1), you can see that after Round #1, each loser would be out $2 (sentences 2 and 3), bringing their totals down to $8 each. Chuck, on the other hand, would be up to $14, having collected $2 from each of the two losers. The second line of the grid shows the situation after Round #2, which was won by Bruce (sentence 4). The third line shows the situation after Round #3, when Chuck is way ahead (sentence 4). Likewise, the fourth line shows the situation after Round #4, when the rules had been changed and Artie won (sentences 5 and 6). Since each of the other two had to give him half their money (sentence 5), he collected $5 from Bruce and $8 from Chuck. His total of $17 was $9 more than

Chuck had at that point. So, the conclusion that Artie ended up with more money than Chuck is proven by the facts given.

21. CORRECT ANSWER: B
The facts prove just the opposite of the conclusion. If <u>all</u> cleaners work part-time (sentence 2), and <u>no</u> part-timers get paid vacations (sentence 1), then <u>no</u> cleaners can get paid vacations. Where *facts* are given in the form, *No A are B, and all C are A,* you can simply substitute C for A, and that will prove that no C are B. (This is much like question 3, except the first fact is all-exclusive rather than all-inclusive. It excludes rather than includes all of something. See the explanation to question 3, if this is not clear.) In this case, *A* is the part-timers, *B* represents recipients of paid vacations, and *C* is cleaners. The facts disprove the conclusion. Since we don't know what Joe's occupation is, sentence 3 is irrelevant to this problem.

22. CORRECT ANSWER: C
In this case, no amount of *following the trail* of facts will lead you to the conclusion given because there is no trail. No fact implies, or leads to, any other; they are simply a collection of statements with no relationship to one another. The facts neither prove nor disprove the conclusion.

23. CORRECT ANSWER: A
Unlike question 22, this question lends itself to *following the trail* of facts. As we've noticed earlier, a good place to begin the trail is with the last fact. It follows from sentence 5 (Dick cleans the house) that Sally goes to the store (sentence 3), which means that Tina also goes to the store (sentence 4). This, in turn, means that Ike goes (sentence 1), and buys the doughnuts (sentence 2). The facts here prove the conclusion.

24. CORRECT ANSWER: A
To decide whether the facts prove the conclusion, you must understand what each fact means. The fact that Joe passed the test (sentence 4) means that Jill didn't apply for the job (sentence 1). Knowing this, all you have to do is reread sentence 3 to see that Jeanne does, indeed, get annoyed. Sentence 2 is not needed to solve this problem, although it may explain why Jeanne got annoyed.

25. CORRECT ANSWER: B
It is helpful to make a list of who's using the machine when, and to fill in the facts you're given. Then you can gradually deduce more information, until you can see whether the conclusion is proved, disproved, or neither. Sentence 2 says Debbie goes first, so your list, at the start, would look something like this:

First - Debbie
Second - ?
Third - ?
Last - ?

It is clear from sentences 3 and 5 that Joan immediately follows May. This also means that Joan cannot be second, May cannot be last, and Mary cannot be third. You may then wish to enter the possibilities to your list:

First - Debbie
Second - May or Mary

15 (#1)

       Third - May or Joan
       Last - Joan or Mary

Now, all we need to know is: Does May go second? If so, the conclusion is proved by the facts; if not, it's disproved. We know from sentence 4 that the person with the most work goes second. That person can't be May, however, because May has been waiting longest (sentence 5), and the longest-waiter is not the person with the most work (sentence 6). So, Debbie is first, Mary is second, May is third, Joan is fourth, and the conclusion is disproved.

       First - Debbie
       Second - Mary
       Third - May
       Last - Joan

EVALUATING CONCLUSIONS IN LIGHT OF KNOWN FACTS
EXAMINATION SECTION
TEST 1

DIRECTIONS: Each question or incomplete statement is followed by several suggested answers or completions. Select the one that BEST answers the question or completes the statement. *PRINT THE LETTER OF THE CORRECT ANSWER IN THE SPACE AT THE RIGHT.*

Questions 1-9.

DIRECTIONS: In Questions 1 through 9, you will read a set of facts and a conclusion drawn from them. The conclusion may be valid or invalid, based on the facts. It is your task to determine the validity of the conclusion.
For each question, select the letter before the statement that BEST expresses the relationship between the given facts and the conclusion that has been drawn from them. Your choices are:
   A. The facts prove the conclusion.
   B. The facts disprove the conclusion; or
   C. The facts neither prove nor disprove the conclusion.

1. FACTS: Lauren must use Highway 29 to get to work. Lauren has a meeting today at 9:00 A.M. If she misses the meeting, Lauren will probably lose a major account. Highway 29 is closed all day today for repairs.

   CONCLUSION: Lauren will not be able to get to work.

   A. The facts prove the conclusion.
   B. The facts disprove the conclusion.
   C. The facts neither prove nor disprove the conclusion.

   1.____

2. FACTS: The Tumbleweed Follies, a traveling burlesque show, is looking for a new line dancer. The position requires both singing and dancing skills. If the show cannot fill the position by Friday, it will begin to look for a magician to fill the time slot currently held by the line dancers. Willa, who wants to audition for the line dancing position, can sing, but cannot dance.

   CONCLUSION: Willa is qualified to audition for the part of line dancer.

   A. The facts prove the conclusion.
   B. The facts disprove the conclusion.
   C. The facts neither prove nor disprove the conclusion.

   2.____

3. FACTS: Terry owns two dogs, Spike and Stan. One of the dogs is short-haired and has blue eyes. One dog as a pink nose. The blue-eyed dog never barks. One of the dogs has white fur on its paws. Sam has long hair.

   CONCLUSION: Spike never barks.

   A. The facts prove the conclusion.
   B. The facts disprove the conclusion.
   C. The facts neither prove nor disprove the conclusion.

4. FACTS: No science teachers are members of the PTA. Some English teachers are members of the PTA. Some English teachers in the PTA also wear glasses. Every PTA member is required to sit on the dunking stool at the student carnival except for those who wear glasses, who will be exempt. Those who are exempt, however, will have to officiate the hamster races. All of the English teachers in the PTA who do not wear glasses are married.

   CONCLUSION: All the married English teachers in the PTA will set on the dunking stool at the student carnival.

   A. The facts prove the conclusion.
   B. The facts disprove the conclusion.
   C. The facts neither prove nor disprove the conclusion.

5. FACTS: If the price of fuel is increased and sales remain constant, oil company profits will increase. The price of fuel was increased, and market experts project that sales levels are likely to be maintained.

   CONCLUSION: The price of fuel will increase.

   A. The facts prove the conclusion.
   B. The facts disprove the conclusion.
   C. The facts neither prove nor disprove the conclusion.

6. FACTS: Some members of the gymnastics team are double-jointed, and some members of the gymnastics team ae also on the lacrosse team. Some double-jointed members of the gymnastics team are also coaches. All gymnastics team members perform floor exercises, except the coaches. All the double-jointed members of the gymnastics team who are not coaches are freshmen.

   CONCLUSION: Some double-jointed freshmen are coaches.

   A. The facts prove the conclusion.
   B. The facts disprove the conclusion.
   C. The facts neither prove nor disprove the conclusion.

7. FACTS: Each member of the International Society speaks at least one foreign language, but no member speaks more than four foreign languages. Five members speak Spanish; three speak Mandarin; four speak French; four speak German; and five speak a foreign language other than Spanish, Mandarin, French, or German.

   CONCLUSION: The lowest possible number of members in the International Society is eight.

   A. The facts prove the conclusion.
   B. The facts disprove the conclusion.
   C. The facts neither prove nor disprove the conclusion.

8. FACTS: Mary keeps seven cats in her apartment. Only three of the cats will eat the same kind of food. Mary wants to keep at least one extra bag of each kind of food.

   CONCLUSION: The minimum number of bags Mary will need to keep as extra is 7.

   A. The facts prove the conclusion.
   B. The facts disprove the conclusion.
   C. The facts neither prove nor disprove the conclusion.

9. FACTS: In Ed and Marie's exercise group, everyone likes the treadmill or the stationary bicycle, or both, but Ed does not like the stationary bicycle. Marie has not expressed a preference, but spends most of her time on the stationary bicycle.

   CONCLUSION: Everyone in the group who does not like the treadmill likes the stationary bicycle.

   A. The facts prove the conclusion.
   B. The facts disprove the conclusion.
   C. The facts neither prove nor disprove the conclusion.

Questions 10-17.

DIRECTIONS: Questions 10 through 17 are based on the following reading passage. It is not your knowledge of the particular topic that is being tested, but your ability to reason based on what you have read. The passage is likely to detail several proposed courses of action and factors affecting these proposals. The reading passage is followed by a conclusion or outcome based on the facts in the passage, or a description of a decision taken regarding the situation. The conclusion is followed by a number of statements that have a possible connection to the conclusion. For each statement, you are to determine whether:

A. The statement proves the conclusion.
B. The statement supports the conclusion but does not prove it.
C. The statement disproves the conclusion.
D. The statement weakens the conclusion but does not disprove it.
E. The statement has no relevance to the conclusion.

Remember that the conclusion after the passage is to be accepted as the outcome of what actually happened, and that you are being asked to evaluate the impact each statement would have had on the conclusion.

PASSAGE

The Owyhee Mission School District's Board of Directors is hosting a public meeting to debate the merits of the proposed abolition of all bilingual education programs within the district. The group that has made the proposal believes the programs, which teach immigrant children academic subjects in their native language until they have learned English well enough to join mainstream classes, inhibit the ability of students to acquire English quickly and succeed in school and in the larger American society. Such programs, they argue, are also a wasteful drain on the district's already scant resources.

At the meeting, several teachers and parents stand to speak out against the proposal. The purpose of an education, they say, should be to build upon, rather than dismantle, a minority child's language and culture. By teaching children in academic subjects in their native tongues, while simultaneously offering English language instruction, schools can meet the goals of learning English and progressing through academic subjects along with their peers.

Hiram Nguyen, a representative of the parents whose children are currently enrolled in bilingual education, stands at the meeting to express the parents' wishes. The parents have been polled, he says, and are overwhelmingly of the opinion that while language and culture are important to them, they are not things that will disappear from the students' lives if they are no longer taught in the classroom. The most important issue for the parents is whether their children will succeed in school and be competitive in the larger American society. If bilingual education can be demonstrated to do that, then the parents are in favor of continuing it.

At the end of the meeting, a proponent of the plan, Oscar Ramos, stands to clarify some misconceptions about the proposal. It does not call for a "sink or swim" approach, he says, but allows for an interpreter to be present in mainstream classes to explain anything a student finds too complex or confusing.

The last word of the meeting is given to Delia Cruz, a bilingual teacher at one of the district's elementary schools. A student is bound to find anything complex or confusing, she says, if it is spoken in a language he has never heard before. It is more wasteful to place children in classrooms where they don't understand anything, she says, than it is to try to teach them something useful as they are learning the English language.

CONCLUSION: After the meeting, the Owyhee Mission School District's Board of Directors votes to terminate all the district's bilingual education programs at the end of the current academic year, but to maintain the current level of funding to each of the schools that have programs cut.

5 (#1)

10. A poll conducted by the *Los Angeles Times* at approximately the same time as the Board's meeting indicated that 75% of the people were opposed to bilingual education; among Latinos, opposition was 84%.
    A. The statement proves the conclusion.
    B. The statement supports the conclusion but does not prove it.
    C. The statement disproves the conclusion.
    D. The statement weakens the conclusion but does not disprove it.
    E. The statement has no relevance to the conclusion.

10.____

11. Of all the studies connected on bilingual education programs, 64% indicate that students learned English grammar better in "sink or swim" classes without any special features than they did in bilingual education classes.
    A. The statement proves the conclusion.
    B. The statement supports the conclusion but does not prove it.
    C. The statement disproves the conclusion.
    D. The statement weakens the conclusion but does not disprove it.
    E. The statement has no relevance to the conclusion.

11.____

12. In the academic year that begins after the Board's vote, Montgomery Burns Elementary, an Owyhee Mission District school, launches a new bilingual program for the children of Somali immigrants.
    A. The statement proves the conclusion.
    B. The statement supports the conclusion but does not prove it.
    C. The statement disproves the conclusion.
    D. The statement weakens the conclusion but does not disprove it.
    E. The statement has no relevance to the conclusion.

12.____

13. In the previous academic year, under severe budget restraints, the Owyhee Mission District cut all physical education, music, and art classes, but its funding for bilingual education classes increased by 18%.
    A. The statement proves the conclusion.
    B. The statement supports the conclusion but does not prove it.
    C. The statement disproves the conclusion.
    D. The statement weakens the conclusion but does not disprove it.
    E. The statement has no relevance to the conclusion.

13.____

14. Before the Board votes, a polling consultant conducts randomly sampled assessments of immigrant students who enrolled in Owyhee District schools at a time when they did not speak any English at all. Ten years after graduating from high school, 44% of those who received bilingual education were professionals – doctors, lawyers, educators, engineers, etc. Of those who did not receive bilingual education, 38% were professionals.
    A. The statement proves the conclusion.
    B. The statement supports the conclusion but does not prove it.
    C. The statement disproves the conclusion.
    D. The statement weakens the conclusion but does not disprove it.
    E. The statement has no relevance to the conclusion.

14.____

15. Over the past several years, the scores of Owyhee District students have gradually declined, and enrollment numbers have followed as anxious parents transferred their children to other schools or applied for a state-funded voucher program.
    A. The statement proves the conclusion.
    B. The statement supports the conclusion but does not prove it.
    C. The statement disproves the conclusion.
    D. The statement weakens the conclusion but does not disprove it.
    E. The statement has no relevance to the conclusion.

15._____

16. California and Massachusetts, two of the most liberal states in the country, have each passed ballot measures banning bilingual education in public schools.
    A. The statement proves the conclusion.
    B. The statement supports the conclusion but does not prove it.
    C. The statement disproves the conclusion.
    D. The statement weakens the conclusion but does not disprove it.
    E. The statement has no relevance to the conclusion.

16._____

17. In the academic year that begins after the Board's vote, no Owyhee Mission Schools are conducting bilingual instruction.
    A. The statement proves the conclusion.
    B. The statement supports the conclusion but does not prove it.
    C. The statement disproves the conclusion.
    D. The statement weakens the conclusion but does not disprove it.
    E. The statement has no relevance to the conclusion.

17._____

Questions 18-25.

DIRECTIONS: Questions 18 through 25 each provide four factual statements and a conclusion based on these statements. After reading the entire question, you will decide whether:
   A. The conclusion is proved by Statements 1-4;
   B. The conclusion is disproved by Statements 1-4;
   C. The facts are not sufficient to prove or disprove the conclusion.

18. FACTUAL STATEMENTS:
    1) Gear X rotates in a clockwise direction if Switch C is in the OFF position.
    2) Gear X will rotate in a counter-clockwise direction if Switch C is ON.
    3) If Gear X is rotating in a clockwise direction, then Gear Y will not be rotating at all.
    4) Switch C is OFF.

    CONCLUSION: Gear Y is rotating.

    A. The conclusion is proved by Statements 1-4;
    B. The conclusion is disproved by Statements 1-4;
    C. The facts are not sufficient to prove or disprove the conclusion.

18._____

19. FACTUAL STATEMENTS:
    1) Mark is older than Jim but younger than Dan.
    2) Fern is older than Mark but younger than Silas.
    3) Dan is younger than Silas but older than Edward.
    4) Edward is older than Mark but younger than Fern.

    CONCLUSION: Dan is older than Fern.

    A. The conclusion is proved by Statements 1-4;
    B. The conclusion is disproved by Statements 1-4;
    C. The facts are not sufficient to prove or disprove the conclusion.

    19.____

20. FACTUAL STATEMENTS:
    1) Each of Fred's three sofa cushions lies on top of four lost coins.
    2) The cushion on the right covers two pennies and two dimes.
    3) The middle cushion covers two dimes and two quarters.
    4) The cushion on the left covers two nickels and two quarters.

    CONCLUSION: To be guaranteed of retrieving at least one coin of each denomination, and without looking at any of the coins, Frank must take three coins each from under the cushions on the right and the left.

    A. The conclusion is proved by Statements 1-4;
    B. The conclusion is disproved by Statements 1-4;
    C. The facts are not sufficient to prove or disprove the conclusion.

    20.____

21. FACTUAL STATEMENTS:
    1) The door to the hammer mill chamber is locked if light 6 is red.
    2) The door to the hammer mill chamber is locked only when the mill is operating.
    3) If the mill is not operating, light 6 is blue.
    4) The door to the hammer mill chamber is locked.

    CONCLUSION: The mill is in operation.

    A. The conclusion is proved by Statements 1-4;
    B. The conclusion is disproved by Statements 1-4;
    C. The facts are not sufficient to prove or disprove the conclusion.

    21.____

22. FACTUAL STATEMENTS:
    1) In a five-story office building, where each story is occupied by a single professional, Dr. Kane's office is above Dr. Assad's.
    2) Dr. Johnson's office is between Dr. Kane's and Dr. Conlon's.
    3) Dr. Steen's office is between Dr. Conlon's and Dr. Assad's.
    4) Dr. Johnson is on the fourth story.

    CONCLUSION: Dr. Steen occupies the second story.

    22.____

A. The conclusion is proved by Statements 1-4;
B. The conclusion is disproved by Statements 1-4;
C. The facts are not sufficient to prove or disprove the conclusion.

23. FACTUAL STATEMENTS:
    1) On Saturday, farmers Hank, Earl, Roy, and Cletus plowed a total of 520 acres.
    2) Hank plowed twice as many acres as Roy.
    3) Roy plowed half as much as the farmer who plowed the most.
    4) Cletus plowed 160 acres.

    CONCLUSION: Hank plowed 200 acres.
    A. The conclusion is proved by Statements 1-4;
    B. The conclusion is disproved by Statements 1-4;
    C. The facts are not sufficient to prove or disprove the conclusion.

24. FACTUAL STATEMENTS:
    1) Four travelers – Tina, Jodie, Alex, and Oscar – each traveled to a different island – Aruba, Jamaica, Nevis, and Barbados – but not necessarily respectively.
    2) Tina did not travel as far to Jamaica as Jodie traveled to her island.
    3) Oscar traveled twice as far as Alex, who traveled the same distance as the traveler who went to Aruba.
    4) Oscar went to Barbados.

    CONCLUSION: Oscar traveled the farthest.

    A. The conclusion is proved by Statements 1-4;
    B. The conclusion is disproved by Statements 1-4;
    C. The facts are not sufficient to prove or disprove the conclusion.

25. FACTUAL STATEMENT:
    1) In the natural history museum, every Native American display that contains pottery also contains beadwork.
    2) Some of the displays containing lodge replicas also contain beadwork.
    3) The display on the Choctaw, a Native American tribe, contains pottery.
    4) The display on the Modoc, a Native American tribe, contains only two of these items.

    CONCLUSION: If the Modoc display contains pottery, it does not contain lodge replicas.

    A. The conclusion is proved by Statements 1-4;
    B. The conclusion is disproved by Statements 1-4;
    C. The facts are not sufficient to prove or disprove the conclusion.

KEY (CORRECT ANSWERS)

1.	A	11.	B
2.	B	12.	C
3.	A	13.	B
4.	A	14.	D
5.	C	15.	E
6.	B	16.	E
7.	B	17.	A
8.	B	18.	B
9.	A	19.	C
10.	B	20.	A

21. A
22. A
23. C
24. A
25. A

TEST 2

DIRECTIONS: Each question or incomplete statement is followed by several suggested answers or completions. Select the one that BEST answers the question or completes the statement. *PRINT THE LETTER OF THE CORRECT ANSWER IN THE SPACE AT THE RIGHT.*

Questions 1-9.

DIRECTIONS: In Questions 1 through 9, you will read a set of facts and a conclusion drawn from them. The conclusion may be valid or invalid, based on the facts. It is your task to determine the validity of the conclusion.
For each question, select the letter before the statement that BEST expresses the relationship between the given facts and the conclusion that has been drawn from them. Your choices are:
   A. The facts prove the conclusion.
   B. The facts disprove the conclusion; or
   C. The facts neither prove nor disprove the conclusion.

1. FACTS: If the maximum allowable income for Medicaid recipients is increased, the number of Medicaid recipients will increase. If the number of Medicaid recipients increases, more funds must be allocated to the Medicaid program, which will require a tax increase. Taxes cannot be approved without the approval of the legislature. The legislature probably will not approve a tax increase.

   CONCLUSION: The maximum allowable income for Medicaid recipients will increase.

   A. The facts prove the conclusion.
   B. The facts disprove the conclusion; or
   C. The facts neither prove nor disprove the conclusion.

2. FACTS: All the dentists on the baseball team are short. Everyone in the dugout is a dentist, but not everyone in the dugout is short. The baseball team is not made up of people of any particular profession.

   CONCLUSION: Some people who are not dentists are in the dugout.

   A. The facts prove the conclusion.
   B. The facts disprove the conclusion; or
   C. The facts neither prove nor disprove the conclusion.

3. FACTS: A taxi company's fleet is divided into two fleets. Fleet One contains cabs A, B, C, and D. Fleet Two contains E, F, G, and H. Each cab is either yellow or green. Five of the cabs are yellow. Cabs A and E are not both yellow. Either Cab C or F, or both, are not yellow. Cabs B and H are either both yellow or both green.

   CONCLUSION: Cab H is green.

A. The facts prove the conclusion.
B. The facts disprove the conclusion; or
C. The facts neither prove nor disprove the conclusion.

4. FACTS: Most people in the skydiving club are not afraid of heights. Everyone in the skydiving club makes three parachute jumps a month.

    CONCLUSION: At least one person who is afraid of heights makes three parachute jumps a month.

    A. The facts prove the conclusion.
    B. The facts disprove the conclusion; or
    C. The facts neither prove nor disprove the conclusion.

    4._____

5. FACTS: If the Board approves the new rule, the agency will move to a new location immediately. If the agency moves, five new supervisors will be immediately appointed. The Board has approved the new proposal.

    CONCLUSION: No new supervisors were appointed.

    A. The facts prove the conclusion.
    B. The facts disprove the conclusion; or
    C. The facts neither prove nor disprove the conclusion.

    5._____

6. FACTS: All the workers at the supermarket chew gum when they sack groceries. Sometimes Lance, a supermarket worker, doesn't chew gum at all when he works. Another supermarket worker, Jenny, chews gum the whole time she is at work.

    CONCLUSION: Jenny always sacks groceries when she is at work.

    6._____

7. FACTS: Lake Lottawatta is bigger than Lake Tacomi. Lake Tacomi and Lake Ottawa are exactly the same size. All lakes in Montana are bigger than Lake Ottawa.

    CONCLUSION: Lake Lottawatta is in Montana.

    A. The facts prove the conclusion.
    B. The facts disprove the conclusion; or
    C. The facts neither prove nor disprove the conclusion.

    7._____

8. FACTS: Two men, Cox and Taylor, are playing poker at a table. Taylor has a pair of aces in his hand. One man is smoking a cigar. One of them has no pairs in his hand and is wearing an eye patch. The man wearing the eye patch is smoking a cigar. One man is bald.

    CONCLUSION: Cox is smoking a cigar.

    8._____

A. The facts prove the conclusion.
B. The facts disprove the conclusion; or
C. The facts neither prove nor disprove the conclusion.

9. FACTS: All Kwakiutls are Wakashan Indians. All Wakashan Indians originated on Vancouver Island. The Nootka also originated on Vancouver Island.

   CONCLUSION: Kwakiutls originated on Vancouver Island.

   A. The facts prove the conclusion.
   B. The facts disprove the conclusion; or
   C. The facts neither prove nor disprove the conclusion.

9.____

Questions 10-17.

DIRECTIONS: Questions 10 through 17 are based on the following reading passage. It is not your knowledge of the particular topic that is being tested, but your ability to reason based on what you have read. The passage is likely to detail several proposed courses of action and factors affecting these proposals. The reading passage is followed by a conclusion or outcome based on the facts in the passage, or a description of a decision taken regarding the situation. The conclusion is followed by a number of statements that have a possible connection to the conclusion. For each statement, you are to determine whether:
A. The statement proves the conclusion.
B. The statement supports the conclusion but does not prove it.
C. The statement disproves the conclusion.
D. The statement weakens the conclusion but does not disprove it.
E. The statement has no relevance to the conclusion.

Remember that the conclusion after the passage is to be accepted as the outcome of what actually happened, and that you are being asked to evaluate the impact each statement would have had on the conclusion.

PASSAGE

The World Wide Web portal and search engine, HipBot, is considering becoming a subscription-only service, locking out nonsubscribers from the content on its web site. HipBot currently relies solely on advertising revenues.

HipBot's content director says that by taking in an annual fee from each customer, the company can both increase profits and provide premium content that no other portal can match.

The marketing director disagrees, saying that there is no guarantee that anyone who now visits the web site for free will agree to pay for the privilege of visiting it again. Most will probably simply use the other major portals. Also, HipBot's advertising clients will not be happy when they learn that the site will be viewed by a more limited number of people.

4 (#2)

CONCLUSION: In January of 2016, the CEO of HipBot decides to keep the portal open to all web users, with some limited "premium content" available to subscribers who don't mind paying a little extra to access it. The company will aim to maintain, or perhaps increase, its advertising revenue.

10. In an independent marketing survey, 62% of respondents said they "strongly agree" with the following statement: "I almost never pay attention to advertisements that appear on the World Wide Web."
    A. The statement proves the conclusion.
    B. The statement supports the conclusion but does not prove it.
    C. The statement disproves the conclusion.
    D. The statement weakens the conclusion but does not disprove it.
    E. The statement has no relevance to the conclusion.

10.____

11. When it learns about the subscription-only debate going on at HipBot, Wernham Hogg Entertainment, one of HipBot's most reliable clients, says it will withdraw its ads and place them on a free web portal if HipBot decides to limit its content to subscribers. Wernham Hogg pays HipBot about $6 million annually – about 12% of HipBot's gross revenues – to run its ads online.
    A. The statement proves the conclusion.
    B. The statement supports the conclusion but does not prove it.
    C. The statement disproves the conclusion.
    D. The statement weakens the conclusion but does not disprove it.
    E. The statement has no relevance to the conclusion.

11.____

12. At the end of the second quarter of FY 2016, after continued stagnant profits, the CEO of HipBot assembles a blue ribbon commission to gather and analyze data on the costs, benefits, and feasibility of adding a limited amount of "premium" content to the HipBot portal.
    A. The statement proves the conclusion.
    B. The statement supports the conclusion but does not prove it.
    C. The statement disproves the conclusion.
    D. The statement weakens the conclusion but does not disprove it.
    E. The statement has no relevance to the conclusion.

12.____

13. In the following fiscal year, Wernham Hogg Entertainment, satisfied with the "hit counts" on HipBot's free web site, spends another $1 million on advertisements that will appear on web pages that are available to HipBot's "premium subscribers.
    A. The statement proves the conclusion.
    B. The statement supports the conclusion but does not prove it.
    C. The statement disproves the conclusion.
    D. The statement weakens the conclusion but does not disprove it.
    E. The statement has no relevance to the conclusion.

13.____

14. HipBot's information technology director reports that the engineers in his department have come up with a feature that will search not only individual web pages, but tie into other web-based search engines, as well, and then comb through all these results to find those most relevant to the user's search.

14.____

A. The statement proves the conclusion.
B. The statement supports the conclusion but does not prove it.
C. The statement disproves the conclusion.
D. The statement weakens the conclusion but does not disprove it.
E. The statement has no relevance to the conclusion.

15. In an independent marketing survey, 79% of respondents said they "strongly agree" with the following statement: "Many web sites are so dominated by advertisements these days that it is increasingly frustrating to find the content I want to read or see."
    A. The statement proves the conclusion.
    B. The statement supports the conclusion but does not prove it.
    C. The statement disproves the conclusion.
    D. The statement weakens the conclusion but does not disprove it.
    E. The statement has no relevance to the conclusion.

15.____

16. After three years of studies at the federal level, the Department of Commerce releases a report suggesting that, in general, the only private "subscriber-only" web sites that do well financially are those with a very specialized user population.
    A. The statement proves the conclusion.
    B. The statement supports the conclusion but does not prove it.
    C. The statement disproves the conclusion.
    D. The statement weakens the conclusion but does not disprove it.
    E. The statement has no relevance to the conclusion.

16.____

17. HipBot's own marketing research indicates that the introduction of premium content has the potential to attract new users to the HipBot portal.
    A. The statement proves the conclusion.
    B. The statement supports the conclusion but does not prove it.
    C. The statement disproves the conclusion.
    D. The statement weakens the conclusion but does not disprove it.
    E. The statement has no relevance to the conclusion.

17.____

Questions 18-25.

DIRECTIONS: Questions 18 through 25 each provide four factual statements and a conclusion based on these statements. After reading the entire question, you will decide whether:
A. The conclusion is proved by Statements 1-4;
B. The conclusion is disproved by Statements 1-4;
C. The facts are not sufficient to prove or disprove the conclusion.

18. **FACTUAL STATEMENTS:**
    1) If the alarm goes off, Sam will wake up.
    2) If Tandy wakes up before 4:00, Linda will leave the bedroom and sleep on the couch.
    3) If Linda leaves the bedroom, she'll check the alarm to make sure it is working.
    4) The alarm goes off.

    CONCLUSION: Tandy woke up before 4:00.

    A. The conclusion is proved by Statements 1-4;
    B. The conclusion is disproved by Statements 1-4;
    C. The facts are not sufficient to prove or disprove the conclusion.

19. **FACTUAL STATEMENTS:**
    1) Four brothers are named Earl, John, Gary, and Pete.
    2) Earl and Pete are unmarried.
    3) John is shorter than the youngest of the four.
    4) The oldest brother is married, and is also the tallest.

    CONCLUSION: Pete is the youngest brother.

    A. The conclusion is proved by Statements 1-4;
    B. The conclusion is disproved by Statements 1-4;
    C. The facts are not sufficient to prove or disprove the conclusion.

20. **FACTUAL STATEMENTS:**
    1) Automobile engines are cooled either by air or by liquid.
    2) If the engine is small and simple enough, air from a belt-driven fan will cool it sufficiently.
    3) Most newer automobile engines are too complicated to be air-cooled.
    4) Air-cooled engines are cheaper and easier to build then liquid-cooled engines.

    CONCLUSION: Most newer automobile engines use liquid coolant.

    A. The conclusion is proved by Statements 1-4;
    B. The conclusion is disproved by Statements 1-4;
    C. The facts are not sufficient to prove or disprove the conclusion.

21. **FACTUAL STATEMENTS:**
    1) Erica will only file a lawsuit if she is injured while parasailing.
    2) If Rick orders Trip to run a rope test, Trip will check the rigging.
    3) If the rigging does not malfunction, Erica will not be injured.
    4) Rick orders Trip to run a rope test.

CONCLUSION: Erica does not file a lawsuit.

A. The conclusion is proved by Statements 1-4;
B. The conclusion is disproved by Statements 1-4;
C. The facts are not sufficient to prove or disprove the conclusion.

22. FACTUAL STATEMENTS:
1) On Maple Street, which is four blocks long, Bill's shop is two blocks east of Ken's shop.
2) Ken's shop is one block west of the only shop on Maple Street with an awning.
3) Erma's shop is one block west of the easternmost block.
4) Bill's shop is on the easternmost block.

CONCLUSION: Bill's shop has an awning.

A. The conclusion is proved by Statements 1-4;
B. The conclusion is disproved by Statements 1-4;
C. The facts are not sufficient to prove or disprove the conclusion.

23. FACTUAL STATEMENTS:
1) Gear X rotates in a clockwise direction if Switch C is in the OFF position.
2) Gear X will rotate in a counter-clockwise direction if Switch C is ON.
3) If Gear X is rotating in a clockwise direction, then Gear Y will not be rotating at all.
4) Gear Y is rotating.

CONCLUSION: Gear X is rotating in a counter-clockwise direction.

A. The conclusion is proved by Statements 1-4;
B. The conclusion is disproved by Statements 1-4;
C. The facts are not sufficient to prove or disprove the conclusion.

24. FACTUAL STATEMENTS:
1) The Republic of Garbanzo's currency system has four basic denominations: the pastor, the noble, the donner, and the rojo.
2) A pastor is worth 2 nobles.
3) 2 donners can be exchanged for a rojo.
4) 3 pastors are equal in value to 2 donners.

CONCLUSION: The rojo is most valuable.

A. The conclusion is proved by Statements 1-4;
B. The conclusion is disproved by Statements 1-4;
C. The facts are not sufficient to prove or disprove the conclusion.

25. **FACTUAL STATEMENTS:**
   1) At Prickett's Nursery, the only citrus trees left are either Meyer lemons or Valencia oranges, and every citrus tree left is either a dwarf or a semidwarf.
   2) Half of the semidwarf trees are Meyer lemons.
   3) There are more semidwarf trees left than dwarf trees.
   4) A quarter of the dwarf trees are Valencia oranges.

   CONCLUSION: There are more Valencia oranges left at Prickett's Nursery than Meyer lemons.

   A. The conclusion is proved by Statements 1-4;
   B. The conclusion is disproved by Statements 1-4;
   C. The facts are not sufficient to prove or disprove the conclusion.

   25.____

KEY (CORRECT ANSWERS)

1.	C		11.	B
2.	B		12.	C
3.	B		13.	A
4.	A		14.	E
5.	B		15.	D
6.	C		16.	B
7.	C		17.	B
8.	A		18.	C
9.	A		19.	C
10.	E		20.	A

21. C
22. B
23. C
24. A
25. B

EVALUATING CONCLUSIONS IN LIGHT OF KNOWN FACTS
EXAMINATION SECTION
TEST 1

DIRECTIONS: Each question or incomplete statement is followed by several suggested answers or completions. Select the one that BEST answers the question or completes the statement. *PRINT THE LETTER OF THE CORRECT ANSWER IN THE SPACE AT THE RIGHT.*

Questions 1-9.

DIRECTIONS: In Questions 1 through 9, you will read a set of facts and a conclusion drawn from them. The conclusion may be valid or invalid, based on the facts—it's your task to determine the validity of the conclusion.

For each question, select the letter before the statement that BEST expresses the relationship between the given facts and the conclusion that has been drawn from them. Your choices are:
   A. The facts prove the conclusion;
   B. The facts disprove the conclusion; or
   C. The facts neither prove nor disprove the conclusion.

1. FACTS: If the supervisor retires, James, the assistant supervisor, will not be transferred to another department. James will be promoted to supervisor if he is not transferred. The supervisor retired.

    CONCLUSION: James will be promoted to supervisor.
       A. The facts prove the conclusion.
       B. The facts disprove the conclusion.
       C. The facts neither prove nor disprove the conclusion.

    1.____

2. FACTS: In the town of Luray, every player on the softball team works at Luray National Bank. In addition, every player on the Luray softball team wear glasses.

    CONCLUSIONS: At least some of the people who work at Luray National Bank wear glasses.
       A. The facts prove the conclusion.
       B. The facts disprove the conclusion.
       C. The facts neither prove nor disprove the conclusion.

    2.____

3. FACTS: The only time Henry and June go out to dinner is on an evening when they have childbirth classes. Their childbirth classes meet on Tuesdays and Thursdays.

    3.____

2 (#1)

CONCLUSION: Henry and June never go out to dinner on Friday or Saturday.
  A. The facts prove the conclusion.
  B. The facts disprove the conclusion.
  C. The facts neither prove nor disprove the conclusion.

4. FACTS: Every player on the field hockey team has at least one bruise. Everyone on the field hockey team also has scarred knees.

   CONCLUSION: Most people with both bruises and scarred knees are field hockey players.
   A. The facts prove the conclusion.
   B. The facts disprove the conclusion.
   C. The facts neither prove nor disprove the conclusion.

4.____

5. FACTS: In the chess tournament, Lance will win his match against Jane if Jane wins her match against Mathias. If Lance wins his match against Jane, Christine will not win her match against Jane.

   CONCLUSION: Christine will not win her match against Jane if Jane wins her match against Mathias.
   A. The facts prove the conclusion.
   B. The facts disprove the conclusion.
   C. The facts neither prove nor disprove the conclusion.

5.____

6. FACTS: No green lights on the machine are indicators for the belt drive status. Not all of the lights on the machine's upper panel are green. Some lights on the machine's lower panel are green.

   CONCLUSION: The green lights on the machine's lower panel may be indicators for the belt drive status.
   A. The facts prove the conclusion.
   B. The facts disprove the conclusion.
   C. The facts neither prove nor disprove the conclusion.

6.____

7. FACTS: At a small, one-room country school, there are eight students: Amy, Ben, Carla, Dan, Elliot, Francine, Greg, and Hannah. Each student is in either the 6th, 7th, or 8th grade. Either two or three students are in each grade. Amy, Dan, and Francine are all in different grades. Ben and Elliot are both in the 7th grade. Hannah and Carl are in the same grade.

   CONCLUSION: Exactly three students are in the 7th grade.
   A. The facts prove the conclusion.
   B. The facts disprove the conclusion.
   C. The facts neither prove nor disprove the conclusion.

7.____

8. FACTS: Two married couples are having lunch together. Two of the four people are German and two are Russian, but in each couple the nationality of the spouse is not necessarily the same as the other's. One person in the group is a teacher, the other a lawyer, one an engineer, and the other a writer. The teacher is a Russian man. The writer is Russian, and her husband is an engineer. One of the people, Mr. Stern, is German.

   CONCLUSION: Mr. Stern's wife is a writer.
   A. The facts prove the conclusion.
   B. The facts disprove the conclusion.
   C. The facts neither prove nor disprove the conclusion.

   8.____

9. FACTS: The flume ride at the county fair is open only to children who are at least 36 inches tall. Lisa is 30 inches tall. John is shorter than Henry, but more than 10 inches taller than Lisa.

   CONCLUSION: Lisa is the only one who can't ride the flume ride.
   A. The facts prove the conclusion.
   B. The facts disprove the conclusion.
   C. The facts neither prove nor disprove the conclusion.

   9.____

Questions 10-17.

DIRECTIONS: Questions 10 through 17 are based on the following reading passage. It is not your knowledge of the particular topic that is being tested, but your ability to reason based on what you have read. The passage is likely to detail several proposed courses of action and factors affecting these proposals. The reading passage is followed by a conclusion or outcome based on the facts in the passage, or a description of a decision taken regarding the situation. The conclusion is followed by a number of statements that have a possible connection to the conclusion. For each statement, you are to determine whether:
   A. The statement proves the conclusion.
   B. The statement supports the conclusion but does not prove it.
   C. The statement disproves the conclusion.
   D. The statement weakens the conclusion but does not disprove it.
   E. The statement has no relevance to the conclusion.

Remember that the conclusion after the passage is to be accepted as the outcome of what actually happened, and that you are being asked to evaluate the impact each statement would have had on the conclusion.

PASSAGE:

   The Grand Army of Foreign Wars, a national veteran's organization, is struggling to maintain its National Home, where the widowed spouses and orphans of deceased members are housed together in a small village-like community. The Home is open to spouses and children who are bereaved for any reason, regardless of whether the member's death was related to military service, but a new global conflict has led to a dramatic surge in the number of members' deaths: many veterans who re-enlisted for the conflict have been killed in action.

The Grand Army of Foreign Wars is considering several options for handling the increased number of applications for housing at the National Home, which has been traditionally supported by membership due. At its national convention, it will choose only one of the following:

The first idea is a one-time $50 tax on all members, above and beyond the dues they pay already. Since the organization has more than a million member, this tax should be sufficient for the construction and maintenance of new housing for applicants on the existing grounds of the National Home. The idea is opposed, however, by some older members who live on fixed incomes. These members object in principle to the taxation of Grand Army members. The Grand Army has never imposed a tax on its members.

The second idea is to launch a national fundraising drive the public relations campaign that will attract donations for the National Home. Several national celebrities are members of the organization, and other celebrities could be attracted to the cause. Many Grand Army members are wary of this approach, however: in the past, the net receipts of some fundraising efforts have been relatively insignificant, given the costs of staging them.

A third approach, suggested by many of the younger members, is to have new applicants share some of the costs of construction and maintenance. The spouses and children would pay an up-front "enrollment" fee, based on a sliding scale proportionate to their income and assets, and then a monthly fee adjusted similarly to contribute to maintenance costs. Many older members are strongly opposed to this idea, as it is in direct contradiction to the principles on which the organization was founded more than a century ago.

The fourth option is simply to maintain the status quo, focus the organization's efforts on supporting the families who already live at the National Home, and wait to accept new applicants based on attrition.

CONCLUSION: At its annual national convention, the Grand Army of Foreign Wars votes to impose a one-time tax of $10 on each member for the purpose of expanding and supporting the National Home to welcome a larger number of applicants. The tax is considered to be the solution most likely to produce the funds needed to accommodate the growing number of applicants.

10. Actuarial studies have shown that because the Grand Army's membership consists mostly of older veterans from earlier wars, the organization's membership will suffer a precipitous decline in numbers in about five years. 10.____
    A. The statement proves the conclusion.
    B. The statement supports the conclusion but does not prove it.
    C. The statement disproves the conclusion.
    D. The statement weakens the conclusion but does not disprove it.
    E. The statement has no relevance to the conclusion.

11. After passage of the funding measure, a splinter group of older members appeals for the "sliding scale" provision to be applied to the tax, so that some members may be allowed to contribute less based on their income. 11.____
    A. The statement proves the conclusion.
    B. The statement supports the conclusion but does not prove it.
    C. The statement disproves the conclusion.
    D. The statement weakens the conclusion but does not disprove it.
    E. The statement has no relevance to the conclusion.

12. The original charter of the Grand Army of Foreign Wars specifically states that the organization will not levy taxes or duties on its members beyond its modest annual dues. It takes a super-majority of attending delegates at the national convention to make alterations to the charter.
    A. The statement proves the conclusion.
    B. The statement supports the conclusion but does not prove it.
    C. The statement disproves the conclusion.
    D. The statement weakens the conclusion but does not disprove it.
    E. The statement has no relevance to the conclusion.

    12.____

13. Six months before Grand Army of Foreign Wars' national convention, the Internal Revenue Service rules that because it is an organization that engages in political lobbying, the Grand Army must no longer enjoy its own federal tax-exempt status.
    A. The statement proves the conclusion.
    B. The statement supports the conclusion but does not prove it.
    C. The statement disproves the conclusion.
    D. The statement weakens the conclusion but does not disprove it.
    E. The statement has no relevance to the conclusion.

    13.____

14. Two months before the national convention, Dirk Rockwell, arguably the country's most famous film actor, announces in a nationally televised interview that he has been saddened to learn of the plight of the National Home, and that he is going to make it his own personal crusade to see that it is able to house and support a greater number of widowed spouses and orphans in the future.
    A. The statement proves the conclusion.
    B. The statement supports the conclusion but does not prove it.
    C. The statement disproves the conclusion.
    D. The statement weakens the conclusion but does not disprove it.
    E. The statement has no relevance to the conclusion.

    14.____

15. The Grand Army's final estimate is that the cost of expanding the National Home to accommodate the increased number of applicants will be about $61 million.
    A. The statement proves the conclusion.
    B. The statement supports the conclusion but does not prove it.
    C. The statement disproves the conclusion.
    D. The statement weakens the conclusion but does not disprove it.
    E. The statement has no relevance to the conclusion.

    15.____

16. Just before the national convention, the Federal Department of Veterans Affairs announces steep cuts in the benefits package that is currently offered to the widowed spouses and orphans of veterans.
    A. The statement proves the conclusion.
    B. The statement supports the conclusion but does not prove it.
    C. The statement disproves the conclusion.
    D. The statement weakens the conclusion but does not disprove it.
    E. The statement has no relevance to the conclusion.

    16.____

17. After the national convention, the Grand Army of Foreign Wars begins charging a modest "start-up" fee to all families who apply for residence at the national home.

    A. The statement proves the conclusion.
    B. The statement supports the conclusion but does not prove it.
    C. The statement disproves the conclusion.
    D. The statement weakens the conclusion but does not disprove it.
    E. The statement has no relevance to the conclusion.

17.____

Questions 18-25.

DIRECTIONS: Questions 18 through 25 each provide four factual statements and a conclusion based on these statements. After reading the entire question, you will decide whether:
    A. The conclusion is proved by statements I-IV;
    B. The conclusion is disproved by statements I-IV.
    C. The facts are not sufficient to prove or disprove the conclusion.

18. FACTUAL STATEMENTS:
    I. In the Field Day high jump competition, Martha jumped higher than Frank.
    II. Carl jumped higher than Ignacio.
    III. Ignacio jumped higher than Frank.
    IV. Dan jumped higher than Carl.

    CONCLUSION: Frank finished last in the high jump competition.
    A. The conclusion is proved by statements I-IV;
    B. The conclusion is disproved by statements I-IV.
    C. The facts are not sufficient to prove or disprove the conclusion.

18.____

19. FACTUAL STATEMENTS:
    I. The door to the hammer mill chamber is locked if light 6 is red.
    II. The door to the hammer mill chamber is locked only when the mill is operating.
    III. If the mill is not operating, light 6 is blue.
    IV. Light 6 is blue.

    CONCLUSION: The door to the hammer mill chamber is locked.
    A. The conclusion is proved by statements I-IV;
    B. The conclusion is disproved by statements I-IV.
    C. The facts are not sufficient to prove or disprove the conclusion.

19.____

20. FACTUAL STATEMENTS:
    I. Ziegfried, the lion tamer at the circus, has demanded ten additional minutes of performance time during each show.
    II. If Ziegfried is allowed his ten additional minutes per show, he will attempt to teach Kimba the tiger to shoot a basketball.
    III. If Kimba learns how to shoot a basketball, then Ziegfried was not given his ten additional minutes.
    IV. Ziegfried was given his ten additional minutes.

20.____

7 (#1)

CONCLUSION: Despite Ziegfried's efforts, Kimba did not learn how to shoot a basketball.
   A. The conclusion is proved by statements I-IV;
   B. The conclusion is disproved by statements I-IV.
   C. The facts are not sufficient to prove or disprove the conclusion.

21. FACTUAL STATEMENTS: 21.____
   I. If Stan goes to counseling, Sara won't divorce him.
   II. If Sara divorces Stan, she'll move back to Texas.
   III. If Sara doesn't divorce Stan, Irene will be disappointed.
   IV. Stan goes to counseling.

   CONCLUSION: Irene will be disappointed.
   A. The conclusion is proved by statements I-IV;
   B. The conclusion is disproved by statements I-IV.
   C. The facts are not sufficient to prove or disprove the conclusion.

22. FACTUAL STATEMENTS: 22.____
   I. If Delia is promoted to district manager, Claudia will have to be promoted to team leader.
   II. Delia will be promoted to district manager unless she misses her fourth-quarter sales quota.
   III. If Claudia is promoted to team leader, Thomas will be promoted to assistant team leader.
   IV. Delia meets her fourth-quarter sales quota.

   CONCLUSION: Thomas is promoted to assistant team leader.
   A. The conclusion is proved by statements I-IV;
   B. The conclusion is disproved by statements I-IV.
   C. The facts are not sufficient to prove or disprove the conclusion.

23. FACTUAL STATEMENTS: 23.____
   I. Clone D is identical to Clone B.
   II. Clone B is not identical to Clone A.
   III. Clone D is not identical to Clone C.
   IV. Clone E is not identical to the clones that are identical to Clone B.

   CONCLUSION: Clone E is identical to Clone D.
   A. The conclusion is proved by statements I-IV;
   B. The conclusion is disproved by statements I-IV.
   C. The facts are not sufficient to prove or disprove the conclusion.

24. FACTUAL STATEMENTS: 24.____
   I. In the Stafford Tower, each floor is occupied by a single business.
   II. Big G Staffing is on a floor between CyberGraphics and MainEvent.
   III. Gasco is on the floor directly below CyberGraphics and three floors above Treehorn Audio.
   IV. MainEvent is five floors below EZ Tax and four floors below Treehorn Audio.

8 (#1)

CONCLUSION: EZ Tax is on a floor between Gasco and MainEvent.
 A. The conclusion is proved by statements I-IV;
 B. The conclusion is disproved by statements I-IV.
 C. The facts are not sufficient to prove or disprove the conclusion.

25. FACTUAL STATEMENTS:
 I. Only county roads lead to Nicodemus.
 II. All the roads from Hill City to Graham County are federal highways.
 III. Some of the roads from Plainville lead to Nicodemus.
 IV. Some of the roads running from Hill City lead to Strong City.

 CONCLUSION: Some of the roads from Plainville are county roads.
 A. The conclusion is proved by statements I-IV;
 B. The conclusion is disproved by statements I-IV.
 C. The facts are not sufficient to prove or disprove the conclusion.

25.____

KEY (CORRECT ANSWERS)

1.	A	11.	A
2.	A	12.	D
3.	A	13.	E
4.	C	14.	D
5.	A	15.	B
6.	B	16.	B
7.	A	17.	C
8.	A	18.	A
9.	A	19.	B
10.	E	20.	A

21. A
22. A
23. B
24. A
25. A

9 (#1)

SOLUTIONS TO PROBLEMS

1. CORRECT ANSWER: A
Given Statement 3, we deduce that James will not be transferred to another department. By Statement 2, we can conclude that James will be promoted.

2. CORRECT ANSWER: A
Since every player on the softball team wears glasses, these individuals compose some of the people who work at the bank. Although not every person who works at the bank plays softball, those bank employees who do play softball wear glasses.

3. CORRECT ANSWER: A
If Henry and June go out to dinner, we conclude that it must be on Tuesday or Thursday, which are the only two days when they have childbirth classes. This implies that if it is not Tuesday or Thursday, then this couple does not go out to dinner.

4. CORRECT ANSWER: C
We can only conclude that if a person plays on the field hockey team, then he or she has both bruises and scarred knees. But there are probably a great number of people who have both bruises and scarred knees but do not play on the field hockey team. The given conclusion can neither be proven or disproven.

5. CORRECT ANSWER: A
From statement 1, if Jane beats Mathias, then Lance will beat Jane. Using statement 2, we can then conclude that Christine will not win her match against Jane.

6. CORRECT ANSWER: B
Statement 1 tells us that no green light can be an indicator of the belt drive status. Thus, the given conclusion must be false.

7. CORRECT ANSWER: A
We already know that Ben and Elliot are in the 7th grade. Even though Hannah and Carl are in the same grade, it cannot be the 7th grade because we would then have at least four students in this 7th grade. This would contradict the third statement, which states that either two or three students are in each grade. Since Amy, Dan, and Francine are in different grade, exactly one of them must be in the 7th grade. Thus, Ben, Elliot, and exactly one of Amy, Dan, and Francine are the three students in the 7th grade.

8. CORRECT ANSWER: A
One man is a teacher, who is Russian. We know that the writer is female and is Russian. Since her husband is an engineer, he cannot be the Russian teacher. Thus, her husband is of German descent, namely Mr. Stern. This means that Mr. Stern's wife is the writer. Note that one couple consists of a male Russian teacher and a female German lawyer. The other couple consists of a male German engineer and a female Russian writer.

9. CORRECT ANSWER: A
Since John is more than 10 inches taller than Lisa, his height is at least 46 inches. Also, John is shorter than Henry, so Henry's height must be greater than 46 inches. Thus, Lisa is the only one whose height is less than 36 inches. Therefore, she is the only one who is not allowed on the flume ride.

18. CORRECT ANSWER: A
Dan jumped higher than Carl, who jumped higher than Ignacio, who jumped higher than Frank. Since Martha jumped higher than Frank, every person jumped higher than Frank. Thus, Frank finished last.

19. CORRECT ANSWER: B
If the light is red, then the door is locked. If the door is locked, then the mill is operating. Reversing the logical sequence of these statements, if the mill is not operating, then the door is not locked, which means that the light is blue. Thus, the given conclusion is disproved.

20. CORRECT ANSWER: A
Using the contrapositive of statement III, Ziegfried was given his ten additional minutes, then Kimba did not learn how to shoot a basketball. Since statement IV is factual, the conclusion is proved.

21. CORRECT ANSWER: A
From Statements IV and I, we conclude that Sara doesn't divorce Stan. Then statement III reveals that Irene will be disappointed. Thus, the conclusion is proved.

22. CORRECT ANSWER: A
Statement II can be rewritten as "Delia is promoted to district manager or she misses her sales quota." Furthermore, this statement is equivalent to "If Delia makes her sales quota, then she is promoted to district manager." From statement I, we conclude that Claudia is promoted to team leader. Finally, by statement III, Thomas is promoted to assistant team leader.

23. CORRECT ANSWER: B
By statement IV, Clone E is not identical to any clones identical to Clone B. Statement I tells us that Clones B and D are identical. Therefore, Clone E cannot be identical to Clone D. The conclusion is disproved.

24. CORRECT ANSWER: A
Based on all four statements, CyberGraphics is somewhere below MainEvent. Gasco is one floor below CyberGraphics. EZ Tax is two floors below Gasco. Treehorn Audio is one floor below EZ Tax. MainEvent is four floors below Treehorn Audio. Thus, EZ Tax is two floors below Gasco and five floors above MainEvent. The conclusion is proved.

25. CORRECT ANSWER: A
From statement III, we know that some of the roads from Plainville lead to Nicodemus. But statement I tells us that only county roads lead to Nicodemus. Therefore, some of the roads from Plainville must be county roads. The conclusion is proved.

TEST 2

DIRECTIONS: Each question or incomplete statement is followed by several suggested answers or completions. Select the one that BEST answers the question or completes the statement. *PRINT THE LETTER OF THE CORRECT ANSWER IN THE SPACE AT THE RIGHT.*

Questions 1-9.

DIRECTIONS: In Questions 1 through 9, you will read a set of facts and a conclusion drawn from them. The conclusion may be valid or invalid, based on the facts—it's your task to determine the validity of the conclusion.

For each question, select the letter before the statement that BEST expresses the relationship between the given facts and the conclusion that has been drawn from them. Your choices are:
  A. The facts prove the conclusion;
  B. The facts disprove the conclusion; or
  C. The facts neither prove nor disprove the conclusion.

1. FACTS: Some employees in the testing department are statisticians. Most of the statisticians who work in the testing department are projection specialists. Tom Wilks works in the testing department.

   CONCLUSION: Tom Wilks is a statistician.
     A. The facts prove the conclusion.
     B. The facts disprove the conclusion.
     C. The facts neither prove nor disprove the conclusion.

2. FACTS: Ten coins are split among Hank, Lawrence, and Gail. If Lawrence gives his coins to Hank, then Hank will have more coins than Gail. If Gail gives her coins to Lawrence, then Lawrence will have more coins than Hank.

   CONCLUSION: Hank has six coins.
     A. The facts prove the conclusion.
     B. The facts disprove the conclusion.
     C. The facts neither prove nor disprove the conclusion.

3. FACTS: Nobody loves everybody. Janet loves Ken. Ken loves everybody who loves Janet.

   CONCLUSION: Everybody loves Janet.
     A. The facts prove the conclusion.
     B. The facts disprove the conclusion.
     C. The facts neither prove nor disprove the conclusion.

4. FACTS: Most of the Torres family lives in East Los Angeles. Many people in East Los Angeles celebrate Cinco de Mayo. Joe is a member of the Torres family.

   CONCLUSION: Joe lives in East Los Angeles.
   A. The facts prove the conclusion.
   B. The facts disprove the conclusion.
   C. The facts neither prove nor disprove the conclusion.

5. FACTS: Five professionals each occupy one story of a five-story office building. Dr. Kane's office is above Dr. Assad's. Dr. Johnson's office is between Dr. Kane's and Dr. Conlon's. Dr. Steen's office is between Dr. Conlon's and Dr. Assad's. Dr. Johnson is on the fourth story.

   CONCLUSION: Dr. Kane occupies the top story.
   A. The facts prove the conclusion.
   B. The facts disprove the conclusion.
   C. The facts neither prove nor disprove the conclusion.

6. FACTS: To be eligible for membership in the Yukon Society, a person must be able to either tunnel through a snowbank while wearing only a T-shirt and short, or hold his breath for two minutes under water that is 50°F. Ray can only hold his breath for a minute and a half.

   CONCLUSION: Ray can still become a member of the Yukon Society by tunneling through a snowbank while wearing a T-shirt and shorts.
   A. The facts prove the conclusion.
   B. The facts disprove the conclusion.
   C. The facts neither prove nor disprove the conclusion.

7. FACTS: A mark is worth five plunks. You can exchange four sharps for a tinplot. It takes eight marks to buy a sharp.

   CONCLUSION: A sharp is the most valuable.
   A. The facts prove the conclusion.
   B. The facts disprove the conclusion.
   C. The facts neither prove nor disprove the conclusion.

8. FACTS: There are gibbons, as well as lemurs, who like to play in the trees at the monkey house. All those who like to play in the trees at the monkey house are fed lettuce and bananas.

   CONCLUSION: Lemurs and gibbons are types of monkeys.
   A. The facts prove the conclusion.
   B. The facts disprove the conclusion.
   C. The facts neither prove nor disprove the conclusion.

9. FACTS: None of the Blackfoot tribes is a Salishan Indian tribe. Salishan Indians came from the northern Pacific Coast. All Salishan Indians live each of the Continental Divide.

9._____

CONCLUSION: No Blackfoot tribes live east of the Continental Divide.
  A. The facts prove the conclusion.
  B. The facts disprove the conclusion.
  C. The facts neither prove nor disprove the conclusion.

Questions 10-17.

DIRECTIONS: Questions 10 through 17 are based on the following reading passage. It is not your knowledge of the particular topic that is being tested, but your ability to reason based on what you have read. The passage is likely to detail several proposed courses of action and factors affecting these proposals. The reading passage is followed by a conclusion or outcome based on the facts in the passage, or a description of a decision taken regarding the situation. The conclusion is followed by a number of statements that have a possible connection to the conclusion. For each statement, you are to determine whether:
  A. The statement proves the conclusion.
  B. The statement supports the conclusion but does not prove it.
  C. The statement disproves the conclusion.
  D. The statement weakens the conclusion but does not disprove it.
  E. The statement has no relevance to the conclusion.

Remember that the conclusion after the passage is to be accepted as the outcome of what actually happened, and that you are being asked to evaluate the impact each statement would have had on the conclusion.

PASSAGE:

On August 12, Beverly Willey reported that she was in the elevator late on the previous evening after leaving her office on the 16th floor of a large office building. In her report, she states that a man got on the elevator at the 11th floor, pulled her off the elevator, assaulted her, and stole her purse. Ms. Willey reported that she had seen the man in the elevators and hallways of the building before. She believes that the man works in the building. Her description of him is as follows: he is tall, unshaven, with wavy brown hair and a scar on his left cheek. He walks with a pronounced limp, often dragging his left foot behind his right.

CONCLUSION: After Beverly Willey makes her report, the police arrest a 43-year-old man, Barton Black, and charge him with her assault.

10. Barton Black is a former Marine who served in Vietnam, where he sustained shrapnel wounds to the left side of his face and suffered nerve damage in his left leg.
    A. The statement proves the conclusion.
    B. The statement supports the conclusion but does not prove it.
    C. The statement disproves the conclusion.
    D. The statement weakens the conclusion but does not disprove it.
    E. The statement has no relevance to the conclusion.

11. When they arrived at his residence to question him, detectives were greeted at the door by Barton Black, who was tall and clean-shaven.
    A. The statement proves the conclusion.
    B. The statement supports the conclusion but does not prove it.
    C. The statement disproves the conclusion.
    D. The statement weakens the conclusion but does not disprove it.
    E. The statement has no relevance to the conclusion.

12. Barton Black was booked into the county jail several days after Beverly Willey's assault.
    A. The statement proves the conclusion.
    B. The statement supports the conclusion but does not prove it.
    C. The statement disproves the conclusion.
    D. The statement weakens the conclusion but does not disprove it.
    E. The statement has no relevance to the conclusion.

13. Upon further investigation, detectives discover that Beverly Willey does not work at the office building.
    A. The statement proves the conclusion.
    B. The statement supports the conclusion but does not prove it.
    C. The statement disproves the conclusion.
    D. The statement weakens the conclusion but does not disprove it.
    E. The statement has no relevance to the conclusion.

14. Upon further investigation, detectives discover that Barton Black does not work at the office building.
    A. The statement proves the conclusion.
    B. The statement supports the conclusion but does not prove it.
    C. The statement disproves the conclusion.
    D. The statement weakens the conclusion but does not disprove it.
    E. The statement has no relevance to the conclusion.

15. In the spring of the following year, Barton Black is convicted of assaulting Beverly Willey on August 11.
    A. The statement proves the conclusion.
    B. The statement supports the conclusion but does not prove it.
    C. The statement disproves the conclusion.
    D. The statement weakens the conclusion but does not disprove it.
    E. The statement has no relevance to the conclusion.

16. During their investigation of the assault, detectives determine that Beverly Willey was assaulted on the 12th floor of the office building.
    A. The statement proves the conclusion.
    B. The statement supports the conclusion but does not prove it.
    C. The statement disproves the conclusion.
    D. The statement weakens the conclusion but does not disprove it.
    E. The statement has no relevance to the conclusion.

17. The day after Beverly Willey's assault, Barton Black fled the area and was never seen again.
    A. The statement proves the conclusion.
    B. The statement supports the conclusion but does not prove it.
    C. The statement disproves the conclusion.
    D. The statement weakens the conclusion but does not disprove it.
    E. The statement has no relevance to the conclusion.

Questions 18-25.

DIRECTIONS: Questions 18 through 25 each provide four factual statements and a conclusion based on these statements. After reading the entire question, you will decide whether:
    A. The conclusion is proved by statements I-IV;
    B. The conclusion is disproved by statements I-IV.
    C. The facts are not sufficient to prove or disprove the conclusion.

18. FACTUAL STATEMENTS:
    I. Among five spice jars on the shelf, the sage is to the right of the parsley.
    II. The pepper is to the left of the basil.
    III. The nutmeg is between the sage and the pepper.
    IV. The pepper is the second spice from the left.

    CONCLUSION: The safe is the farthest to the right.
    A. The conclusion is proved by statements I-IV;
    B. The conclusion is disproved by statements I-IV.
    C. The facts are not sufficient to prove or disprove the conclusion.

19. FACTUAL STATEMENTS:
    I. Gear X rotates in a clockwise direction if Switch C is in the OFF position.
    II. Gear X will rotate in a counter-clockwise direction is Switch C is ON.
    III. If Gear X is rotating in a clockwise direction, then Gear Y will not be rotating at all.
    IV. Switch C is ON.

    CONCLUSION: Gear X is rotating in a counter-clockwise direction.
    A. The conclusion is proved by statements I-IV;
    B. The conclusion is disproved by statements I-IV.
    C. The facts are not sufficient to prove or disprove the conclusion.

6 (#2)

20. FACTUAL STATEMENTS:
    I. Lane will leave for the Toronto meeting today only if Terence, Rourke, and Jackson all file their marketing reports by the end of the work day.
    II. Rourke will file her report on time only if Ganz submits last quarter's data.
    III. If Terence attends the security meeting, he will attend it with Jackson, and they will not file their marketing reports by the end of the work day.

    CONCLUSION: Lane will leave for the Toronto meeting today.
    A. The conclusion is proved by statements I-IV;
    B. The conclusion is disproved by statements I-IV.
    C. The facts are not sufficient to prove or disprove the conclusion.

21. FACTUAL STATEMENTS:
    I. Bob is in second place in the Boston Marathon.
    II. Gregory is winning the Boston Marathon.
    III. There are four miles to go in the race, and Bob is gaining on Gregory at the rate of 100 yards every minute.
    IV. There are 1760 yards in a mile and Gregory's usual pace during the Boston Marathon is one mile every six minutes.

    CONCLUSION: Bob wins the Boston Marathon.
    A. The conclusion is proved by statements I-IV;
    B. The conclusion is disproved by statements I-IV.
    C. The facts are not sufficient to prove or disprove the conclusion.

22. FACTUAL STATEMENTS:
    I. Four brothers are named Earl, John, Gary, and Pete.
    II. Earl and Pete are unmarried.
    III. John is shorter than the youngest of the four.
    IV. The oldest brother is married, and is also the tallest.

    CONCLUSION: Gary is the oldest brother.
    A. The conclusion is proved by statements I-IV;
    B. The conclusion is disproved by statements I-IV.
    C. The facts are not sufficient to prove or disprove the conclusion.

23. FACTUAL STATEMENTS:
    I. Brigade X is ten miles from the demilitarized zone.
    II. If General Woundwort gives the order, Brigade X will advance to the demilitarized zone, but not quickly enough to reach the zone before the conflict begins.
    III. Brigade Y, five miles behind Brigade X, will not advance unless General Woundwort gives the order.
    IV. Brigade Y advances.

7 (#2)

CONCLUSION: Brigade X reaches the demilitarized zone before the conflict begins.
   A. The conclusion is proved by statements I-IV;
   B. The conclusion is disproved by statements I-IV.
   C. The facts are not sufficient to prove or disprove the conclusion.

24. FACTUAL STATEMENTS: 24.____
   I. Jerry has decided to take a cab from Fullerton to Elverton.
   II. Chubby Cab charges $5 plus $3 a mile.
   III. Orange Cab charges $7.50 but gives free mileage for the first 5 miles.
   IV. After the first 5 miles, Orange Cab charges $2.50 a mile.

   CONCLUSION: Orange Cab is the cheaper fare from Fullerton to Elverton.
   A. The conclusion is proved by statements I-IV;
   B. The conclusion is disproved by statements I-IV.
   C. The facts are not sufficient to prove or disprove the conclusion.

25. FACTUAL STATEMENTS: 25.____
   I. Dan is never in class when his friend Lucy is absent.
   II. Lucy is never absent unless her mother is sick.
   III. If Lucy is in class, Sergio is in class also.
   IV. Sergio is never in class when Dalton is absent.

   CONCLUSION: If Lucy is absent, Dalton may be in class.
   A. The conclusion is proved by statements I-IV;
   B. The conclusion is disproved by statements I-IV.
   C. The facts are not sufficient to prove or disprove the conclusion.

KEY (CORRECT ANSWERS)

1.	C	11.	E
2.	B	12.	B
3.	B	13.	D
4.	C	14.	E
5.	A	15.	A
6.	A	16.	E
7.	B	17.	C
8.	C	18.	B
9.	C	19.	A
10.	B	20.	C

21. C
22. A
23. B
24. A
25. B

SOLUTIONS TO PROBLEMS

1. CORRECT ANSWER: C
   Statement 1 only tells us that some employees who work in the Testing Department are statisticians. This means that we need to allow the possibility that at least one person in this department is not a statistician. Thus, if a person works in the Testing Department, we cannot conclude whether or not this individual is a statistician.

2. CORRECT ANSWER: B
   If Hank had six coins, then the total of Gail's collection and Lawrence's collection would be four. Thus, if Gail gave all her coins to Lawrence, Lawrence would only have four coins. Thus, it would be impossible for Lawrence to have more coins than Hank.

3. CORRECT ANSWER: B
   Statement 1 tells us that nobody loves everybody. If everybody loved Janet, then Statement 3 would imply that Ken loves everybody. This would contradict statement 1. The conclusion is disproved.

4. CORRECT ANSWER: C
   Although most of the Torres family lives in East Los Angeles, we can assume that some members of this family do not live in East Los Angeles. Thus, we cannot prove or disprove that Joe, who is a member of the Torres family, lives in East Los Angeles.

5. CORRECT ANSWER: A
   Since Dr. Johnson is on the 4th floor, either (a) Dr. Kane is on the 5th floor and Dr. Conlon is on the 3rd floor, or (b) Dr. Kane is on the 3rd floor and Dr. Conlon is on the 5th floor. If option (b) were correct, then since Dr. Assad would be on the 1st floor, it would be impossible for Dr. Steen's office to be between Dr. Conlon and Dr. Assad's office. Therefore, Dr. Kane's office must be on the 5th floor. The order of the doctors' offices, from 5th floor down to the 1st floor is: Dr. Kane, Dr. Johnson, Dr. Conlon, Dr. Steen, Dr. Assad.

6. CORRECT ANSWER: A
   Ray does not satisfy the requirement of holding his breath for two minutes under water, since he can only hold is breath for one minute in that setting. But if he tunnels through a snowbank with just a T-shirt and shorts, he will satisfy the eligibility requirement. Note that the eligibility requirement contains the key word "or." So only one of the two clauses separated by "or" need to be fulfilled.

7. CORRECT ANSWER: B
   Statement 2 says that four sharps is equivalent to one tinplot. This means that a tinplot is worth more than a sharp. The conclusion is disproved. We note that the order of these items, from most valuable to least valuable are: tinplot, sharp, mark, plunk.

8. CORRECT ANSWER: C
   We can only conclude that gibbons and lemurs are fed lettuce and bananas. We can neither prove nor disprove that these animals are types of monkeys.

9. CORRECT ANSWER: C
We know that all Salishan Indians live east of the Continental Divide. But some non-members of this tribe of Indians may also live east of the Continental Divide. Since none of the members of the Blackfoot tribe belong to the Salishan Indian tribe, we cannot draw any conclusion about the location of the Blackfoot tribe with respect to the Continental Divide.

18. CORRECT ANSWER: B
Since the pepper is second from the left and the nutmeg is between the sage and the pepper, the positions 2, 3, and 4 (from the left) are pepper, nutmeg, sage. By statement II, the basil must be in position 5, which implies that the parsley is in position 1. Therefore, the basil, not the sage, is farthest to the right. The conclusion disproved.

19. CORRECT ANSWER: A
Statement II assures us that if switch C is ON, then Gear X is rotating in a counterclockwise direction. The conclusion is proved.

20. CORRECT ANSWER: C
Based on Statement IV, followed by Statement II, we conclude that Ganz and Rourke will file their reports on time. Statement III reveals that if Terence and Jackson attend the security meeting, they will fail to file their reports on time. We have no further information if Terence and Jackson attended the security meeting, so we are not able to either confirm or deny that their reports were filed on time. This implies that we cannot know for certain that Lane will leave for his meeting in Toronto.

21. CORRECT ANSWER: C
Although Bob is in second place behind Gregory, we cannot deduce how far behind Gregory he is running. At Gregory's current pace, he will cover four miles in 24 minutes. If Bob were only 100 yards behind Gregory, he would catch up to Gregory in one minute. But if Bob were very far behind Gregory, for example 5 miles, this is the equivalent of (5)(1760) = 8800 yards. Then Bob would need 8800/100 = 88 minutes to catch up to Gregory. Thus, the given facts are not sufficient to draw a conclusion.

22. CORRECT ANSWER: A
Statement II tells us that neither Earl nor Pete could be the oldest; also, either John or Gary is married. Statement IV reveals that the oldest brother is both married and the tallest. By Statement III, John cannot be the tallest. Since John is not the tallest, he is not the oldest. Thus, the oldest brother must be Gary. The conclusion is proved.

23. CORRECT ANSWER: B
By Statements III and IV, General Woundwort must have given the order to advance. Statement II then tells us that Brigade X will advance to the demilitarized zone, but not soon enough before the conflict begins. Thus, the conclusion is disproved.

11 (#2)

24. CORRECT ANSWER: A
If the distance is 5 miles or less, then the cost for the Orange Cab is only $7.50, whereas the cost for the Chubby Cab is $5 + 3x$, where x represents the number of miles traveled. For 1 to 5 miles, the cost of the Chubby Cab is between $8 and $20. This means that for a distance of 5 miles, the Orange Cab costs $7.50, whereas the Chubby Cab costs $20. After 5 miles, the cost per mile of the Chubby Cab exceeds the cost per mile of the Orange Cab. Thus, regardless of the actual distance between Fullerton and Elverton, the cost for the Orange Cab will be cheaper than that of the Chubby Cab.

25. CORRECT ANSWER: B
It looks like "Dalton" should be replaced by "Dan" in the conclusion. Then by statement I, if Lucy is absent, Dan is never in class. Thus, the conclusion is disproved.

READING COMPREHENSION
UNDERSTANDING AND INTERPRETING WRITTEN MATERIAL
EXAMINATION SECTION
TEST 1

DIRECTIONS: All questions are to be answered SOLELY on the basis of the information contained in the passage. Each question or incomplete statement is followed by several suggested answers or completions. Select the one that BEST answers the question or completes the statement. *PRINT THE LETTER OF THE CORRECT ANSWER IN THE SPACE AT THE RIGHT.*

Questions 1-3.

The equipment in a mail room may include a mail-metering machine. This machine simultaneously stamps, postmarks, seals, and counts letters as fast as the operator can feed them. It can also print the proper postage directly on a gummed strip to be affixed to bulky items. It is equipped with a meter which is removed from the machine and sent to the postmaster to be set for a given number of stampings of any denomination. The setting of the meter must be paid for in advance. One of the advantages of metered mail is that it bypasses the cancellation operation and, thereby, facilitates handling by the post office. Mail metering also makes the pilfering of stamps impossible, but does not prevent the passage of personal mail in company envelopes through the meters unless there is established a rigid control or censorship over outgoing mail.

1. According to this statement, the postmaster
   A. is responsible for training new clerks in the use of mail-metering machines
   B. usually recommends that both large and small firms adopt the use of mail metering machines
   C. is responsible for setting the meter to print a fixed number of stampings
   D. examines the mail-metering machines to see that they are properly installed in the mail room

1.____

2. According to this statement, the use of mail-metering machines
   A. requires the employment of more clerks in a mail room than does the use of postage stamps
   B. interferes with the handling of large quantities of outgoing mail
   C. does not prevent employees from sending their personal letters at company expense
   D. usually involves smaller expenditures for mail room equipment than does the use of postage stamps

2.____

3. On the basis of this statement, it is MOST accurate to state that
   A. mail-metering machines are often used for opening envelopes
   B. postage stamps are generally used when bulky packages are to be mailed
   C. the use of metered mail tends to interfere with rapid mail handling by the post office
   D. mail-metering machines can seal and count letters at the same time

3.____

Questions 4-8.

It is the Housing Administration's policy that all tenants, whether new or transferring from one housing development to another, shall be required to pay a standard security deposit of one month's rent based on the rent at the time of admission. There are, however, certain exceptions to this policy. Employees of the Administration shall not be required to pay a security deposit if they secure an apartment in an Administration development. Where the payment of a full security deposit may present a hardship to a tenant, the development's manager may allow a tenant to move into an apartment upon payment of only part of the security deposit. In such cases, however, the tenant must agree to gradually pay the balance of the deposit. If a tenant transfers from one apartment to another within the same project, the security deposit originally paid by the tenant for his former apartment will be acceptable for his new apartment, even if the rent in the new apartment is greater than the rent in the former one. Finally, tenants who receive public assistance need not pay a security deposit before moving into an apartment if the appropriate agency states, in writing, that it will pay the deposit. However, it is the responsibility of the development's manager to make certain that payment shall be received within one month of the date the tenant moves into the apartment.

4. According to the above passage, when a tenant transfers from one apartment to another in the same development, the Housing Administration will
   A. accept the tenant's old security deposit as the security deposit for his new apartment
   B. refund the tenant's old security deposit and not require him to pay a new deposit
   C. keep the tenant's old security deposit and require him to pay a new deposit
   D. require the tenant to pay a new security deposit based on the difference between his old rent and his new rent

5. On the basis of the above passage, it is INCORREC to state that a tenant who receives public assistance may move into an Administration development if
   A. he pays the appropriate security deposit
   B. the appropriate agency gives a written indication that it will pay the security deposit before the tenant moves in
   C. the appropriate agency states, by telephone, that it will pay the security deposit
   D. the appropriate agency writes the manager to indicate that the security deposit will be paid within one month but not less than two weeks from the date the tenant moves into the apartment

6. On the basis of the above passage, a tenant who transfers from an apartment in one development to an apartment in a different department will
   A. forfeit his old security deposit and be required to pay another deposit
   B. have his old security deposit refunded and not have to pay a new deposit
   C. pay the difference between his old security deposit and the new one
   D. have to pay a security deposit based on the new apartment's rent

7. The Housing Administration will NOT require payment of a security deposit if a tenant
    A. is an Administration employee
    B. is receiving public assistance
    C. claims that payment will present a hardship
    D. indicates, in writing, that he will be responsible for any damage done to his apartment

8. Of the following, the BEST title for the above passage is:
    A. Security Deposits – Transfers
    B. Security Deposits – Policy
    C. Exemptions and Exceptions – Security Deposits
    D. Amounts – Security Deposits

Questions 9-11.

Terrazzo flooring will last a very long time if it is cared for properly. Lacquers, shellac or varnish preparations should never be used on terrazzo. Soap cleaners are not recommended, since they dull the appearance of the floor. Alkaline solutions are harmful, so neutral cleaner or non-alkaline synthetic detergents will give best results. If the floor is very dirty, it may be necessary to scrub it. The same neutral cleaning solution should be used for scrubbing as for mopping. Scouring powder may be sprinkled at particularly dirty spots. Do not use steel wool for scrubbing. Small pieces of steel filings left on the floor will rust and discolor the terrazzo. Non-woven nylon or open-mesh fabric abrasive pads are suitable for scrubbing terrazzo floors.

9. According to the above passage, the BEST cleaning agent for terrazzo flooring is a(n)
    A. soap cleaner   B. varnish preparation
    C. neutral cleaner   D. alkaline solution

10. According to the above passage, terrazzo floors should NOT be scrubbed with
    A. non-woven nylon abrasive pads   B. steel wool
    C. open-mesh fabric abrasive pads D. scouring powder

11. As used in the above passage, the word *discolor* means MOST NEARLY
    A. crack   B. scratch   C. dissolve   D. stain

Questions 12-15.

Planning for the unloading of incoming trucks is not easy since generally little or no advance notice of truck arrivals is received. The height of the floor of truck bodies and loading platforms sometimes are different; this makes necessary the use of special unloading methods. When available, hydraulic ramps compensate for the differences in platform and truck floor levels. When hydraulic ramps are not available, forklift equipment can sometimes be used, if the truck sprigs are strong enough to support such equipment. In a situation like this, the unloading operation does not differ much from unloading a railroad box car in the cases where the forklift truck or a hydraulic pallet jack cannot be used inside the truck, a pallet dolly should be placed inside the truck, so that the empty pallet can be loaded close to the truck contents and rolled easily to the truck door and platform.

12. According to the above passage, unloading trucks are
    A. easy to plan since the time of arrival is usually known beforehand
    B. the same as loading a railroad box car
    C. hard to plan since trucks arrive without notice
    D. a very normal thing to do

13. According to the above passage, which materials-handling equipment can make up for the difference in platform and truck floor levels?
    A. Hydraulic jacks
    B. Hydraulic ramps
    C. Forklift trucks
    D. Conveyors

14. According to the above passage, what materials-handling equipment can be used when a truck cannot support the weight of forklift equipment?
    A. A pallet dolly
    B. A hydraulic ramp
    C. Bridge plates
    D. A warehouse tractor

15. Which of the following is the BEST title for the above passage?
    A. Unloading Railroad Box Cars
    B. Unloading Motor Trucks
    C. Loading Rail Box
    D. Loading Motor Trucks

Questions 16-19.

Ventilation, as used in firefighting operations, means opening up a building or structure in which a fire is burning to release the accumulated heat, smoke, and gases. Lack of knowledge of the principle of ventilation on the part of firemen may result in unnecessary punishment due to ventilation being neglected or improperly handled. While ventilation itself extinguishes no fires, when used in an intelligent manner, it allows firemen to get at the fire more quickly, easily, and with less danger and hardship.

16. According to the above passage, the MOST important result of failure to apply the principles of ventilation at a fire may be
    A. loss of public confidence
    B. disciplinary action
    C. waste of water
    D. excessive use of equipment
    E. injury to fireman

17. It may be inferred from the above passage that the CHIEF advantage of ventilation is that it
    A. eliminates the need for gas masks
    B. reduces smoke damage
    C. permits firemen to work closer to the fire
    D. cools the fire
    E. enables firemen to use shorter hose lines

18. Knowledge of the principles of ventilation, as defined in the above passage, would be LEAST important in a fire in a
    A. tenement house
    B. grocery store
    C. ship's hold
    D. lumberyard
    E. office building

5 (#1)

19. We may conclude from the above passage that, for the well-trained and equipped fireman, ventilation is 19.____
    A. a simple matter
    B. rarely necessary
    C. relatively unimportant
    D. a basic tool
    E. sometimes a handicap

Questions 20-22.

Many public service and industrial organizations are becoming increasingly insistent that supervisors at the work level be qualified instructors. The reason for this is that technological improvements and overall organizational growth require the acquisition of new skills and knowledge by workers. These skills and knowledge can be acquired in two ways. They can be gained either by absorption-rubbing shoulders with the job or through planned instruction. Permitting the acquisition of new skills and knowledge is to be haphazard and uncertain is too costly. At higher supervisory levels, the need for instructing subordinate is not so obvious, but it is just as important as at the lowest work level. A high-ranking supervisor accomplishes the requirements of his position only if his subordinate supervisors perform their work efficiently. Regardless of one's supervisory position, the ability to instruct easily and efficiently helps to insure well-qualified and thoroughly-trained subordinates. There exists an unfounded but rather prevalent belief that becoming a competent instructor is a long, arduous, and complicated process. This belief arises partially as a result of the requirement of a long period of college preparation involved in preparing teachers for our school system. This time is necessary because teachers must learn a great deal of subject matter. The worker who advances to a supervisory position generally has superior skill and knowledge; therefore, he has only to learn the techniques by which he can impart his knowledge in order to become a competent instructor.

20. According to the above passage, a prolonged period of preparation for instructing is NOT generally necessary for a worker who is advanced to a supervisory position because 20.____
    A. he may already possess some of the requirements of a competent instructor
    B. his previous job knowledge is generally sufficient to enable him to begin instructing immediately
    C. in his present position there is less need for the specific job knowledge of the ordinary worker
    D. the ability to instruct follows naturally from superior skill and knowledge

21. According to the above passage, it is important for the higher-level supervisor to be a good instructor because 21.____
    A. at this level there is a tendency to overlook the need for instruction of both subordinate supervisors and workers
    B. good training practices will then be readily adopted by lower-level supervisors
    C. the need for effective training is more critical at the higher levels of responsibility
    D. training can be used to improve the supervisory performance of his subordinate supervisors

22. According to the above passage, the acquisition of new skills and knowledge by workers is BEST accomplished when
    A. the method of training allows for the use of absorption
    B. organizational growth and technological improvement indicate a need for further training
    C. such training is the result of careful planning
    D. the cost factor involved in training can be readily justified

Questions 23-25.

The organization of any large agency falls into three broad general zones: top management, middle management, and rank-and-file operations. The normal task of middle management is to supervise, direct, and control the performance of operations within the scope of law, policy, and regulations already established. Where policy is settled and well defined, middle management is basically a set of standard operations, although they may call for high-developed skills. Where, however, policy is not clearly stated, is ambiguous, or is rapidly shifting, middle management is likely to have an important influence upon emergency policy trends. Persons working in the zone of middle management usually become specialists. They need specialist knowledge of law, rules, and regulations, and court decisions governing their organization if they are to discharge their duties effectively. They will also have acquired specialist knowledge of relationships and sequences in the normal flow of business. Further, their attention is brought to bear on a particular administrative task, in a particular jurisdiction, with a particular clientele. The importance of middle management is obviously great. The reasons for such importance are not difficult to find: Here it is that the essential action of government in behalf of citizens is taken; here it is that citizens deal with government when they pass beyond their first contacts; here is a training ground from which a considerable part of top management emerges; and here it is that the spirit and temper of the public service and its reputation are largely made.

23. According to the above passage, the critical importance of middle management is due to the fact that it is at this level that
    A. formal executive training can be most useful
    B. the greatest amount of action is taken on the complaints of the general public
    C. the official actions taken have the greatest impact on general attitudes towards the public service
    D. the public most frequently comes in contact with governmental operations and agencies

24. According to the above passage, the one of the following statements which is NOT offered as an explanation of the tendency for middle management responsibility to produce specialists is that
    A. middle-management personnel frequently feel that their work is the most important in an organization
    B. specialized knowledge is acquired during the course of everyday work
    C. specialized knowledge is necessary for effective job performance
    D. their work assignments are directed to specific problems in specific situations

25. According to the above passage, the GREATEST impact of middle management in policy determination would be likely to be felt in the situation in which
    A. middle management possesses highly developed operational skills
    B. several policy directives from top management are subject to varying interpretations
    C. the authority of middle management to supervise, direct, and control operations has been clearly established
    D. top management has neglected to consider the policy views of middle management

25.____

KEY (CORRECT ANSWERS)

1. C
2. C
3. D
4. A
5. C

6. D
7. A
8. B
9. C
10. B

11. D
12. C
13. B
14. A
15. B

16. E
17. C
18. D
19. D
20. A

21. D
22. C
23. C
24. A
25. B

TEST 2

DIRECTIONS: All questions are to be answered SOLELY on the basis of the information contained in the passage. Each question or incomplete statement is followed by several suggested answers or completions. Select the one that BEST answers the question or completes the statement. *PRINT THE LETTER OF THE CORRECT ANSWER IN THE SPACE AT THE RIGHT.*

Questions 1-2.

Metal spraying is used for many purposes. Worn bearings on shafts and spindles can be readily restored to original dimensions with any desired metal or alloy. Low-carbon steel shafts may be supplied with high-carbon steel journal surfaces, which can then be ground to size after spraying. By using babbitt wire, bearings can be lined or babbited while rotating. Pump shafts and impellers can be coated with any desired metal to overcome wear and corrosion. Valve seats may be re-surfaced. Defective castings can be repaired by filling in blowholes and checks. The application of metal spraying to the field of corrosion resistance is growing, although the major application in this field is in the use of sprayed zinc. Tin, lead, and aluminum have been used considerably. The process is used for structural and tank applications in the field as well as in the shop.

1. According to the above passage, worn bearing surface on shafts are metal-sprayed in order to   1.____
   A. prevent corrosion of the shaft
   B. fit them into larger-sized impellers
   C. returns them to their original sizes
   D. replaces worn babbitt metal

2. According to the above passage, rotating bearings can be metal-sprayed using   2.____
   A. babbitt wire   B. high-carbon steel
   C. low-carbon steel   D. any desired metal

Questions 3-5.

The method of cleaning which should generally be used is the space assignment method. Under this method, the buildings to be cleaned are divided into different sections. Within each section, each crew of Custodial Assistants is assigned to do one particular cleaning job. For example, within a section, one crew may be assigned to cleaning offices, another to scrubbing floors, a third to collecting trash, and so on. Other methods which may be used are the post-assignment methods and the gang-cleaning method. Under the post-assignment method, a Custodial Assistant is assigned to one area of a building and performs all cleaning jobs in that area. This method is seldom used except where buildings are so small and distant from each other that it is not economical to use the space-assigned method. Under the gang-cleaning method, a Custodial Foreman takes a number of Custodial Assistants through a section of the building. These Custodial Assistants work as a group and complete the various cleaning jobs as they go. This method is generally used only where the building contains very large open areas.

3. According to the above passage, under the space-assignment method, each crew generally
    A. works as a group and does a variety of different cleaning jobs
    B. is assigned to one area and performs all cleaning jobs in that area
    C. does one particular cleaning job within a section of a building
    D. follows the Custodial Foreman through a building containing large, open areas

4. According to the above passage, the post-assignment method is used mostly where the buildings to be cleaned are _____ in size and situated _____.
    A. large; close together   B. small; close together
    C. large; far apart   D. small; far apart

5. As used in the above passage, the word *economical* means MOST NEARLY
    A. thrifty   B. agreed   C. unusual   D. wasteful

Questions 6-9.

The desirability of complete refuse collection by municipalities is becoming generally accepted. In many cases, however, such ideal service is economically impractical and certain limits must be imposed. Some municipal authorities find it necessary to regulate the quantity of refuse, by weight or volume, which will be collected from a single residence or place of business at one collection. The purpose of the regulations is twofold: First, to maintain the degree of service rendered on a somewhat uniform basis; and, second, to insure a more or less constant collection from week to week. If left unregulated, careless producers might permit large quantities of refuse to accumulate on their premises over long periods and place abnormal amounts out for collection at irregular intervals, thus upsetting the collection schedule. Regulation is especially applied to large wholesale, industrial, and manufacturing enterprises which, in the great majority of cases, are required to dispose of all or part of their refuse themselves, at their own expense. The maximum quantities permitted by regulation should obviously be sufficient to take care of a normal accumulation at a household over the established interval between regular collections. In commercial districts, the maximum quantity limitations are often fixed on arbitrary bases rather than on normal production.

6. According to the above passage, many municipalities do not have complete refuse collections because
    A. it costs too much   B. it is difficult to regulate
    C. it is not a municipal function   D. they don't consider it desirable

7. According to the above passage, regulation by municipalities of the amount of refuse collected per collection from any one place of business does NOT contribute to
    A. accumulation of refuse by careless producers
    B. maintenance of collection schedules
    C. steady collection from one week to the next
    D. uniform service

8. According to the above passage, regulations by municipalities of refuse collection from certain enterprises helps to cut down
   A. accumulation of refuse for private collection
   B. the amount of refuse produced
   C. variation in the volume of refuse produced
   D. variation in collection service

9. According to the above passage, municipalities limit the amount of refuse collected in commercial districts on an arbitrary basis rather than on the basis of a normal accumulation. This is probably done because
   A. arbitrary standards are easy to establish and enforce
   B. normal accumulation is different for each district
   C. normal accumulation would require the collection of too much refuse
   D. there is no such thing as a normal accumulation

Questions 10-13.

The following passage is adapted from an old office manual:

Modern office methods, geared to ever higher speeds and aimed at ever greater efficiency, are largely the result of the typewriter. The typewriter is a substitute for handwriting and, in the hands of a skilled typist, not only turns out letters and other documents at least three times faster than a penman can do the work, but turns out the greater volume more uniformly and legibly. With the use of carbon paper and onionskin paper, identical copies can be made at the same time.

The typewriter, besides its effect on the conduct of business and government, has had a very important effect on the position of women. The typewriter has done much to bring women into business and government and today there are vastly more women than men typists. Many women have used the keys of the typewriter to climb the ladder to responsible managerial positions.

The typewriter, as its name implies, employs type to make an ink impression on paper. For many years, the manual typewriter was the standard machine used. Today, the electric typewriter is dominant, and completely automatic typewriters are coming into wider use.

The mechanism of the office manual typewriter includes a set of keys arranged systematically in rows; a semicircular frame of type, connected to the keys by levers; the carriage, or paper carrier; a rubber roller, called a platen, against which the type strikes; and an inked ribbon which makes the impression of the type character when the key strikes it.

10. The above passage mentions a number of good features of the combination of a skilled typist and a typewriter. Of the following, the feature which is NOT mentioned in the passage is
    A. speed   B. uniformity   C. reliability   D. legibility

11. According to the above passage, a skilled typist can
    A. turn out at least five carbon copies of typed matter
    B. type at least three times faster than a penman can write
    C. type more than 80 words a minute
    D. readily move into a managerial position

12. According to the above passage, which of the following is NOT part of the mechanism of a manual typewriter?
    A. Carbon paper
    B. Paper carrier
    C. Platen
    D. Inked ribbon

13. According to the above passage, the typewriter has helped
    A. men more than women in business
    B. women in career advancement into management
    C. men and women equally, but women have taken better advantage of it
    D. more women than men, because men generally dislike routine typing work

Questions 14-18.

Reductions in pipe size of a building heating system are made with eccentric fittings and are pitched downward. The ends of mains with gravity return shall be at least 18" above the water line of the boiler. As condensate flows opposite to the steam, run outs are one size larger than the vertical pipe and are pitched upward. In a one-pipe system, an automatic air vent must be provided at each main to relieve air pressure and to let steam enter the radiator. As steam enters the radiator, a *thermal* device causes the vent to close, thereby holding the steam. Steam mains should not be less than two inches in diameter. The end of the steam main should have a minimum size of one-half of its greatest diameter. Small steam systems should be sized for a 2-oz. pressure drop. Large steam systems should be sized for a 4-oz. pressure drop.

14. The word *thermal*, as used in the above passage, means MOST NEARLY
    A. convector   B. heat   C. instrument   D. current

15. According to the above passage, the one of the following that is one size larger than the vertical pipe is the
    A. steam main   B. valve   C. water line   D. run out

16. According to the above paragraph, small steam systems should be sized for a pressure drop of _____ oz.
    A. 2   B. 3   C. 4   D. 5

17. According to the above passage, ends of mains with gravity return shall be AT LEAST
    A. 18" above the water line of the boiler
    B. one-quarter of the greatest diameter of the main
    C. twice the size of the vertical pipe in the main
    D. 18" above the steam line of the boiler

18. According to the above passage, the one of the following that is provided at each main to relieve air pressure is a(n)
    A. gravity return   B. convector   C. eccentric   D. vent

Questions 19-21.

The bearings of all electrical equipment should be subjected to careful inspection at scheduled periodic intervals in order to secure maximum life. The newer type of sleeve bearing requires very little attention since the oil does not become contaminated and oil leakage is negligible. Maintenance of the correct oil level is frequently the only upkeep required for years of service with this type of bearing.

19. According to the above passage, the MAIN reason for making periodic inspections of electrical equipment is to
    A. reduce waste of lubricants
    B. prevent injury to operators
    C. make equipment last longer
    D. keeps operators "on their toes"

20. According to the above passage, the bearings of electrical equipment should be inspected
    A. whenever the equipment isn't working properly
    B. whenever there is time for inspections
    C. at least once a year
    D. at regular times

21. According to the above passage, when using the newer type of sleeve bearings,
    A. oil leakage is slight
    B. the oil level should be checked every few years
    C. oil leakage is due to carelessness
    D. oil soon becomes dirty

Questions 22-25.

There is hardly a city in the country that is not short of fire protection in some areas within its boundaries. These municipalities have spread out and have re-shuffled their residential, business, and industrial districts without readjusting the existing protective fire forces; or creating new protection units. Fire stations are still situated according to the needs of earlier times and have not been altered or improved to house modern firefighting equipment. They are neither efficient for carrying out their tasks nor livable for the men who must occupy them.

22. Of the following, the title which BEST describes the central idea of the above passage is:
    A. The Dynamic Nature of Contemporary Society
    B. The Cost of Fire Protection
    C. The Location and Design of Fire Stations
    D. The Design and Use of Firefighting Equipment
    E. The Growth of American Cities

23. According to the above passage, fire protection is inadequate in the United Sates in
    A. most areas of some cities
    B. some areas of most cities
    C. some areas in all cities
    D. all areas in some cities
    E. most areas in most cities

24. The one of the following criteria for planning of fire stations which is NOT mentioned in the above passage is:
    A. Comfort of Firemen
    B. Proper Location
    C. Design for Modern Equipment
    D. Efficiency of Operation
    E. Cost of Construction

24.____

25. Of the following suggestions for improving the fire service, the one which would BEST deal with the problem discussed in the above passage would involve
    A. specialized training in the use of modern fire apparatus
    B. replacement of obsolete fire apparatus
    C. revision of zoning laws
    D. longer basic training for probationary firemen
    E. reassignment of fire districts

25.____

Questions 26-30.

Stopping, standing, and parking of motor vehicles is regulated by law to keep the public highways open for a smooth flow of traffic, and to keep stopped vehicles from blocking intersections, driveways, signs, fire hydrants, and other areas that must be kept clear. These established regulations apply in all situations, unless otherwise indicated by signs. Other local restrictions are posted in the areas to which they apply. Three examples of these other types of restrictions, which may apply singly or in combination with one another are:
NO STOPPING: This means that a driver may not stop a vehicle for any purpose except when necessary to avoid interference with other vehicles, or in compliance with directions of a police officer or signal.
NO STANDING: This means that a driver may stop a vehicle only temporarily to actually receive or discharge passengers.
NO PARKING: This means that a driver may stop a vehicle only temporarily to actually load or unload merchandise or passengers. When stopped, it is advisable to turn on warning flashers, if equipped with them. However, one should never use a directional signal for this purpose, because it may confuse other drivers. Some NO PARKING signs prohibit parking between certain hours on certain days. For example, the sign may read NO PARKING 8 A.M. to 11 A.M., MONDAY, WEDNESDAY, FRIDAY. These signs are usually utilized on streets where cleaning operations take place on alternate days.

26. The parking regulation that applies to fire hydrants is an example of _____ regulations.
    A. local   B. established   C. posted   D. temporary

26.____

27. When stopped in a NO PARKING zone, it is advisable to
    A. turn on the right directional signal to indicate to other drivers that you will remain stopped
    B. turn on the left directional signal to indicate to other drivers that you may be leaving the curb after a period of time
    C. turn on the warning flashers if your car is equipped with them
    D. put the vehicle in reverse so that the backup lights will be on to warn approaching cars that you have temporarily stopped

27.____

28. You may stop a vehicle temporarily to discharge passengers in an area under the restriction of a _____ zone.
    A. NO STOPPING – NO STANDING
    B. NO STANDING – NO PARKING
    C. NO PARKING – NO STOPPING
    D. NO STOPPING – NO STANDING – NO PARKING

28._____

29. A sign reads "NO PARKING 8 A.M. to 11 A.M., MONDAY, WEDNESDAY, FRIDAY."
    Based on this sign, an enforcement officer would issue a summons to a car that is parked on a
    A. Tuesday at 9:30 A.M.   B. Wednesday at 12:00 A.M.
    C. Friday at 10:30 A.M.   D. Saturday at 8:00 A.M.

29._____

30. NO PARKING signs prohibiting parking between certain hours, on certain days, are usually utilized on streets where
    A. vehicles frequently take on and discharge passengers
    B. cleaning operations take place on alternate days
    C. NO STOPPING signs have been ignored
    D. commercial vehicles take on and unload merchandise

30._____

KEY (CORRECT ANSWERS)

1.	C	11.	B	21.	A
2.	A	12.	A	22.	C
3.	C	13.	B	23.	B
4.	D	14.	B	24.	E
5.	A	15.	D	25.	E
6.	A	16.	A	26.	B
7.	A	17.	A	27.	C
8.	D	18.	D	28.	B
9.	C	19.	C	29.	C
10.	C	20.	D	30.	B

PREPARING WRITTEN MATERIAL

PARAGRAPH REARRANGEMENT
COMMENTARY

The sentences that follow are in scrambled order. You are to rearrange them in proper order and indicate the letter choice containing the correct answer at the space at the right.

Each group of sentences in this section is actually a paragraph presented in scrambled order. Each sentence in the group has a place in that paragraph; no sentence is to be left out. You are to read each group of sentences and decide upon the best order in which to put the sentences so as to form a well-organized paragraph.

The questions in this section measure the ability to solve a problem when all the facts relevant to its solution are not given.

More specifically, certain positions of responsibility and authority require the employee to discover connection between events sometimes, apparently, unrelated. In order to do this, the employee will find it necessary to correctly infer that unspecified events have probably occurred or are likely to occur. This ability becomes especially important when action must be taken on incomplete information.

Accordingly, these questions require competitors to choose among several suggested alternatives, each of which presents a different sequential arrangement of the events. Competitors must choose the MOST logical of the suggested sequences.

In order to do so, they may be required to draw on general knowledge to infer missing concepts or events that are essential to sequencing the given events. Competitors should be careful to infer only what is essential to the sequence. The plausibility of the wrong alternatives will always require the inclusion of unlikely events or of additional chains of events which are NOT essential to sequencing the given events.

It's very important to remember that you are looking for the best of the four possible choices, and that the best choice of all may not even be one of the answers you're given to choose from.

There is no one right way to solve these problems. Many people have found it helpful to first write out the order of the sentences, as they would have arranged them, on their scrap paper before looking at the possible answers. If their optimum answer is there, this can save them some time. If it isn't, this method can still give insight into solving the problem. Others find it most helpful to just go through each of the possible choices, contrasting each as they go along. You should use whatever method feels comfortable and works for you.

While most of these types of questions are not that difficult, we've added a higher percentage of the difficult type, just to give you more practice. Usually there are only one or two questions on this section that contain such subtle distinctions that you're unable to answer confidently. And you then may find yourself stuck deciding between two possible choices, neither of which you're sure about.

PREPARING WRITTEN MATERIAL
EXAMINATION SECTION
TEST 1

DIRECTIONS: The following groups of sentences need to be arranged in an order that makes sense. Select the letter preceding the sequence that represents the BEST sentence order. *PRINT THE LETTER OF THE CORRECT ANSWER IN THE SPACE AT THE RIGHT.*

1.
   I. A large Naval station on Alameda Island, near Oakland, held many warships in port, and the War Department was worried that if the bridge were to be blown up by the enemy, passage to and from the bay would be hopelessly blocked.
   II. Though many skeptics were opposed to the idea of building such an enormous bridge, the most vocal opposition came from a surprising source: the United States War Department.
   III. The War Department's concerns led to a showdown at San Francisco City Hall between Strauss and the Secretary of War, who demanded to know what would happen if a military enemy blew up the bridge.
   IV. In 1933, by submitting a construction cost estimate of $17 million, an engineer named Joseph Strauss won the contract to build the Golden Gate Bridge of San Francisco, which would then become one of the world's largest bridges.
   V. Strauss quickly ended the debate by explaining that the Golden Gate Bridge was to be a suspension bridge, whose roadway would hang in the air from cables strung between two huge towers, and would immediately sink into three hundred feet of water if it were destroyed.

   The BEST order is:
   A. II, III, I, IV, V   B. I, II, III, V, IV   C. IV, II, I, III, V   D. IV, I, III, V, II

   1.____

2.
   I. Plastic surgeons have already begun to use virtual reality to map out the complex nerve and tissue structures of a particular patient's face, in order to prepare for delicate surgery.
   II. A virtual reality program responds to these movements by adjusting the images that a person sees on a screen or through goggles, thereby creating an "interactive" world in which a person can see and touch three-dimensional graphic objects.
   III. No more than a computer program that is designed to build and display graphic images, the virtual reality program takes graphic programs a step further by sensing a person's head and body movements.
   IV. The computer technology known as virtual reality, now in its very first stages of development, is already revolutionizing some aspects of contemporary life.
   V. Virtual reality computers are also being used by the space program, most recently to simulate conditions for the astronauts who were launched on a repair mission to the Hubble telescope.

   2.____

The BEST order is:
A. IV, II, I, V, III   B. III, I, V, II, IV   C. IV, III, II, I, V   D. III, I, II, IV, V

3.   I. Before you plant anything, the soil in your plant bed should be carefully raked level, a small section at a time, and any clods or rocks that can't be broken up should be removed.
     II. Your plant should be placed in a hole that will position it at the same level it was at the nursery, and a small indentation should be pressed into the soil around the plant in order to hold water near its roots.
     III. Before placing the plant in the soil, lightly separate any roots that may have been matted together in the container, cutting away any thick masses that can't be separated, so that the remaining roots will be able to grow outward.
     IV. After the bed is ready, remove your plant from its container by turning it upside down and tapping or pushing on the bottom —never remove it by pulling on the plant.
     V. When you bring home a small plant in an individual container from the nursery, there are several things to remember while preparing to plant it in your own garden.

   The BEST order is:
   A. V, IV, III, II, I   B. V, II, IV, III, II   C. I, IV, II, III, V   D. I, IV, V, II, III

4.   I. The motte and its tower were usually built first, so that sentries could use it as a lookout to warn the castle workers of any danger that might approach the castle.
     II. Though the moat and palisade offered the bailey a good deal of protection, it was linked to the motte by a set of stairs that led to a retractable drawbridge at the motte's gate, to enable people to evacuate onto the motte in case of an attack.
     III. The motte of these early castles was a fortified hill, sometimes as high as one hundred feet, on which stood a palisade and tower.
     IV. The bailey was a clear, level spot below the motte, also enclosed by a palisade, which in turn was surrounded by a large trench or moat.
     V. The earliest castles built in Europe were not the magnificent stone giants that still tower over much of the European landscape, but simpler wooden constructions called motte-and-bailey castles.

   The BEST order is:
   A. V, III, I, IV, II   B. V, IV, I, II, III   C. I, IV, III, II, V   D. I, III, II, IV, V

5.   I. If an infant is left alone or abandoned for a short while, its immediate response is to cry loudly, accompanying its screams with aggressive flailing of its legs and limbs.
     II. If a child has been abandoned for a longer period of time, it becomes completely still and quiet, as if realizing that now its only chance for survival is to shut its mouth and remain motionless.
     III. Along with their intense fear of the dark, the crying behavior of human infants offers insights into how prehistoric newborn children might have evolved instincts that would prevent them from becoming victims of predators.

IV. This behavior often surprises people who enter a hospital's maternity ward for the first time and encounter total silence from a roomful of infants.
V. This violent screaming response is quite different from an infant's cries of discomfort or hunger, and seems to serve as either the child's first line of defense against an unwanted intruder, or a desperate attempt to communicate its position to the mother.
The BEST order is:
   A. III, II, IV, I, V   B. III, I, V, II, IV   C. I, V, IV, II, III   D. II, IV, I, V, III

6. I. When two cats meet who are strangers, their first actions and gestures determine who the "dominant" cat will be, at least for the time being.
   II. Unlike dogs, cats are typically a solitary animal species who avoid social interaction, but they do display specific social responses to each other upon meeting.
   III. This is unlikely, however; before such a point of open hostility is reached, one of the cats will usually take the "submissive" position of crouching down while looking away from the other dat.
   IV. If a cat desires dominance or sees the other cat as a threat to its territory, it will stare directly at the intruder with a lowered tail.
   V. If the other cat responds with a similar gesture, or with the strong defensive posture of an arched back, laid-back ears and raised tail, a fight or chase is likely if neither cat gives in.
   The BEST order is:
      A. IV, II, I, V, III   B. I, II, IV, V, III   C. I, IV, V, III, II   D. II, I, IV, V, III

7. I. A star or planet's gravitational force can best be explained in this way: anything passing through this "dent" in space will veer toward the star or planet as if it were rolling into a hole.
   II. Objects that are massive or heavy, such as stars or planets, "sink" into this surface, creating a sort of dent or concavity in the surrounding space.
   III. Black holes, the most massive objects known to exist in space, create dents so large and deep that the space surrounding them actually folds in on itself, preventing anything that falls in —even light —from ever escaping again.
   IV. The sort of dent a star or planet makes depends on how massive it is; planets generally have weak gravitational pulls, but stars, which are larger and heavier, make a bigger "dent" that will attract more matter.
   V. In outer space, the force of gravity works as if the surrounding space is a soft, flat surface.
   The BEST order is:
      A. III, V, II, I, IV   B. III, IV, I, V, II   C. V, II, I, IV, III   D. I, V, II, IV, III

8. I. Eventually, the society of Kyoto gave the world one of its first and greatest novels when Japan's most promising writer, Lady Murasaki Shikibu, wrote her chronicle of Kyoto's society, *The Tale of Genji*, which preceded the first European novels by more than 500 years.
   II. The society of Kyoto was dedicated to the pleasures of art; the courtiers experimented with new and colorful methods of sculpture, painting, writing, decorative gardening, and even making clothes.

III. Japanese culture began under the powerful authority of Chinese Buddhism, which influenced every aspect of Japanese life from religion to politics and art.
IV. This new, vibrant culture was so sophisticated that all the people in Kyoto's imperial court considered themselves poets, and the line between life and art hardly existed —lovers corresponded entirely through written verses, and even government officials communicated by writing poems to each other.
V. In the eighth century, when the emperor established the town of Kyoto as the capital of the Japanese empire, Japanese society began to develop its own distinctive style.

The BEST order is:
  A. V, II, IV, I, III   B. II, I, V, IV, III   C. V, III, IV, I, II   D. III, V, II, IV, I

9.
I. Instead of wheels, the HSST uses two sets of magnets, one which sits on the track, and another that is carried by the train; these magnets generate an identical magnetic field which forces the two sets apart.
II. In the last few decades, railway travel has become less popular throughout the world, because it is much slower than travel by airplane, and not much less expensive.
III. The HSST's designers say that the train can take passengers from one town to another as quickly as a jet plane —while consuming less than half the energy.
IV. This repellent effect is strong enough to lift the entire train above the trackway, and the train, literally traveling on air, rockets along at speeds of up to 300 miles per hour.
V. The revolutionary technology of magnetic levitation, currently being tested by Japan's experimental HSST (High Speed Surface Transport), may yet bring passenger trains back from the dead.

The BEST order is:
  A. II, V, I, IV, III   B. II, I, IV, III, V   C. V, II, III, I, IV   D. V, I, III, IV, II

9.____

10.
I. When European countries first began to colonize the African continent, their impression of the African people was of a vast group of loosely organized tribal societies, without any great centralized source of power or wealth.
II. The legend of Timbuktu persisted until the nineteenth century, when a French adventurer visited Timbuktu and found that raids by neighboring tribesmen had made the city a shadow of its former self.
III. In the fifteenth century, when the stories of travelers who had traveled Africa's Sudan region began circulating around Europe, this impression began to change.
IV. In 1470, an Italian merchant named Benedetto Dei traveled to Timbuktu and confirmed these rumors, describing a thriving metropolis where rich and poor people worshipped together in the city's many ornate mosques — there was even a university in Timbuktu, much like its European counterparts, where African scholars pursued their studies in the arts and sciences.

10.____

V. The travelers' legends told of an enormous city in the western Sudan, Timbuktu, where the streets were crowded with goods brought by faraway caravans, and where there was a stone palace as large as any in Europe.

The BEST order is:
A. III, V, I, IV, II   B. I, II, IV, III, V   C. I, III, V, IV, II   D. II, I, III, IV, V

11. I. Also, our reference points in sighting the moon make us believe that its size is changing; when the moon is rising through the trees, it seems huge, because our brains unconsciously compare the size of the moon with the size of the trees in the foreground.
II. To most people, the sky itself appears more distant at the horizon than directly overhead, and if the moon's size—which remains constant—is projected from the horizon, the apparent distance of the horizon makes the moon look bigger.
III. Up higher in the sky, the moon is set against tiny stars in the background, which will make the moon seem smaller.
IV. People often wonder why the moon becomes bigger when it approaches the horizon, but most scientists agree that this is a complicated optical illusion, produced by at least three factors.
V. The moon illusion may also be partially explained by a phenomenon that has nothing to do with errors in our perception—light that enters the earth's atmosphere is sometimes refracted, and so the atmosphere may act as a kind of magnifying glass for the moon's image.

The BEST order is:
A. IV, III, V, II, I   B. IV, II, I, III, V   C. V, II, I, III, IV   D. II, I, III, IV, V

11.____

12. I. When the Native Americans were introduced to the horses used by white explorers, they were amazed at their new alternative—here was an animal that was strong and swift, would patiently carry a person or other loads on its back, and they later discovered, was right at home on the plains.
II. Before the arrival of European explorers to North America, the natives of the American plains used large dogs to carry their travois-long lodgepoles loaded with clothing, gear, and food.
III. These horses, it is now known, were not really strangers to North America; the very first horses originated here, on this continent, tens of thousands of years ago, and migrated into Asia across the Bering Land Bridge, a strip of land that used to link our continent with the Eastern world.
IV. At first, the natives knew so little about horses that at least one tribe tried to feed their new animals pieces of dried meat and animal fat, and were surprised when the horses turned their heads away and began to eat the grass of the prairie.
V. The American horse eventually became extinct, but its Asian cousins were reintroduced to the New World when the European explorers brought them to live among the Native Americans.

The BEST order is:
A. II, I, IV, III, V   B. II, IV, I, III, V   C. I, II, IV, III, V   D. I, III, V, II, IV

12.____

13.
   I. The dress worn by the dancer is believed to have been adorned in the past by shells which would strike each other as the dancer performed, creating a lovely sound.
   II. Today's jingle-dress is decorated with the tin lids of snuff cans, which are rolled into cones and sewn onto the dress,
   III. During the jingle-dress dance, the dancer must blend complicated footwork with a series of gentle hos that cause the cones to jingle in rhythm to a drumbeat.
   IV. When contemporary Native American tribes meet for a pow-wow, one of the most popular ceremonies to take place is the women's jingle-dress dance.
   V. Besides being more readily available than shells, the lids are thought by many dancers to create a softer, more subtle sound.
   The BEST order is:
   A. II, IV, V, I, III   B. IV, II, I, III, V   C. II, I, III, V, IV   D. IV, I, II, V, III

14.
   I. If a homeowner lives where seasonal climates are extreme, deciduous shade trees—which will drop their leaves in the winter and allow sunlight to pass through the windows—should be planted near the southern exposure in order to keep the house cool during the summer.
   II. This trajectory is shorter and lower in the sky than at any other time of year during the winter, when a house most requires heating; the northern-facing parts of a house do not receive any direct sunlight at all.
   III. In designing an energy-efficient house, especially in colder climates, it is important to remember that most of the house's windows should face south.
   IV. Though the sun always rises in the east and sets in the west, the sun of the northern hemisphere is permanently situated in the southern portion of the sky.
   V. The explanation for why so many architects and builders want this "southern exposure" is related to the path of the sun in the sky.
   The BEST order is:
   A. III, I, V, IV, II   B. III, V, IV, II, I   C. I, III, IV, II, V   D. I, II, V, IV, III

15.
   I. His journeying lasted twenty-four years and took him over an estimated 75,000 miles, a distance that would not be surpassed by anyone other than Magellan—who sailed around the world—for another six hundred years.
   II. Perhaps the most far-flung of these lesser-known travelers was Ibn Batuta, an African Moslem who left his birthplace of Tangier in the summer of 1325.
   III. Ibn Batuta traveled all over Africa and Asia, from Niger to Peking, and to the islands of Maldive and Indonesia.
   IV. However, a few explorers of the Eastern world logged enough miles and adventures to make Marco Polo's voyage look like an evening stroll.
   V. In America, the most well-known of the Old World's explorers are usually Europeans such as Marco Polo, the Italian who brought many elements of Chinese culture to the Western world.
   The BEST order is:
   A. V, IV, II, III, I   B. V, IV, III, II, I   C. III, II, I, IV, V   D. II, III, I, IV, V

16. I. In the rainforests of South America, a rare species of frog practices a reproductive method that is entirely different from this standard process.
 II. She will eventually carry each of the tadpoles up into the canopy and drop each into its own little pool, where it will be easy to locate and safe from most predators.
 III. After fertilization, the female of the species, who lives almost entirely on the forest floor, lays between 2 and 16 eggs among the leaf litter at the base of a tree, and stands watch over these eggs until they hatch.
 IV. Most frogs are pond-dwellers who are able to deposit hundreds of eggs in the water and then leave them alone, knowing that enough eggs have been laid to insure the survival of some of their offspring.
 V. Once the tadpoles emerge, the female backs in among them, and a tadpole will wriggle onto her back to be carried high into the forest canopy, where the female will deposit it in a little pool of water cupped in the leaf of a plant.
 The BEST order is:
 A. I, IV, III, II, V   B. I, III, V, II, IV   C. IV, III, II, V, I   D. IV, I, III, V, II

16.____

17. I. Eratosthenes had heard from travelers that at exactly noon on June 21, in the ancient city of Aswan, Egypt, the sun cast no shadow in a well, which meant that the sun must be directly overhead.
 II. He knew the sun always cast a shadow in Alexandria, and so he figured that if he could measure the length of an Alexandria shadow at the time when there was no shadow in Aswan, he could calculate the angle of the sun, and therefore the circumference of the earth.
 III. The evidence for a round earth was not new in 1492; in fact, Eratosthenes, an Alexandrian geographer who lived nearly sixteen centuries before Columbus's voyage (275-195 B.C.), actually developed a method for calculating the circumference of the earth that is still in use today.
 IV. Eratosthenes's method was correct, but his result—28,700 miles—was about 15 percent too high, probably because of the inaccurate ancient methods of keeping time, and because Aswan was not due south of Alexandria, as Eratosthenes had believed.
 V. When Christopher Columbus sailed across the Atlantic Ocean for the first time in 1492, there were still some people in the world who ignored scientific evidence and believed that the earth was flat, rather than round.
 The BEST order is:
 A. I, II, V, III, IV   B. V, III, IV, I, II   C. V, III, I, II, IV   D. III, V, I, II, IV

17.____

18. I. The first name for the child is considered a trial naming, often impersonal and neutral, such as the Ngoni name *Chabwera*, meaning "it has arrived."
 II. This sort of name is not due to any parental indifference to the child, but is a kind of silent recognition of Africa's sometimes high infant death rate; most parents ease the pain of losing a child with the belief that it is not really a person until it has been given a final name.
 III. In many tribal African societies, families often give two different names to their children, at different periods in time.
 IV. After the trial naming period has subsided and it is clear that the child will survive, the parents choose a final name for the child, an act that symbolically completes the act of birth.

18.____

V. In fact, some African first-given names are explicitly uncomplimentary, translating as "I am dead" or "I am ugly," in order to avoid the jealousy of ancestral spirits who might wish to take a child that is especially healthy or attractive.

The BEST order is:
A. III, I, II, V, IV   B. III, IV, II, I, V   C. IV, III, I, II, V   D. IV, V, III, I, II

19. I. Though uncertain of the definite reasons for this behavior, scientists believe the birds digest the clay in order to counteract toxins contained in the seeds of certain fruits that are eaten by macaws.
  II. For example, all macaws flock to riverbanks at certain times of the year to eat the clay that is found in river mud.
  III. The macaws of South America are not only among the largest and most beautifully colored of the world's flying birds, but they are also one of the smartest.
  IV. It is believed that macaws are forced to resort to these toxic fruits during the dry season, when foods are more scarce.
  V. The macaw's intelligence has led to intense study by scientists, who have discovered some macaw behaviors that have not yet been explained.

The BEST order is:
A. III, IV, I, II, V   B. III, V, II, I, IV   C. V, II, I, IV, III   D. IV, I, II, III, V

20. I. Although Maggie Kuhn has since passed away, the Gray Panthers are still waging a campaign to reinstate the historical view of the elderly as people whose experience allows them to make their greatest contribution in their later years.
  II. In 1972, an elderly woman named Maggie Kuhn responded to this sort of treatment by forming a group called the Gray Panthers, an organization of both old and young adults with the common goal of creating change.
  III. This attitude is reflected strongly in the way elderly people are treated by our society; many are forced into early retirement, or are placed in rest homes in which they are isolated from their communities.
  IV. Unlike most other cultures around the world, Americans tend to look upon old age with a sense of dread and sadness.
  V. Kuhn believed that when the elderly are forced to withdraw into lives that lack purpose, society loses one of its greatest resources: people who have a lifetime of experience and wisdom to offer their communities.

The BEST order is:
A. IV, III, II, V, I   B. IV, II, I, III, V   C. II, IV, III, V, I   D. II, I, IV, III, V

21. I. The current theory among most anthropologists is that humans evolved from apes who lived in trees near the grasslands of Africa.
  II. Still, some anthropologists insist that such an invention was necessary for the survival of early humans, and point to the Kung Bushmen of central Africa as a society in which the sling is still used in this way.
  III. Two of these inventions—fire, and weapons such as spears and clubs—were obvious defenses against predators, and there is archaeological evidence to support the theory of their use.

IV. Once people had evolved enough to leave the safety of trees and walk upright, they needed the protection of several inventions in order to survive.
V. But another invention, a feather or fiber sling that allowed mothers to carry children while leaving their hands free to gather roots or berries, would certainly have decomposed and left behind no trace of itself.
The BEST order is:
  A. I, II, III, V, IV   B. IV, I, II, III, V   C. I, IV, III, V, II   D. IV, III, V, II, I

22. I. The person holding the bird should keep it in hot water up to its neck, and the person cleaning should work a mild solution of dishwashing liquid into the bird's plumage, paying close attention to the head and neck.
II. When rinsing the bird, after all the oil has been removed, the running water should be directed against the lay of its feathers, until water begins to bead off the surface of the feathers—a sign that all the detergent has been rinsed out.
III. If you have rescued a sea bird from an oil spill and want to restore it to clean and normal living, you need a large sink, a constant supply of running hot water (a little over 100°F), and regular dishwashing liquid.
IV. This cleaning with detergent solution should be repeated as many times as it takes to remove all traces of oil from the bird's feathers, sometime over a period of several days.
V. But before you begin to clean the bird, you must find a partner because cleaning an oiled bird is a two-person job.
The BEST order is:
  A. III, I, II, IV, V   B. III, V, I, IV, II   C. III, I, IV, V, II   D. III, IV, V, I, II

23. I. The most difficult time of year for the Tsaatang is the spring calving, when the reindeer leave their wintering ground and rush to their accustomed calving place, without stopping by night or by day.
II. Reindeer travel in herds, and though some animals are tamed by the Tsaatang for riding or milking, the herds are allowed to roam free.
III. This journey is hard for the Tsaatang, who carry all their possessions with them, but once it's over it proves worthwhile; the Tsaatang can immediately begin to gather milk from reindeer cows who have given birth.
IV. The Tsaatang, a small tribe who live in the far northwest corner of Mongolia, practice a lifestyle that is completely dependent on the reindeer, their main resource for food, clothing, and transport.
V. The people must follow their yearly migrations, living in portable shelters that resemble Native American tepees.
The BEST order is:
  A. I, III, II, V, IV   B. I, IV, II, V, III   C. IV, I, III, V, II   D. IV II, V, I, III

24. I. The Romans later improved this system by installing these heated pipe networks throughout walls and ceilings, supplying heat to even the uppermost floors of a building—a system that, to this day, hasn't been much improved.
II. Air-conditioning, the method by which humans control indoor temperatures, was practiced much earlier than most people think.

III. The earliest heating devices other than open fires were used in 350 B.C. by the ancient Greeks, who directed air that had been heated by underground fires into baked clay pipes that ran under the floor.
IV. Ironically, the first successful cooling system, patented in England in 1831, used fire as its main energy source—fires were lit in the attic of a building, creating an updraft of air that drew cool air into the building through ducts that had underground openings near the river Thames.
V. Cooling buildings was more of a challenge, and wasn't attempted until 1500: a water-based system, designed by Leonardo da Vinci, does not appear to have been successful, since it was never used again.

The BEST order is:
  A. III, V, IV, I, II   B. III, I, II, V, IV   C. II, III, I, V, IV   D. IV, II, III, I, V

25. I. Cold, dry air from Canada passes over the Rocky Mountains and sweeps down onto the plains, where it collides with warm, moist air from the waters of the Gulf of Mexico, and when the two air masses meet, the resulting disturbance sometimes forms a violent funnel cloud that strikes the earth and destroys virtually everything in its path.
II. Hurricanes, storms which are generally not this violent and last much longer, are usually given names by meteorologists, but this tradition cannot be applied to tornados, which have a life span measured in minutes and disappear in the same way as they are born—unnamed.
III. A tornado funnel forms rotating columns of air whose speed reaches three hundred miles an hour—a speed that can only be estimated, because no wind-measuring devices in the direct path of a storm have ever survived.
IV. The natural phenomena known as tornados occur primarily over the Midwestern grasslands of the United States.
V. It is here, meteorologists tell us, that conditions for the formation of tornados are sometimes perfect during the spring months.

The BEST order is:
  A. II, IV, V, I, III   B. II, III, I, V, IV   C. IV, V, I, III, II   D. IV, III, I, V, II

25._____

KEY (CORRECT ANSWERS)

1.	C		11.	B
2.	C		12.	A
3.	B		13.	D
4.	A		14.	B
5.	B		15.	A
6.	D		16.	D
7.	C		17.	C
8.	D		18.	A
9.	A		19.	B
10.	C		20.	A

21. C
22. B
23. D
24. C
25. C

ENGLISH EXPRESSION
CHOICE OF EXPRESSION
COMMENTARY

One special form of the English Expression multiple-choice question in current use requires the candidate to select from among five (5) versions of a particular part of a sentence (or of an entire sentence), the one version that expresses the idea of the sentence most clearly, effectively, and accurately. Thus, the candidate is required not only to recognize errors, but also to choose the best way of phrasing a particular part of the sentence.

This is a test of choice of expression, which assays the candidate's ability to express himself correctly and effectively, including his sensitivity to the subtleties and nuances of the language.

SAMPLE QUESTIONS

DIRECTIONS: In each of the following sentences, some part of the sentence or the entire sentence is underlined. The underlined part presents a problem in the appropriate use of language. Beneath each sentence you will find five ways of writing the underlined part. The first of these indicates no change (that is, it repeats the original), but the other four are all different. If you think the original sentence is better than any of the suggested changes, you should choose answer A; otherwise you should mark one of the other choices. Select the BEST answer and print the letter in the space at the right.

This is a test of correctness and effectiveness of expression. In choosing answers, follow the requirements of standard written English; that is, pay attention to acceptable usage in grammar, diction (choice of words), sentence construction, and punctuation. Choose the answer that produces the most effective sentence—clear and exact, without awkwardness or ambiguity. Do not make a choice that changes the meaning of the original sentence.

SAMPLE QUESTION 1

Although these states now trade actively with the West, and although they are willing to exchange technological information, their arts and thoughts and social structure <u>remains substantially similar to what it has always been</u>.
- A. remains substantially similar to what it has always been
- B. remain substantially unchanged
- C. remains substantially unchanged
- D. remain substantially similar to what they have always been
- E. remain substantially without being changed

The purpose of questions of this type is to determine the candidate's ability to select the clearest and most effective means of expressing what the statement attempts to say. In this example, the phrasing in the statement, which is repeated in A, presents a problem of agreement between a subject and its verb (<u>their arts and thought and social structure</u> and <u>remains</u>), a problem of agreement between a pronoun and its antecedent (<u>their arts and thought and social structure</u> and <u>it</u>), an a problem of precise and concise phrasing (<u>remains</u>

substantially similar to what it has always been for remains substantially unchanged). Each of the four remaining choices in some way corrects one or more of the faults in the sentence, but only one deals with all three problems satisfactorily. Although C presents a more careful and concise wording of the phrasing of the statement and, in the process, eliminates the problem of agreement between pronoun and antecedent, it fails to correct the problem of agreement between the subject and its verb. In D, the subject agrees with its verb and the pronoun agrees with its antecedent, but the phrasing is not so accurate as it should be. The same difficulty persists in E. Only in B are all the problems presented corrected satisfactory. The question is not difficult.

SAMPLE QUESTION 2

Her latest novel is the largest in scope, the most accomplished in technique, and it is more significant in theme than anything she has written.
 A. it is more significant in theme than anything
 B. It is most significant in theme of anything
 C. more significant in theme than anything
 D. the most significant in theme than anything
 E. the most significant in theme of anything

This question is of greater difficulty than the preceding one. The problem posed in the sentence and repeated in A is essentially one of parallelism; Does the underlined portion of the sentence follow the pattern established by the first two elements of the series (the largest...the most accomplished)? It does not, for it introduces a pronoun and verb (it is) that the second term of the series indicates should be omitted and a degree of comparison (more significant) that is not in keeping with the superlatives used earlier in the sentence. B uses the superlative degree of significant but retains the unnecessary it is; C removes the it is, but retains the faulty comparative form of the adjective. D corrects both errors in parallelism, but introduces an error in idiom (the most...than). Only E corrects all the problems without introducing another fault.

SAMPLE QUESTION 3

Desiring to insure the continuity of their knowledge, magical lore is transmitted by the chiefs to their descendants.
 A. magical lore is transmitted by the chiefs
 B. transmission of magical lore is made by the chiefs
 C. the chiefs' magical lore is transmitted
 D. the chiefs transmit magical lore
 E. the chiefs make transmission of magical lore
The CORRECT answer is D.

SAMPLE QUESTION 4

As Malcolm walks quickly and confident into the purser's office, the rest of the crew wondered whether he would be charged with the theft.
 A. As Malcolm walks quickly and confident
 B. As Malcolm was walking quick and confident
 C. As Malcom walked quickly and confident

D. As Malcolm walked quickly and confidently
E. As Malcolm walks quickly and confidently
The CORRECT answer is D.

SAMPLE QUESTION 5

The chairman, <u>granted the power to assign any duties to whoever he</u> wished, was still unable to prevent bickering.
A. granted the power to assign any duties to whoever he wished
B. granting the power to assign any duties to whoever he wished
C. being granted the power to assign any duties to whoever he wished
D. having been granted the power to assign any duties to whosoever he wished
E. granted the power to assign any duties to whomever he wished
The CORRECT answer is E.

SAMPLE QUESTION 6

Certainly, well-seasoned products are more expensive, <u>but those kinds prove chaper</u> in the end.
A. but those kinds prove cheaper
B. but these kinds prove cheaper
C. but that kind proves cheaper
D. but those kind prove cheaper
E. but this kind proves cheaper
The CORRECT answer is A.

SAMPLE QUESTION 7

"We shall not," he shouted, "whatever the <u>difficulties." "lose faith in the success of our plan!!</u>"
A. difficulties," "lose faith in the success of our plan!"
B. difficulties, "lose faith in the success of our plan"!
C. "difficulties, lose faith in the success of our plan!"
D. difficulties, lose faith in the success of our plan"!
E. difficulties, lose faith in the success of our plan!"

SAMPLE QUESTION 8

<u>Climb up the tree</u>, the lush foliage obscured the chattering monkeys.
A. Climbing up the tree
B. Having climbed up the tree
C. Clambering up the tree
D. After we had climbed up the tree
E. As we climbed up the tree
The CORRECT answer is E.

EXAMINATION SECTION

TEST 1

DIRECTIONS: See DIRECTIONS for Sample Questions on Page 1. *PRINT THE LETTER OF THE CORRECT ANSWER IN THE SPACE AT THE RIGHT.*

1. At the opening of the story, Charles Gilbert <u>has just come</u> to make his home with his two unmarried aunts.
   - A. No change
   - B. hadn't hardly come
   - C. has just came
   - D. had just come
   - E. has hardly came

   1._____

2. The sisters, who are no longer young, <u>are use to living</u> quiet lives.
   - A. No change
   - B. are used to live
   - C. are use'd to living
   - D. are used to living
   - E. are use to live

   2._____

3. They <u>willingly except</u> the child.
   - A. No change
   - B. willingly eccepted
   - C. willingly accepted
   - D. willingly acepted
   - E. willingly accept

   3._____

4. As the months pass, Charles' presence <u>affects many changes</u> in their household.
   - A. No change
   - B. affect many changes
   - C. effects many changes
   - D. effect many changes
   - E. affected many changes

   4._____

5. These changes <u>is not all together</u> to their liking.
   - A. No change
   - B. is not altogether
   - C. are not all together
   - D. are not altogether
   - E. is not alltogether

   5._____

6. In fact, they have some difficulty in adapting <u>theirselves</u> to these changes
   - A. No change
   - B. in adopting theirselves
   - C. in adopting themselves
   - D. in adapting theirselves
   - E. in adapting themselves

   6._____

7. That is the man <u>whom I believe</u> was the driver of the car.
   - A. No change
   - B. who I believed
   - C. whom I believed
   - D. who to believe
   - E. who I believe

   7._____

8. John's climb to fame was more rapid <u>than his brother's</u>.
   - A. No change
   - B. than his brother
   - C. than that of his brother's
   - D. than for his brother
   - E. than the brother

   8._____

9. We knew that he had formerly swam on an Olympic team. 9.____
   A. No change   B. has formerly swum
   C. did formerly swum   D. had formerly swum
   E. has formerly swam

10. Not one of us loyal supporters ever get a pass to a game. 10.____
    A. No change   B. ever did got a pass
    C. ever has get a pass   D. ever had get a pass
    E. ever gets a pass

11. He was complemented on having done a fine job. 11.____
    A. No change   B. was compliminted
    C. was compleminted   D. was complimented
    E. did get complimented

12. This play is different from the one we had seen last night. 12.____
    A. No change   B. have seen
    C. had saw   D. have saw
    E. saw

13. A row of trees was planted in front of the house. 13.____
    A. No change   B. was to be planted
    C. were planted   D. were to be planted
    E. are planted

14. The house looked its age in spite of our attempts to beautify it. 14.____
    A. No change   B. looks its age
    C. looked its' age   D. looked it's age
    E. looked it age

15. I do not know what to council in this case. 15.____
    A. No change   B. where to council
    C. when to councel   D. what to counsel
    E. what to counsil

16. She is more capable than any other girl in the office. 16.____
    A. No change   B. than any girl
    C. than any other girls   D. than other girl
    E. than other girls

17. At the picnic the young children behaved very good. 17.____
    A. No change   B. behave very good
    C. behaved better   D. behave very well
    E. behaved very well

18. I resolved to go irregardless of the consequences. 18.____
    A. No change   B. to depart irregardless of
    C. to go regarding of   D. to go regardingly of
    E. to go regardless of

19. The new movie has a number of actors <u>which have been famous</u> on Broadway.
    A. No change
    B. which had been famous
    C. who had been famous
    D. that are famous
    E. who have been famous

20. I am certain that these books <u>are not our's</u>.
    A. No change
    B. have not been ours'
    C. have not been our's
    D. are not ours
    E. are not ours'

21. <u>Each of your papers is filed</u> for future reference.
    A. No change
    B. Each of your papers are filed
    C. Each of your papers have been filed
    D. Each of your papers are to be filed
    E. Each of your paper is filed

22. I wish that <u>he would take his work more serious</u>.
    A. No change
    B. he took his work more serious
    C. he will take his work more serious
    D. he shall take his work more seriously
    E. he would take his work more seriously

23. <u>After the treasurer report had been read</u>, the chairman called for the reports of the committees.
    A. No change
    B. After the treasure's report had been read
    C. After the treasurers' report had been read
    D. After the treasurerer's report had been read
    E. After the treasurer's report had been read

24. Last night the stranger <u>lead us down the mountain</u>.
    A. No change
    B. leaded us down the mountain
    C. let us down the mountain
    D. led us down the mountain
    E. had led us down the mountain

25. It would not be safe <u>for either you or I</u> to travel in Viet Nam.
    A. No change
    B. for either you or me
    C. for either I or you
    D. for either of you or I
    E. for either of I or you

KEY (CORRECT ANSWERS)

1.	A	11.	D
2.	D	12.	E
3.	E	13.	A
4.	C	14.	A
5.	D	15.	D
6.	E	16.	A
7.	E	17.	E
8.	A	18.	E
9.	D	19.	E
10.	E	20.	D

21. A
22. E
23. E
24. D
25. B

TEST 2

DIRECTIONS: See DIRECTIONS for Sample Questions on Page 1. *PRINT THE LETTER OF THE CORRECT ANSWER IN THE SPACE AT THE RIGHT.*

1. Both the body and the mind <u>needs exercise</u>.
    - A. No change
    - B. have needs of exercise
    - C. is needful of exercise
    - D. needed exercise
    - E. need exercise

    1.____

2. <u>It's paw injured</u>, the animal limped down the road.
    - A. No change
    - B. It's paw injured
    - C. Its paw injured
    - D. Its' paw injured
    - E. Its paw injure

    2.____

3. The butter <u>tastes rancidly</u>.
    - A. No change
    - B. tastes rancid
    - C. tasted rancidly
    - D. taste rancidly
    - E. taste rancid

    3.____

4. <u>Who do you think</u> has sent me a letter?
    - A. No change
    - B. Whom do you think
    - C. Whome do you think
    - D. Who did you think
    - E. Whom can you think

    4.____

5. If more nations <u>would have fought</u> against tyranny, the course of history would have been different.
    - A. No change
    - B. would fight
    - C. could have fought
    - D. fought
    - E. had fought

    5.____

6. Radio and television programs, along with other media of communication, <u>helps us to appreciate the arts and to keep informed</u>.
    - A. No change
    - B. helps us to appreciate the arts and to be informed
    - C. helps us to be appreciative of the arts and to keep informed
    - D. helps us to be appreciative of the arts and to be informed
    - E. help us to appreciate the arts and to keep informed

    6.____

7. Music, <u>for example most always</u> has listening and viewing audiences numbering in the hundreds of thousands.
    - A. No change
    - B. for example, most always
    - C. for example, almost always
    - D. for example nearly always
    - E. for example, near always

    7.____

8. When operas are performed on radio or television, <u>they effect the listener</u>.
    - A. No change
    - B. they inflict the listener
    - C. these effect the listeners
    - D. they affects the listeners
    - E. they affect the listener

    8.____

2 (#2)

9. After hearing then the listener wants to buy recordings of the music.   9.____
   A. No change
   B. After hearing them, the listener wants
   C. After hearing them, the listener want
   D. By hearing them the listener wants
   E. By hearing them, the listener wants

10. To we Americans the daily news program has become important.   10.____
    A. No change   B. To we the Americans
    C. To us Americans   D. To us the Americans
    E. To we and us Americans

11. This has resulted from it's coverage of a days' events.   11____
    A. No change
    B. from its coverage of a days' events
    C. from it's coverage of a day's events
    D. from its' coverage of a day's events
    E. from its coverage of a day's events

12. In schools, teachers advice their students to listen to or to view certain programs.   12.____
    A. No change
    B. teachers advise there students
    C. teachers advise their students
    D. the teacher advises their students
    E. teachers advise his students

13. In these ways we are preceding toward the goal of an educated and an informed public.   13.____
    A. No change
    B. we are preeceding toward the goal
    C. we are proceeding toward the goal
    D. we are preceding toward the goal
    E. we are proceeding toward the goal

14. The cost of living is raising again.   14.____
    A. No change   B. are raising again
    C. is rising again   D. are rising again
    E. is risen again

15. We did not realize that the boys' father had forbidden them to keep there puppy.   15.____
    A. No change
    B. had forbade them to keep there puppy
    C. had forbade them to keep their puppy
    D. has forbidden them to keep their puppy
    E. had forbidden them to keep their puppy

16. Her willingness to help others' was her outstanding characteristic.　　　　　　　　　　16.____
    A. No change
    B. Her willingness to help other's,
    C. Her willingness to help others's
    D. Her willingness to help others
    E. Her willingness to help each other

17. Because he did not have an invitation, the girls objected to him going.　　　　　　　　17.____
    A. No change
    B. the girls object to him going
    C. the girls objected to him's going
    D. the girls objected to his going
    E. the girls object to his going

18. Weekly dances have become a popular accepted feature of the summer schedule.　　　18.____
    A. No change
    B. have become a popular accepted feature
    C. have become a popular excepted feature
    D. have become a popularly excepted feature
    E. have become a popularly accepted feature

19. I couldn't hardly believe that he would desert our party.　　　　　　　　　　　　　　19.____
    A. No change　　　　　　　　　　　B. would hardly believe
    C. didn't hardly believe　　　　　　 D. should hardly believe
    E. could hardly believe

20. I found the place in the book more readily than she.　　　　　　　　　　　　　　　20.____
    A. No change　　　　　　　　　　　B. more readily than her
    C. more ready than she　　　　　　 D. more quickly than her
    E. more ready than her

21. A good example of American outdoor activities are sports.　　　　　　　　　　　　21.____
    A. No change　　　　　　　　　　　B. is sports
    C. are sport　　　　　　　　　　　　D. are sports events
    E. are to be found in sports

22. My point of view is much different from your's.　　　　　　　　　　　　　　　　22.____
    A. No change　　　　　　　　　　　B. much different from your's
    C. much different than yours　　　　D. much different from yours
    E. much different than yours'

23. The cook was suppose to use two spoonfuls of dressing for each serving.　　　　　　23.____
    A. No change
    B. was supposed to use two spoonful
    C. was suppose to use two spoonsful
    D. was supposed to use two spoonsfuls
    E. was supposed to use two spoonfuls

24. If anyone has any doubt about the values of the tour, <u>refer him to me</u>. 24._____
    A. No change
    B. refer him to I
    C. refer me to he
    D. refer them to me
    E. refer he to I

25. We expect that the affects of <u>the trip will be neneficial</u>. 25._____
    A. No change
    B. the effects of the trip will be beneficial
    C. the effects of the trip should be beneficial
    D. the affects of the trip would be beneficial
    E. the effects of the trip will be benificial

KEY (CORRECT ANSWERS)

1.	E	11.	E
2.	C	12.	C
3.	B	13.	E
4.	A	14.	C
5.	E	15.	E
6.	E	16.	D
7.	C	17.	D
8.	E	18.	E
9.	B	19.	E
10.	C	20.	A

21. B
22. D
23. E
24. A
25. B

TEST 3

DIRECTIONS: See DIRECTIONS for Sample Questions on Page 1. *PRINT THE LETTER OF THE CORRECT ANSWER IN THE SPACE AT THE RIGHT.*

1. <u>That, my friend</u> is not the proper attitude.
   A. No change
   B. That my friend
   C. That my fried,
   D. That—my friend
   E. That, my friend,

   1.____

2. The girl refused to admit <u>that the note was her's</u>.
   A. No change
   B. that the note were her's
   C. that the note was hers'
   D. that the note was hers
   E. that the note might be hers

   2.____

3. There <u>were fewer candidates that we had been lead</u> to expect
   A. No change
   B. was fewer candidates than we had been lead
   C. were fewer candidates than we had been lead
   D. was fewer candidates than we had been led
   E. were fewer candidates than we had been led

   3.____

4. When I first saw the car, <u>its steering wheel was broke</u>.
   A. No change
   B. its' steering wheel was broken
   C. it's steering wheel had been broken
   D. its steering wheel were broken
   E. its steering wheel was broken

   4.____

5. I find that the essential spirit for <u>we beginners is missing</u>.
   A. No change
   B. we who begin are missing
   C. us beginners are missing
   D. us beginners is missing
   E. we beginners are missing

   5.____

6. I believe that <u>you had ought</u> to study harder.
   A. No change
   B. you should have ought
   C. you had better
   D. you ought to have
   E. you ought

   6.____

7. This is <u>Tom, whom I am sure</u>, will be glad to help you.
   A. No change
   B. Tom whom, I am sure,
   C. Tom, whom I am sure
   D. Tom who I am sure,
   E. Tom, who, I am sure,

   7.____

8. His father or his mother <u>has read to him</u> every night since he was very small.
   A. No change
   B. did read to him
   C. have been reading to him
   D. had read to him
   E. have read to him

   8.____

9. He become an authority
   A. No change
   B. becomed an authority
   C. become the authority
   D. became an authority
   E. becamed an authority

10. I know of no other reason in the club who is more kind-hearted than her.
    A. No change
    B. who are more kind-hearted than they
    C. who are more kind-hearted than them
    D. whom are more kind-hearted than she
    E. who is more kind-hearted than she

11. After Bill had ran the mile, he was breathless.
    A. No change
    B. had runned the mile
    C. has ran the mile
    D. had ranned the mile
    E. had run the mile

12. Wilson has scarcely no equal as a pitcher.
    A. No change
    B. has scarcely an equal
    C. has hardly no equal
    D. had scarcely no equal
    E. has scarcely any equals

13. It was the worse storm that the inhabitants of the island could remember.
    A. No change
    B. were the worse storm
    C. was the worst storm
    D. was the worsest storm
    E. was the most worse storm

14. If only we had began before it was too late.
    A. No change
    B. we had began
    C. we would have begun
    D. we had begun
    E. we had beginned

15. Lets evaluate our year's work.
    A. No change
    B. Let us' evaluate
    C. Lets' evaluate
    D. Lets' us evaluate
    E. Let's evaluate

16. This is an organization with which I wouldn't want to be associated with.
    A. No change
    B. with whom I wouldn't want to be associated with
    C. that I wouldn't want to be associated
    D. with which I would want not to be associated with
    E. with which I wouldn't want to be associated

17. The enemy fled in many directions, leaving there weapons on the field.
    A. No change
    B. leaving its weapons
    C. letting their weapons
    D. leaving alone there weapons
    E. leaving their weapons

18. I hoped that John could effect a compromise between the approved forces.　18.____
    A. No change
    B. could accept a compromise between
    C. could except a compromise between
    D. would have effected a compromise among
    E. could effect a compromise among

19. I was surprised to learn that he has not always spoke English fluently.　19.____
    A. No change
    B. that he had not always spoke English
    C. that he did not always speak English
    D. that he has not always spoken English
    E. that he could not always speak English

20. The lawyer promised to notify my father and I of his plans for a new trial.　20.____
    A. No change					B. to notify I and my father
    C. to notify me and our father	D. to notify my father and me
    E. to notify mine father and me

21. The most important feature of the series of tennis lessons were the large amount of strokes taught.　21.____
    A. No change					B. were the large number
    C. was the large amount			D. was the largeness of the amount
    E. was the large number

22. That the prize proved to be beyond her reach did not surprise him.　22.____
    A. No change
    B. has not surprised him
    C. had not ought to have surprised him
    D. should not surprise him
    E. would not have surprised him

23. I am not all together in agreement with the author's point of view.　23.____
    A. No change					B. all together of agreement
    C. all together for agreement	D. altogether with agreement
    E. altogether in agreement

24. Windstorms have recently established a record which meteorologists hope will not be equal for many years to come.　24.____
    A. No change					B. will be equal
    C. will not be equalized		D. will be equaled
    E. will not be equaled

25. A large number of Shakespeare's soliloquies must be considered <u>as representing thought</u>, not speech.   25._____
    A. No change
    B. as representative of speech, not thought
    C. as represented by thought, not speech
    D. as indicating thought, not speech
    E. as representative of thought, more than speech

KEY (CORRECT ANSWERS)

1. E
2. D
3. E
4. E
5. D

6. E
7. E
8. A
9. D
10. E

11. E
12. B
13. C
14. D
15. E

16. E
17. E
18. A
19. D
20. D

21. E
22. A
23. E
24. E
25. A

TEST 4

DIRECTIONS: See DIRECTIONS for Sample Questions on Page 1. *PRINT THE LETTER OF THE CORRECT ANSWER IN THE SPACE AT THE RIGHT.*

1. A sight to inspire fear <u>are wild animals on the lose</u>.
    A. No change
    B. are wild animals on the loose
    C. is wild animals on the loose
    D. is wild animals on the lose
    E. are wild animals loose

    1.____

2. For many years, the settlers <u>had been seeking to workship as they please</u>.
    A. No change
    B. had seeked to workship as they pleased
    C. sought to workship as they please
    D. sought to have worshiped as they pleased
    E. had been seeking to worship as they pleased

    2.____

3. The girls stated that the dresses were <u>their's</u>.
    A. No change
    B. there's
    C. theirs
    D. theirs'
    E. there own

    3.____

4. <u>Please fellows</u> don't drop the ball.
    A. No change
    B. Please, fellows
    C. Please fellows;
    D. Please, fellows,
    E. Please! fellows

    4.____

5. Your sweater <u>has laid</u> on the floor for a week.
    A. No change
    B. has been laying
    C. has been lying
    D. laid
    E. has been lain

    5.____

6. I wonder whether <u>you're sure that scheme of yours'</u> will work.
    A. No change
    B. your sure that scheme of your's
    C. you're sure that scheme of yours
    D. your sure that scheme of yours
    E. you're sure that your scheme's

    6.____

7. Please let <u>her and me</u> do it.
    A. No change
    B. she and I
    C. she and me
    D. her and I
    E. her and him

    7.____

8. I expected him to be angry <u>and to scold</u> her.
    A. No change
    B. and that he would scold
    C. and that he might scold
    D. and that he should scold
    E. , scolding

    8.____

105

9. Knowing little about algebra, it was difficult to solve the equation.
    A. No change
    B. the equation was difficult to solve
    C. the solution to the equation was difficult to find
    D. I found it difficult to solve the equation
    E. it being difficult to solve the equation

10. He worked more diligent now that he had become vice president of the company.
    A. No change
    B. works more diligent
    C. works more diligently
    D. began to work more diligent
    E. worked more diligently

11. Flinging himself at the barricade he pounded on it furiously.
    A. No change
    B. Flinging himself at the barricade: he
    C. Flinging himself at the barricade—he
    D. Flinging himself at the barricade; he
    E. Flinging himself at the barricade, he

12. When he begun to give us advise, we stopped listening.
    A. No change
    B. began to give us advise
    C. begun to give us advice
    D. began to give us advice
    E. begin to give us advice

13. John was only one of the boys whom as you know was not eligible.
    A. No change
    B. who as you know were
    C. whom as you know were
    D. who as you know was
    E. who as you know is

14. Why was Jane and he permitted to go?
    A. No change
    B. was Jane and him
    C. were Jane and he
    D. were Jane and him
    E. weren't Jane and he

15. Take courage Tom: we all make mistakes.
    A. No change
    B. Take courage Tom—we
    C. Take courage, Tom; we
    D. Take courage, Tom we
    E. Take courage! Tom: we

16. Henderson, the president of the class and who is also captain of the team, will lead the rally.
    A. No change
    B. since he is captain of the team
    C. captain of the team
    D. also being captain of the team
    E. who be also captain of the team

17. Our car has always run good on that kind of gasoline.
    A. No change
    B. run well
    C. ran good
    D. ran well
    E. done good

18. There was a serious difference of opinion among her and I.
    A. No change
    B. among she and I
    C. between her and I
    D. between her and me
    E. among her and me

    18.____

19. "This is most unusual," said Helen, "the mailman has never been this late before."
    A. No change
    B. Helen, "The
    C. Helen—"The
    D. Helen; "The
    E. Helen." The

    19.____

20. The three main characters in the story are Johnny Hobart a teenager, his mother a widow, and the local druggist.
    A. No change
    B. teenager; his mother, a widow; and
    C. teenager; his mother a widow; and
    D. teenager, his mother, a widow and
    E. teenager, his mother, a widow; and

    20.____

21. How much has food costs raised during the past year?
    A. No change
    B. have food costs rose
    C. have food costs risen
    D. has food costs risen
    E. have food costs been raised

    21.____

22. "Will you come too" she pleaded?
    A. No change
    B. too,?"she pleaded
    C. too?" she pleaded
    D. too," she pleaded?
    E. too, she pleaded?"

    22.____

23. If he would have drank more milk, his health would have been better.
    A. No change
    B. would drink
    C. had drank
    D. had he drunk
    E. had drunk

    23.____

24. Jack had no sooner laid down and fallen asleep when the alarm sounded.
    A. No change
    B. no sooner lain down and fallen asleep than
    C. no sooner lay down and fell asleep when
    D. no sooner laid down and fell asleep than
    E. no sooner lain down than he fell asleep when

    24.____

25. Jackson is one of the few Sophomores, who has ever made the varsity team.
    A. No change
    B. one of the few Sophomores, who have
    C. one of the few sophomores, who has
    D. one of the few sophomores who have
    E. one of the few sophomores who has

    25.____

KEY (CORRECT ANSWERS)

1.	C		11.	E
2.	E		12.	D
3.	C		13.	B
4.	D		14.	C
5.	C		15.	C
6.	C		16.	C
7.	A		17.	B
8.	A		18.	D
9.	D		19.	E
10.	E		20.	B

21. C
22. C
23. E
24. B
25. D

TEST 5

DIRECTIONS: See DIRECTIONS for Sample Questions on Page 1. *PRINT THE LETTER OF THE CORRECT ANSWER IN THE SPACE AT THE RIGHT.*

1. The lieutenant had ridden almost a kilometer when the scattering shells <u>begin landing</u> uncomfortably close.
   A. No change
   B. beginning to land
   C. began to land
   D. having begun to land
   E. begin to land

   1.____

2. <u>Having studied eight weeks</u>, he now feels sufficiently prepared for the examination.
   A. No change
   B. For eight weeks he studies so
   C. Due to eight weeks of study
   D. After eight weeks of studying
   E. Since he's been spending the last eight weeks in study

   2.____

3. <u>Coming from the Greek, and the word "democracy" means government by the people</u>.
   A. No change
   B. "Democracy," the word which comes from the Greek, means government by the people.
   C. Meaning government by the people, the word "democracy" comes from the Greek.
   D. Its meaning being government by the people in Greek, the word is "democracy."
   E. The word "democracy" comes from the Greek and means government by the people.

   3.____

4. Moslem universities were one of the chief agencies <u>in the development</u> and spreading Arabic civilization.
   A. No change
   B. in the development of
   C. to develop
   D. in developing
   E. for the developing of

   4.____

5. The water of Bering Strait <u>were closing</u> to navigation by ice early in the fall.
   A. No change
   B. has closed
   C. have closed
   D. had been closed
   E. closed

   5.____

6. The man, <u>since he grew up</u> on the block, felt sentimental when returning to it.
   A. No change
   B. having grown up
   C. growing up
   D. since he had grown up
   E. whose growth had been

   6.____

109

7. <u>Jack and Jill watched the canoe to take their parents out of sight round the bend of the creek</u>.
   A. No change
   B. The canoe, taking their parents out of sight, rounds the bend as Jack and Jill watch.
   C. Jack and Jill watched the canoe round the bend of the creek, taking their parents out of sight,
   D. The canoe rounded the bend of the creek as it took their parents out of sight, Jack and Jill watching.
   E. Jack and Jill watching, the canoe is rounding the bend of the creek to take their parents out of sight.

7.____

8. Chaucer's best-known work is THE CANTERBURY TALES, a collection of stories <u>which he tells</u> with a group of pilgrims as they travel to the town of Canterbury.
   A. No change
   B. which he tells through
   C. who tell
   D. told by
   E. told through

8.____

9. The Estates-General, the old feudal assembly of France, <u>had not met</u> for one hundred and seventy-five years when it convened in 1789.
   A. No change
   B. has not met
   C. has not been meeting
   D. had no meeting
   E. has no meeting

9.____

10. Just forty years ago, <u>there had been</u> fewer than one hundred symphony orchestras in the United States.
    A. No change
    B. there had
    C. there were
    D. there was
    E. there existed

10.____

11. Mrs. Smith complained that her son's temper tantrums <u>aggravated her</u> and caused her to have a headache.
    A. No change
    B. gave her aggravation
    C. were aggravating to her
    D. aggravated her condition
    E. instigated

11.____

12. A girl <u>like I</u> would never be seen in a place like that.
    A. No change   B. as I   C. as me
    D. like I am   E. like me

12.____

13. <u>Between you and me,</u> my opinion is that this room is certainly nicer than the first one we saw.
    A. No change
    B. between you and I
    C. among you and me
    D. betwixt you and I
    E. between we

13.____

14. It is important to know for <u>what kind of a person you are working</u>. 14.____
    A. No change
    B. what kind of a person for whom you are working
    C. what kind of person you are working
    D. what kind of person you are working for
    E. what kind of a person you are working for

15. I had <u>all ready</u> finished the book before you came in. 15.____
    A. No change   B. already   C. previously
    D. allready   E. all

16. <u>Ask not for who the bell tolls, it tolls for thee.</u> 16.____
    A. No change
    B. Ask not for whom the bell tolls, it tolls for thee.
    C. Ask not whom the bell tolls for; it tolls for thee.
    D. Ask not for whom the bell tolls; it tolls for thee.
    E. As not who the bell tolls for: It tolls for thee.

17. It is a far better thing I do, than <u>ever I did</u> before. 17.____
    A. No change   B. never I did
    C. I have ever did   D. I have ever been done
    E. ever have I done

18. <u>Ending a sentence with a preposition is something up with which I will not put</u>. 18.____
    A. No change
    B. Ending a sentence with a preposition is something with which I will not put up.
    C. To end a sentence with a preposition is that which I will not put up with.
    D. Ending a sentence with a preposition is something of which I will not put up.
    E. Something I will not put up with is ending a sentence with a preposition.

19. Everyone <u>took off their hats and stand up</u> to sing the national anthem. 19.____
    A. No change
    B. took off their hats and stood up
    C. take off their hats and stand up
    D. took off his hat and stood up
    E. have taken off their hats and standing up

20. <u>She promised me that if she had the opportunity she would have came irregardless of the weather</u>. 20.____
    A. No change
    B. She promised me that if she had the opportunity she would have come regardless of the weather.
    C. She assured me that had she had the opportunity he would have come regardless of the weather.
    D. She assured me that if she would have had the opportunity she would have come regardless of the weather.

E. She promised me that if she had had the opportunity she would have came irregardless of the weather.

21. The man decided it would be advisable to marry a girl <u>somewhat younger than him</u>.
    A. No change
    B. somehow younger than him
    C. some younger than him
    D. somewhat younger from him
    E. somewhat younger than he

21._____

22. Sitting near the campfire, the old man told <u>John and I about many exciting adventures he had had</u>.
    A. No change
    B. John and me about many exciting adventures he had,
    C. John and I about much exciting adventure which he'd had
    D. John and me about many exciting adventures he had had
    E. John and me about many exciting adventures he has had.

22._____

23. <u>If you had stood at home and done your homework</u>, you would not have failed the course.
    A. No change
    B. If you had stood at home and done you're homework,
    C. If you had staid at home and done your homework,
    D. Had you stayed at home and done your homework,
    E. Had you stood at home and done your homework,

23._____

24. The children didn't, as a rule, <u>do anything beyond</u> what they were told to do.
    A. No change
    B. do hardly anything beyond
    C. do anything except
    D. do hardly anything except for
    E. do nothing beyond

24._____

25. <u>Either the girls or him is</u> right.
    A. No change
    B. Either the girls or he is
    C. Either the girls or him are
    D. Either the girls or he are
    E. Either the girls nor he is

25._____

KEY (CORRECT ANSWERS)

1.	C		11.	D
2.	A		12.	E
3.	E		13.	A
4.	D		14.	C
5.	D		15.	B
6.	B		16.	D
7.	C		17.	E
8.	D		18.	E
9.	A		19.	D
10.	C		20.	C

21.	E
22.	D
23.	D
24.	A
25.	B

ENGLISH EXPRESSION
ERROR RECOGNITION

COMMENTARY

Tests of English grammar and usage or, better, tests of English Expression are designed to measure the ability of a candidate to express himself in clear and effective, standard written English.

The test of English Expression may contain several sets of multiple choice questions.

One popular kind of multiple-choice question directs the candidate to select, from among the three (3) options given, the reason why, for the sentences presented, some cannot be accepted in standard written English. This is a (restrictive) test of error recognition.

The object of this test is to measure the candidate's technical and mechanical writing ability.

The candidate is presented with a number of sentences which he is to examine and classify, in accordance with the stated directions, which confine his evaluation specifically to one of three (3) given types of error for each sentence. (Some sentences have no error.)

This is a fairly straightforward question-type and should present only a reasonable amount of difficulty to the well-prepared candidate.

The best preparation for this test is, of course, to answer the questions in the *SAMPLE* and *Test* exercises and then to compare your answers with the Answer Keys.

In addition, as a further aid to the candidate, the corrections (for the errors) have been appended to the keys so that learning is concretized and reinforced.

The directions for the test of error recognition are as follows:

DIRECTIONS: Among the sentences in this group are some which cannot be accepted in formal, written English for one or another of the following reasons:

POOR DICTION: The use of a word which is improper either because its meaning does not fit the sentence or because it is not acceptable in formal writing. *Example:* The audience was strongly <u>effected</u> by the senator's speech.

VERBOSITY: Repetitious elements adding nothing to the meaning of the sentence and not justified by any need for special emphasis. *Example:* At that time there was <u>then</u> no right of petition.

FAULTY GRAMMAR: Word forms and expressions which do not conform to the grammatical and structural usages required by formal written English (errors in case, number, parallelism, and the like). *Example:* Everyone in the delegation had <u>their</u> reasons for opposing the measure.

No sentence has more than one kind of error. Some sentences have no errors. Read each sentence carefully; then on your answer sheet blacken the box under:

    D if the sentence contains an error in <u>diction</u>,
    V if the sentence is <u>verbose</u>,
    G if the sentence contains <u>faulty grammar</u>,
    O if the sentence contains none of these errors.

SAMPLE TEST A

1. In the last decade movie production has advanced forward with great strides.
2. It was easy to see the reason for Nancy's success as an organizer; she had an almost unlimited capacity for hard work and was not afraid to ask her subordinates to get a move on when they fell behind in their efforts.
3. Neither of the men was seriously hurt in the accident.
4. The commission decided to reimburse the property owners, to readjust the rates, and that they would extend the services in the near future.
5. Who it was that invented the wheel has never been determined and is not known.
6. The new judge was a brilliant conversationalist and a fine cellist, having studied it for many years.
7. The dean made an illusion to the Boer War in his talk.
8. All things considered, he did unusual well.
9. The worried boy takes everything to heart too seriously.
10. Our club sent two delegates, Mary and I, to the convention.

KEY (CORRECT ANSWERS)

QUESTION	ANSWER	CORRECTION
1.	V	Eliminate forward.
2.	D	Replace to get a move on by "to work (strive) harder."
3.	O	
4.	G	Substitute, in the interest of parallelism, "and to extend" for and that they would extend.
5.	V	Eliminate and is not known.
6.	G	It is singular and, apparently, here, refers to two subjects. In this case, substitute "diction and music" for it.
7.	D	"Allusion," not illusion.
8.	G	"Unusually," adverb, not unusual, adjective.
9.	V	Eliminate too seriously.
10.	G	Substitute "me," for I

SAMPLE TEST B

1. I like him better than her.
2. His eccentricities and peculiarities continually made good newspaper copy.
3. Between you and I, I think Paul is wrong.
4. This is the more exciting of the two books.
5. This is the most careful written letter of all.
6. During the opening course I read not only four plays but also three historical novels.
7. This assortment of candies, nuts, and fruits are excellent.
8. Nothing would satisfy him but that I bow to his wishes.
9. The two companies were hopeful of eventually affecting a merger if the government didn't object.
10. The ore, pitchblende, is an important source of radium, which is found in many parts of the world.

KEY (CORRECT ANSWERS)

QUESTION	ANSWER	CORRECTION
1.	O	
2.	V	Eliminate and peculiarities.
3.	G	"Between you and me."
4.	D	"Interesting," not exciting.
5.	G	"Carefully," not careful.
6.	O	
7.	G	"Is," not are.
8.	G	"Bowed," not bow.
9.	D	"Effecting," not affecting.
10.	G	The clause, "which is found in many parts of the world," has been misplaced and brings in a measure of confusion. Rewrite: The ore, pitchblende, which is found in many parts of the world, is an important source of radium.

SAMPLE TEST C

1. The ideal college for a student is one for which he is best fitted and most aptly suited.
2. If you would have considered all the alternatives logically, you would have chosen another course of study.
3. Coming in on the bus, we can see the new atomic reactor plant.
4. Due to the mechanic's carelessness or a fault in the construction of the plane, sixty lives were lost.
5. The language in Faulkner is somewhat like Proust, although Faulkner is much more inclined to sesquipedalianism.
6. Asia is as valuable and more fully developed than Africa.
7. The gourmet eagerly awaited the vapid food, a feature of this fine restaurant.
8. He tried to soften the sodden mass by calcifying it slowly.
9. Neither the diplomats nor our president were to blame for the international fiasco.
10. Under the regime of military life, some gain weight; others lose it.

KEY (CORRECT ANSWERS)

QUESTION	ANSWER	CORRECTION
1.	V	Eliminate and most aptly suited.
2.	G	Substitute "Had you considered" for If you would have considered.
3.	O	
4.	G	Substitute "Because of" for Due to.
5.	G	"Like that in (of) Proust," *not* like Proust.
6.	G	Use "as valuable as" for as valuable.
7.	D	"Sapid" (food), not vapid food.
8.	D	"Emulsifying," *not* calcifying, which means "hardening."
9.	G	"Was to blame." *not* were to blame.
10.	D	"Regimen," *not* regime.

TESTS IN ERROR RECOGNITION

DIRECTIONS: Among the sentences in this section are some which cannot be accepted in formal, written English for one or another of the following reasons:

POOR DICTION: The use of a word which is improper either because its meaning does not fit the sentence or because it is not acceptable in formal writing.

EXAMPLE: The audience was strongly <u>effected</u> by the senator's speech.

VERBOSITY: Repetitious elements adding nothing to the meaning of the sentence and not justified by any need for special emphasis.

EXAMPLE: At that time there was <u>then</u> no right of petition.

FAULTY GRAMMAR: Word forms and expressions which do not conform to the grammatical and structural usages required by formal written English (errors in case, number, parallelism, and the like).

EXAMPLE: Everyone in the delegation had <u>their</u> reasons for opposing the measure.

No sentence has more than one kind of error. Some sentences have no errors. Read each sentence carefully; then on your answer sheet blacken the box under:

D if the sentence contains an error in <u>diction</u>.
V if the sentence is <u>verbose</u>.
G if the sentence contains <u>faulty grammar</u>.
O if the sentence contains <u>none</u> of these errors.

EXAMINATION SECTION
TEST 1

1. Neither of the applicants had had the requisite or required experience. 1.____
2. That child is standing there waiting since three o'clock. 2.____
3. Unbelievable as it sounds, waiters here do not accept gratuities in this restaurant. 3.____
4. "We men, he declared, have never learned to dress for comfort." 4.____
5. I think they, on the average, are much heavier than us. 5.____
6. The officers of the new company protested that their services were complementary rather than competitive. 6.____
7. Largely because of Joe's chicanery, we felt we could trust him to make an honest presentation of the facts. 7.____
8. After his graduation from Central High School, he went down to college. 8.____
9. When he was warned about the dangers of eating green apples, he merely replied that he liked those kind best. 9.____
10. The boys liked Ivanhoe as a character, but being more interested in the gory plot in "Macbeth." 10.____

TEST 2

1. The winters were hard and dreary, nothing could live without shelter. 1.____
2. Not one in a thousand readers take the matter seriously. 2.____
3. This tire has so many defections that it is worthless. 3.____
4. The jury were divided in their views. 4.____
5. He was so credulous that his friends found it hard to deceive him 5.____
6. The emperor's latest ukase is sure to stir up such resentment that the people will revolt. 6.____
7. When you go to the library tomorrow, please bring this book to the librarian in the reference room. 7.____
8. His speech is so precise as to seem infected. 8.____
9. I had sooner serve overseas before I remain inactive at home. 9.____
10. We read each other's letters together. 10.____

TEST 3

1. Returning to the spot after dark, the old house looked sinister in the pale moonlight.   1._____
2. "Try to come early," she said, "and be sure to bring your bathing suit."   2._____
3. Everyone but Francis and I was given a ticket.   3._____
4. They were convinced by Ben's elusive answers that he intended to tell the whole story.   4._____
5. Within an hour of the sounding of the alarm, the fire was distinguished.   5._____
6. I never looked well in that type dress.   6._____
7. Send it to the person whom you think has lost it.   7._____
8. If we cannot borrow a car, we shall remain at home.   8._____
9. They insisted on him going.   9._____
10. Despite the beggar's lack of hunger, he became more and more unimpassioned in his demands for food.   10._____

TEST 4

1. The coffee grounds left a sedentary deposit in the cup.   1._____
2. I can but do my best.   2._____
3. I cannot help but comparing him with his predecessor.   3._____
4. Many of Aesop's Fables are parodies from which we can profit.   4._____
5. I wish that I was in Florida now.   5._____
6. I like this kind of grapes better than any other.   6._____
7. The remainder of the time was spent in prayer.   7._____
8. Immigration is when people come into a foreign country to live.   8._____
9. He coughed continuously last winter.   9._____
10. The method is different than the one that was formerly used.   10._____

TEST 5

1. The study of the changes that have taken place and the reason for them are fascinating. 1._____
2. The reason he declined the invitation was because he didn't have a tuxedo. 2._____
3. Neither of the boys was willing or wanted to go. 3._____
4. That politician has a facile tongue, and his statements are generally halting and uncertain. 4._____
5. From the history of the case, I see no reason to infer his dishonesty. 5._____
6. Even though the pump seemed damaged beyond repair, they should of made some attempt to salvage it. 6._____
7. I found the play exciting (and gruesome), but the audience seemed unmoved by it. 7._____
8. The storm had knocked down scores of trees on the tundra. 8._____
9. Whom do you think will be selected from among the applicants? 9._____
10. I wish I were the only person alone on the platform at this moment. 10._____

TEST 6

1. The flowers smelled so sweet that the whole house was perfumed. 1._____
2. When either or both habits becomes fixed, the student improves. 2._____
3. Neither his words nor his action were justifiable. 3._____
4. A calm almost always comes before a storm. 4._____
5. The gallery with all its pictures were destroyed. 5._____
6. Those trees which are not deciduous remain green and attractive all winter. 6._____
7. Whom did they say won? 7._____
8. The man whom I thought was my friend deceived me. 8._____
9. Send whoever will do the work. 9._____
10. The question of who should be leader arose and the power he should have. 10._____

TEST 7

1. You garbled that quotation so exactly that I did not recognize it, even though I clearly heard you.   1.____
2. The disadvantage of the machine he bought is that it is stationery; a mobile unit would be better.   2.____
3. He is the only one of the boys who have never been late.   3.____
4. Let John and I help you with the mowing.   4.____
5. The prize flower was so flawed in its symmetry as to seem artificial.   5.____
6. The sentinel who slept on post was shot for his dereliction despite his previous flagrant record.   6.____
7. Baker, finally despired of the help which, even if it came, would be too late, and weary of the long vigil, started down the mountain.   7.____
8. Howard is a friend of my brother.   8.____
9. When she graduated college, she was only nineteen.   9.____
10. The assortment in the store on Thirty-fourth Street is preferable to, and better than, that in the one on Thirty-ninth.   10.____

TEST 8

1. Did you enjoy sailing in the Harrisons' catch?   1.____
2. I saw on the bulletin board where the committee appropriated the money for a new flag.   2.____
3. If we install the boiler tomorrow, we would have completed half the project.   3.____
4. What a gregarious blunder I made when I added those figures!   4.____
5. I had never seen anybody so angry and so irate.   5.____
6. The jury was in disagreement for three days, but finally reached a verdict.   6.____
7. Our opponent's diffident manner confirmed our hopes for a peaceful settlement of the conflict.   7.____
8. If he had not neglected to drain the pipes, they would not have burst.   8.____
9. She cooked the fish which he had caught in a chafing dish.   9.____
10. By the time they reached the shelter, it had begun to rain and pour.   10.____

TEST 9

1. Having torn his shoe, the boy's toe stuck out. 1._____
2. The spectators agreed that the winner was a remarkable fine swimmer. 2._____
3. Oranges grown while still green in California are packed and shipped to the New York market. 3._____
4. My father, who was taken ill suddenly, is making good progress satisfactorily. 4._____
5. Any dissatisfied subscriber may have his money refunded promptly. 5._____
6. What kind of a teacher would you like to be? 6._____
7. There are certain cuts of meat that the chef always brazes and that make most attractive dishes. 7._____
8. The temperature has dropped so much that it is likely to snow and it might hail. 8._____
9. The improvements in the plan enable the teacher to save much time. 9._____
10. To offer people advice is often wasting one's breath. 10._____

TEST 10

1. Never before, to the best of my recollection, has there been such promising students. 1._____
2. It is only because your manners are so objectionable that you are not invited to the party. 2._____
3. An altruistic proverb is: "God helps those who help themselves." 3._____
4. I fully expected that the children would be at their desks and to find them ready to begin work. 4._____
5. A complete system of railroads covers and crisscrosses the entire country. 5._____
6. Our vacation being over, I am sorry to say. 6._____
7. It is so dark that I can't hardly see. 7._____
8. Either you or I am right; we cannot both be right. 8._____
9. After it had laid in the rain all night, it was not fit for use again. 9._____
10. Although the meaning was implicit, the statement required further explanation. 10._____

TEST 11

1. Where but America is there greater prosperity? 1._____
2. The door opens, and in walks John and Mary. 2._____
3. Due to bad weather, the game was postponed. 3._____
4. There are very good and sufficient grounds for such a decision. 4._____
5. Amalgamating their forces helped the two generals to defeat the enemy. 5._____
6. America is the greatest nation, and of all other nations England is the greater. 6._____
7. Chicago is larger than any city in Illinois. 7._____
8. The omniscient clap of thunder was not followed by a storm. 8._____
9. Of London and Paris, the former is the wealthiest. 9._____
10. The town consists of three distinct sections, of which the western one is by far the larger. 10._____

TEST 12

1. Of the two, I think he is the most reliable. 1._____
2. What kind of a heating system does Bert plan to install? 2._____
3. I had sooner live in a shack here in the country than a penthouse here in the city. 3._____
4. Let us confine ourselves to remarks tangential to the issue at hand. 4._____
5. He should be hungry by now: he ate one egg only for breakfast. 5._____
6. Wilton never has and never will do a good day's work. 6._____
7. We might have had better results and products from the planting if we had prepared the ground differently. 7._____
8. This book is so recondite that even a child could understand it. 8._____
9. I didn't see why he should feel so badly about his loss; he is far from impoverished. 9._____
10. The children's room, not having been painted for some years, was given priority in the repair schedule. 10._____

TEST 13

1. Realizing I had forgotten my gloves, I returned to the theatre, using a flashlight and turned down every seat.   1._____

2. We walked as long as there was any light to guide us.   2._____

3. Speaking from practical experience, I advise you to give up those unquestionably quixotic schemes.   3._____

4. A spiritual person is usually deeply concerned with mundane affairs.   4._____

5. My younger brother insists that he is as tall as me.   5._____

6. As long as you are ready, you may as well start promptly and on time.   6._____

7. Please come here and try and help me finish this piece of work.   7._____

8. She acts like her feelings were hurt.   8._____

9. The pilot shouted decisive orders to his assistant as the plane burst into flames.   9._____

10. I will not go unless I receive a special invitation.   10._____

TEST 14

1. He is not so competent as we thought him to be.   1._____

2. The merchant ship carried a refectory of rifles and ammunition.   2._____

3. In Brooklyn lives a man who has never been in Manhattan.   3._____

4. He was able to earn little during the summer, having had scarcely three weeks work.   4._____

5. I always had the feeling that he was helpful only when he couldn't hardly avoid doing so.   5._____

6. As president, he had the authority and the power to commit the organization to the plan.   6._____

7. Their love of flowers was not an affectation, for they use to walk many miles just to see a well-known garden.   7._____

8. Even though the dormitory had an adequate supply of bedrooms, he preferred to sleep in a cabana.   8._____

9. Because the data submitted was incomplete, we could not compile the report.   9._____

10. The large attendance was probably due to the interest aroused by the advance publicity.   10._____

TEST 15

1. With a great sigh, he lay down and fell asleep at once.   1.____
2. The demand for the transatlantic passage continues unabated; there is no evidence that it will diminish.   2.____
3. Conditions here are much better than Europe.   3.____
4. Whoever is ready, irregardless of his place on line, may come up now.   4.____
5. I think he is the man who's responsible for the disaster.   5.____
6. After having rested all day, Tom felt enervated.   6.____
7. "What we must determine first," he said, "is on whose side we are on."   7.____
8. In that he offered no protest, he was as responsible for the child's injury as those who inflicted it.   8.____
9. In that region, lakes abound in fish, the woods in wild life, and the fields are full of flowers.   9.____
10. There's the man whose watch was robbed during the Easter parade.   10.____

TEST 16

1. If you are not iridescent in mathematics, you should not be interested in engineering.   1.____
2. But for Heath's intervention, Bryan would have been discharged.   2.____
3. He is not so skillful or clever as his opponent.   3.____
4. It is abhorrent to me to see children victimized.   4.____
5. Hoping for the best is not as effective as to work hard.   5.____
6. If he would have waited, I could easily have met him.   6.____
7. The new expressway, with its miles of straight road, made the journey a pleasant but tortuous one.   7.____
8. The leader, with all his scores of followers, was arrested.   8.____
9. Did any of the applicants bring their tools?   9.____
10. Dinner being over, let us discuss the matter right now and here.   10.____

TEST 17

1. The large tips he received made the job a highly lucid one despite its long hours. 1.____
2. If you would have studied the problem carefully you would have found the solution more quickly. 2.____
3. His testimony today is completely and radically different from that of yesterday. 3.____
4. We found his captious suggestions to be friendly and constructive. 4.____
5. It was superior in every way to the book previously read. 5.____
6. The egg business is only incidental to the regular business of the general store. 6.____
7. Honor as well as profit are to be gained by those studies. 7.____
8. The happiness or misery of men's lives depend on their early training. 8.____
9. She admired the cavalier manner with which her husband treated her. 9.____
10. Neither Tom nor John were present for the rehearsal. 10.____

TEST 18

1. Do you want us to assimilate friendship and loyalty that we do not really feel? 1.____
2. He seen only the first chapter when he made his decision. 2.____
3. Owing to the fortunes of war, thousands and myriads of innocent children are hungry. 3.____
4. Silver and gold have I none, but such as I have I give thee. 4.____
5. Many a youthful iconoclast becomes a dissenter in later years. 5.____
6. He plays a first-rate, excellent game of golf. 6.____
7. Except a living man, there is nothing more wonderful than a book. 7.____
8. I expect that you want to see me. 8.____
9. Books of various kinds should be within easy reach of the pupils. 9.____
10. Chattering endlessly, the laconic gossip bored us all. 10.____

TEST 19

1. The administrator's unconscionable demands elated the workers.   1._____
2. Diamonds are more desired than any precious stones.   2._____
3. There goes the last piece of cake and the last spoonful of ice cream.   3._____
4. Neither Charles or his broker finished his assignment.   4._____
5. A box of choice figs was sent him for Christmas.   5._____
6. We had no sooner entered the room when the bell rang.   6._____
7. You always look devastating in that sort of clothes.   7._____
8. Invidious smokers usually find it difficult to break the habit.   8._____
9. Home is home, be it ever so humble and so plain.   9._____
10. Choose an author as you choose a friend.   10._____

TEST 20

1. His efforts were feeble, the results were poor.   1._____
2. There's no reason to object to John being at the meeting.   2._____
3. Only a quack would maintain that he has an indefatigable remedy for rheumatism.   3._____
4. He was eager to go to high school, but refused to go to Allenby High School, because   4._____
   there were girls there as well as boys there.
5. Since the installation of the traffic light, there have been less accidents at that crossing. 5._____
6. While holding the valence, Uncle Ray fell off the ladder.   6._____
7. He has failed only because he has not assayed the task.   7._____
8. Do you want that I should tell him?   8._____
9. "Shall it be admitted that we have given up the struggle," he asked.   9._____
10. "Does he insist that we report? I asked."   10._____

KEY (CORRECT ANSWERS)
TEST 1

QUESTION	ANSWER	CORRECTION
1.	V	Eliminate or required.
2.	G	Replace is standing there waiting by "has been waiting there."
3.	V	Eliminate here.
4.	G	Add quotation marks (") after men and before have.
5.	G	Replace us by "we."
6.	O	
7.	D	"Integrity," not chicanery.
8.	D	"Went on" instead of went down.
9.	G	"That kind" for those kind.
10.	G	Restore parallelism by replacing being more with "were more."

TEST 2

QUESTION	ANSWER	CORRECTION
1.	G	Semi-colon (;) after dreary, instead of comma(,).
2.	G	"Takes," not take.
3.	D	"Defects," not defections.
4.	O	
5.	D	"Easy," not hard.
6.	O	
7.	D	"Take," not bring.
8.	D	"Affected," not infected.
9.	G	Replace before I by "than."
10.	V	Eliminate "together."

TEST 3

QUESTION	ANSWER	CORRECTION
1.	G	Replace the dangling participle, Returning, with "On my return."
2.	O	
3.	G	Use "me," for I.
4.	D	Not elusive: "voluntary" or "full" would be in accord with the sense of this sentence.
5.	D	"Extinguished." not distinguished.
6.	D, G	Substitute "good" for well.
7.	G	Use "who" for whom.
8.	O	
9.	G	"His" for him.
10.	D	"Impassioned" for unimpassioned.

TEST 4

QUESTION	ANSWER	CORRECTION
1.	D	"Sedimentary," not sedentary.
2.	O	
3.	G	Eliminate but.
4.	D	"Parables," not parodies.
5.	G	"Were," not was.
6.	O	
7.	O	
8.	G	Rewrite": "Immigration denotes people coming into..."
9.	D	"Continually " not continuously.
10.	G	"From," not than.

TEST 5

QUESTION	ANSWER	CORRECTION
1.	G	Replace are by "is."
2.	G	Replace because by "that."
3.	V	Eliminate or wanted.
4.	D	Replace facile by "clumsy. "
5.	O	
6.	G	Replace should of by "should have."
7.	O	
8.	D	Replace on the tundra (a treeless plain) by "in the forest."
9.	G	Replace whom by "who."
10.	V	Eliminate alone.

TEST 6

QUESTION	ANSWER	CORRECTION
1.	O	
2.	G	"Become," not becomes.
3.	G	Use "was" instead of were.
4.	O	
5.	G	"Was destroyed," not were destroyed.
6.	O	
7.	G	"Who," not whom.
8.	G	"Who," not whom.
9.	O	
10.	G	Attain parallelism by placing arose at the end of this sentence.

TEST 7

QUESTION	ANSWER	CORRECTION
1.	D	Replace exactly by "badly."
2.	D	Use "stationary" instead of stationery.
3.	O	
4.	G	Replace I by "me."
5.	D	Replace flawed by "flawless."
6.	D	"Excellent," not flagrant.
7.	G	Use "despairing" instead of despaired to restore parallelism.
8.	G	"Brother's," not brother.
9.	G	Add "from" after graduated.
10.	V	Eliminate and better than.

TEST 8

QUESTION	ANSWER	CORRECTION
1.	D	Substitute "ketch" for catch.
2.	G	Substitute "that" for where.
3.	G	Substitute "shall have" for would have.
4.	D	Substitute "egregious" for gregarious.
5.	V	Eliminate and so irate.
6.	G	Use "The jury were" since they are reaching a verdict as individuals.
7.	D	"Sanguine" should be substituted for diffident.
8.	G	Replace If he had not by "Had he not."
9.	G	Place in a chafing dish immediately after She cooked.
10.	V	Eliminate and pour.

TEST 9

QUESTION	ANSWER	CORRECTION
1.	G	Rewrite: "The boy having torn his shoe, his toe stuck out."
2.	D, G	Use the adverbial form, "remarkably."
3.	G	Place the phrase, while still green, after are packed.
4.	V	Eliminate satisfactorily.
5.	O	
6.	G	Eliminate a.
7.	G	"Braises," not brazes.
8.	D	Faulty parallelism: reword as .... "and hail."
9.	O	
10.	G	"Offering" for To offer.

TEST 10

QUESTION	ANSWER	CORRECTION
1.	G	"Have," not has.
2.	O	
3.	D	Not altrustic, "selfish."
4.	G	To assure parallelism and balance, place comma(,) after desks, and eliminate and to find them.
5.	V	Eliminate and crisscrosses.
6.	G	Replace being by "is."
7.	G	"Can hardly see," not can't hardly see.
8.	O	
9.	D, G	"Lain," not laid.
10.	O	

TEST 11

QUESTION	ANSWER	CORRECTION
1.	G	Insert "in" before America.
2.	G	"Walk," not walks.
3.	G	"Because of," not due to
4.	V	Eliminate and sufficient.
5.	O	
6.	G	"Greatest" should replace greater at the end of this sentence.
7.	G	Insert "other" before city.
8.	D	"Ominous," not omniscient.
9.	G	"Wealthier" for wealthiest.
10.	G	"Largest" for larger.

TEST 12

QUESTION	ANSWER	CORRECTION
1.	G	Replace most by "more."
2.	G	Remove a.
3.	V	Replace both heres.
4.	D	Replace tangential by "germane."
5.	G	Place only BEFORE one egg instead of after it.
6.	G	Add "done" after never has.
7.	V	Eliminate and products.
8.	D	Substitute "clear" for recondite.
9.	D,G	Replace badly by "bad."
10.	O	

TEST 13

QUESTION	ANSWER	CORRECTION
1.	G	To achieve parallelism and balance, rewrite as follows: "... and, using a flashlight, turned down every seat."
2.	O	
3.	O	
4.	D	Mundane means worldly; what is needed here is "religious" or "ethereal."
5.	G	"I" instead of me.
6.	V	Eliminate and on time.
7.	V	Eliminate and try.
8.	G	Use "as though" instead of like.
9.	V	Eliminate decisive.
10.	O	

TEST 14

QUESTION	ANSWER	CORRECTION
1.	O	
2.	D	"Cargo," not refectory (which means, a dinner hall).
3.	O	
4.	G	"Weeks'," not weeks.
5.	V	Eliminate hardly.
6.	V	Eliminate and the power.
7.	D,G	"Used to," not use to.
8.	D	"Cubicle," not cabana.
9.	G	Use "were" instead of was.
10.	O	

TEST 15

QUESTION	ANSWER	CORRECTION
1.	O	
2.	O	
3.	G	Insert "in" before Europe.
4.	D	Substitute "regardless" for irregardless.
5.	O	
6.	D	Substitute "invigorated" for enervated.
7.	V	Eliminate second on.
8.	O	
9.	G	Restore parallelism by having last clause read, "and the fields in flowers."
10.	D	Replace robbed by "stolen."

TEST 16

QUESTION	ANSWER	CORRECTION
1.	D	Substitute "proficient" for <u>iridescent</u>.
2.	O	
3.	V	Eliminate <u>or clever</u>.
4.	O	
5.	D	"So" for <u>as</u> (effective).
6.	G	"Had he waited," instead of <u>If he would have waited</u>.
7.	D	"Boring," not <u>tortuous</u> (which means twisting or winding).
8.	O	
9.	G	Use "his" instead of <u>their</u>.
10.	V	Eliminate <u>right now and here</u>.

TEST 17

QUESTION	ANSWER	CORRECTION
1.	D	"Lucrative," not <u>lucid</u>.
2.	G	"Had you studied ..." is to be substituted.
3.	V	Eliminate <u>completely and radically</u>.
4.	D	"Careful," not <u>captious</u>.
5.	O	
6.	O	
7.	G	"Is" for <u>are</u>.
8.	G	"Depends" for <u>depend</u>.
9.	D	Hardly! Rather, "resented" for <u>admired</u>.
10.	G	"Was," not <u>were</u>.

TEST 18

QUESTION	ANSWER	CORRECTION
1.	D	"Simulate," not <u>assimilate</u>.
2.	G	Use "had read" for <u>seen</u>.
3.	V	Eliminate <u>and myriads</u>.
4.	O	
5.	D	The sense would seem to require "conformist," not <u>dissenter</u>.
6.	V	Eliminate <u>excellent</u>.
7.	O	
8.	D	Use "suppose," for <u>expect</u>.
9.	O	
10.	D	"Garrulous," not <u>laconic</u>.

TEST 19

QUESTION	ANSWER	CORRECTION
1.	D	"Embittered," not elated.
2.	G	Insert "other" after any.
3.	G	"Go," for goes.
4.	G	"Nor," for or.
5.	O	
6.	G	"Than," for well.
7.	D	"Well," not devastating.
8.	D	"Inveterate," not invidious.
9.	V	Eliminate and so plain.
10.	O	

TEST 20

QUESTION	ANSWER	CORRECTION
1.	O	
2.	G	Replace John by "John's."
3.	D	Substitute "infallible" for indefatigable.
4.	V	Eliminate "there" after girls.
5.	D	Substitute "fewer" for less.
6.	D	Substitute "valance" for valence.
7.	D	Substitute "essayed" for assayed.
8.	G	Replace that I should by "me to."
9.	G	Replace comma (,) after struggle with a question mark (?).
10.	G	Quotation marks (") should be removed after asked and placed after report, thus: report?"

ENGLISH EXPRESSION
CHANGE IN CONSTRUCTION

COMMENTARY

A searching type of multiple-choice question requires the candidate to revise a sentence according to the directions provided for that sentence and choose the word or phrase that will appear in the best revision.

Fundamentally, this question attempts to measure the candidate's ability to re-write or to manipulate a sentence or statement with grammatical correctness, felicity of expression, flexibility in construction, and facility of substitution.

This is actually a subtle method of employing the multiple-choice question to achieve the evaluations ordinarily directly obtained through the traditional essay-writing question.

SAMPLE QUESTIONS

DIRECTIONS: In questions 1 and 2, you are given a complete sentence which you are to rewrite in your mind, starting with the words given just below it.

Make whatever changes the new sentence plan requires, but no others; do not change the overall meaning of the sentence.

Note that you are not correcting a mistake in the original sentence; you are simply changing the construction. The revised sentence should be grammatically correct, but it need not necessarily be a better way of expressing the meaning.

There may be more than one way of recasting the sentence but only one will enable you to answer the question.

Read the directions for each question carefully. They may specify that the missing word or expression appear somewhere in the rewritten sentence; they may ask for the next word in the rewritten sentence, the word following a specific word, etc.

1. Most people acquire about 75 percent of what they learn through the sense of sight.
   REWRITTEN: About 75 percent ....
   Somewhere in the part of the rewritten sentence indicated by dots is the word

   A. them   B. acquired   C. a   D. learning   E. study

   ACCEPTABLY REWRITTEN, the above sentence would read:
   About 75 percent of what most people learn is acquired through the sense of sight.
   You would, therefore, mark B on your answer sheet.

2. Various studies show that a great amount of the absenteeism in factories is caused by preventable accidents.
   REWRITTEN: According to various studies, preventable accidents ...
   The NEXT WORDS in the rewritten sentence are

   A. result from   B. could be   C. are caused by
   D. are related to   E. account for

   ACCEPTABLY REWRITTEN, the above sentence would read:
   According to various studies, preventable accidents account for the great amount of absenteeism in factories.
   You would, therefore, mark E on your answer sheet.

EXAMINATION SECTION
TEST 1

DIRECTIONS: In the following questions, you are given a complete sentence which you are to rewrite in your mind, starting with the words given just below it. Make whatever changes the new sentence plan requires, but no others; do not change the overall meaning of the sentence.

Note that you are not correcting a mistake in the original sentence; you are simply changing the construction. The revised sentence should be grammatically correct, but it need not necessarily be a better way of expressing the meaning. There may be more than one way of recasting the sentence but only one will enable you to answer the question.

Read the directions for each question carefully. They may specify that the missing word or expression appear somewhere in the rewritten sentence; they may ask for the next word in the rewritten sentence, the word following a specific word, etc.

1. As a literary genre, the messianic drama falls into the category of myth or romance, for its central figure conforms to the definitions supplied by Northrup Frye, in THE ANATOMY OF CRITICISM, of the mythic hero.
   REWRITTEN:
   Because its central figure conforms to the definitions of the mythic hero supplied by Northrup Frye, in THE ANATOMY OF CRITICISM, the messianic drama is ....
   The *NEXT* word in the rewritten sentence is

   A. into   B. literary   C. categorized
   D. categorically E. a

1.____

2. In THE EMPEROR JULIAN, the second part of the drama, Ibsen reveals Julian to be a false Messiah.
   REWRITTEN:
   Julian is .....
   Somewhere in the part of the rewritten sentence indicated by dots is the word

   A. reveals   B. by   C. falsified
   D. in which   E. messianic

2.____

3. More interesting, because more subtly hidden, is Chekhov's use of melodrama.
   REWRITTEN:
   Because it is more .....
   The *NEXT* word in the rewritten sentence is

   A. subtly   B. interesting   C. melodramatic
   D. used   E. hidden

3.____

4. Shaw's response to this is to withdraw, partially, from his public concerns into a more personal, private, and poetic form of expression.
   REWRITTEN:
   Shaw responded to this with a ..... .
   Somewhere in the part of the rewritten sentence indicated by dots is the word

   A. partially B. is to   C. withdraws
   D. publicly   E. withdrawal

4.____

5. But life draws him back again, against his will, in the form of uncontrollable instinct.
   REWRITTEN:
   He is ...
   The NEXT word in the rewritten sentence is

   A. uncontrollable   B. instinctive   C. back
   D. drawn   E. willful

6. Such destructive criticism accounts, in part, for the unpopularity of this drama, for the modern world wants affirmations.
   REWRITTEN:
   This drama is ....
   The NEXT word in the rewritten sentence is

   A. unpopular   B. accounted   C. criticized
   D. in part   E. destructive

7. Shaw is just as unable to accept the concept of a malevolent or determined man as to accept the concept of a determined and mindless universe.
   REWRITTEN:
   It is equally difficult ...
   Somewhere in the part of the rewritten sentence indicated by dots is (are) the word(s)

   A. unable   B. for him   C. just
   D. to conceive E. to understand

8. We know from his descriptions that Leeuwenhoek saw both plant and animal microorganisms and that among them may have been some bacteria.
   REWRITTEN:
   Among the plant and animal microorganisms which we ...
   The NEXT word in the rewritten sentence is

   A. saw   B. described   C. know
   D. assume E. discovered

9. The Japanese quickly overcame the Russian fleet and then landed troops on the mainland of Asia.
   REWRITTEN:
   The Russian fleet ...
   Somewhere in the part of the rewritten sentence indicated by dots is(are) the word(s)

   A. overcame   B. and then   C. defeated
   D. retreated E. who

10. Napoleon would not tolerate such an arrangement and sent an army of twenty thousand men to suppress the movement.
    REWRITTEN:
    The movement .....
    The NEXT word in the rewritten sentence is

    A. was   B. suppressed   C. would
    D. sent   E. of

11. To have the program succeed, Marx realized he would need the united support of workingmen all over the world.
    REWRITTEN:
      Marx realized that the success .....
    Somewhere in the part of the rewritten sentence indicated by dots is the word

    A. he   B. would   C. have
    D. required   E. to

12. His beautiful descriptions of nature reflect the poet's deep belief in the closeness of nature to the human soul.
    REWRITTEN:
      One reflection of .....
    The *NEXT* word(s) in the rewritten sentence is(are)

    A. beauty   B. the poet's   C. poetry
    D. the descriptions   E. closeness

13. The extraordinary play is a chronicle of O'Neill's own spiritual metamorphosis from a messianic into an existential rebel.
    REWRITTEN:
      O'Neill had undergone .....
    The *NEXT* word in the rewritten sentence is

    A. extraordinary   B. existentialism   C. rebelliousness
    D. spirituality   E. a

14. Considering its great influence, Europe is surprisingly small.
    REWRITTEN:
      The smallness of Europe is surprising when one ...
    The *NEXT* word in the rewritten sentence is

    A. influences   B. is   C. considers
    D. knows   E. consideration

15. Until late in the 1800's we knew nothing of a remarkable civilization which was old when the Greeks arrived.
    REWRITTEN:
      One remarkable civilization which was old when the Greeks arrived .....
    Somewhere in the part of the rewritten sentence indicated by dots is the word

    A. we   B. unknown   C. knew
    D. nothing   E. of

16. Our knowledge of Aegean civilization comes largely from the work of two men.
    REWRITTEN:
      The work of two men ....
    The *NEXT* word in the rewritten sentence is

    A. comes   B. teaches   C. acknowledges
    D. enhances   E. contributes

17. Twelve of the most important deities formed a council, which was supposed to meet on snowcapped Mount Olympus, in northern Thessaly.
    REWRITTEN:
    Mount Olympus, in northern Thessaly, was supposed to be the..........
    The NEXT word(s) in the rewritten sentence is (are)

    A. meeting place B. council C. most important
    D. epitome E. deities

18. In the United States the states and local governments regulate the public schools and supply them with funds.
    REWRITTEN:
    Public schools in the United States are .....
    Somewhere in the part of the rewritten sentence indicated by dots is the word

    A. them B. regulate C. subsidized
    D. governed E. supplied

19. The obstacle of distance was partly overcome by the invention of the steamship and the building of the Suez Canal.
    REWRITTEN:
    The invention of the steamship and the building of the Suez Canal helped
    Somewhere in the part of the rewritten sentence indicated by dots is the word

    A. was B. overcoming C. overcome
    D. partly E. shorten

20. Although cotton has been used for cloth since ancient times, It was not known in England until the seventeenth century when the East India Company brought *calico* (named for Calicut) from India.
    REWRITTEN:
    When the East India Company brought *calico* (named for Calicut) from India in the seventeenth century, it was England's first .....
    Somewhere in the part of the rewritten sentence indicated by dots is the word

    A. known B. knowledge C. was
    D. although E. until

21. In the eighteenth century weaving was still done on the hand loom.
    REWRITTEN:
    The hand loom .....
    Somewhere in the part of the rewritten sentence indicated by dots is the word

    A. done B. on C. for
    D. remained E. weaves

22. When rubbed with wool, amber accumulates a charge of static electricity and will then attract small pieces of pith or paper.
    REWRITTEN:
    Small pieces of pith or paper can .....
    The NEXT word in the rewritten sentence is

    A. accumulate B. be C. attract
    D. charge E. then

23. As a result of the Second World War, cities were devastated and millions were left homeless.
    REWRITTEN:
        The Second World War resulted .....
        Somewhere in the part of the rewritten sentence indicated by dots is the word

    A. leaving   B. devastating   C. were
    D. deprivation   E. devastated

24. With the growing urbanization and mechanization of modern life has come increasing recognition of the evils of drunkenness.
    REWRITTEN:
        The evils of drunkenness have become .....
    Somewhere in the part of the rewritten sentence indicated by dots is the word

    A. recognition   B. recognized   C. come
    D. increasing   E. increased

25. Chekhov dilutes the melodramatic pathos by qualifying our sympathy for the victims.
    REWRITTEN:
        The result of Chekhov's .....
    The *NEXT* word in the rewritten sentence is

    A. dilution   B. diluting   C. melodramatic
    D. qualification   E. qualifying

KEYS (CORRECT ANSWERS)

1.	C	11.	D
2.	B	12.	B
3.	A	13.	E
4.	E	14.	C
5.	D	15.	B
6.	A	16.	E
7.	B	17.	A
8.	C	18.	E
9.	E	19.	C
10.	A	20.	D

21. C
22. B
23. A
24. B
25. E

6 (#1)

ACCEPTABLY REWRITTEN

1. Because its central figure conforms to the definitions of the mythic hero supplied by Northrup Frye, in THE ANATOMY OF CRITICISM, the messianic drama is <u>categorized</u> in the literary genre of myth or romance.

2. Julian is revealed <u>by</u> Ibsen to be a false Messiah, in THE EMPEROR JULIAN, the second part of the drama.

3. Because it is more <u>subtly</u> hidden, Chekhov's use of melodrama is more interesting.

4. Shaw responded to this with a partial <u>withdrawal</u> from his public concerns into a more personal, private, and, poetic form of expression.

5. He is <u>drawn</u> back again by life, against his will, in the form of uncontrollable instinct.

6. This drama is <u>unpopular</u> partly because it receives such destructive criticism when the modern world wants affirmations.

7. It is equally difficult for Shaw to accept the concept of a malevolent or determined man as it is <u>for him</u> to accept the concept of a determined and mindless universe.

8. Among the plant and animal microorganisms which we <u>know</u> that Leewen-hoek saw because of his descriptions, there may have been some bacteria.

9. The Russian fleet was quickly overcome by the Japanese <u>who</u> then landed troops on the mainland of Asia.

10. The movement <u>was</u> suppressed by an army of twenty thousand men sent by Napoleon who would not tolerate such an arrangement.

11. Marx realized that the success of the program <u>required</u> the united support of workingmen all over the world.

12. One reflection of <u>the poet's</u> deep belief in the closeness of nature to the human soul can be found in his beautiful descriptions of nature.

13. O'Neill had undergone <u>a</u> spiritual metamorphosis from a messianic into an existential rebel, of which this play is an extraordinary chronicle.

14. The smallness of Europe is surprising when one <u>considers</u> its great influence.

15. One remarkable civilization which was old when the Greeks arrived was <u>unknown</u> to us until late in the 1800's.

16. The work of two men <u>contributes</u> largely to our knowledge of Aegean civilization.

17. Snowcapped Mount Olympus, in northern Thessaly, was supposed to be the <u>meeting place</u> for a council formed by twelve of the most important deities.

18. Public schools in the United States are regulated and <u>supplied</u> with funds by the states and local government.

19. The invention of the steamship and the building of the Suez Canal helped to <u>overcome</u> the obstacle of distance.

20. When the East India Company brought *calico* (named for Calicut) from India in the seventeenth century, it was England's first introduction to cotton, <u>although</u> it has been used for cloth since ancient times.

21. The hand loom was still used <u>for</u> weaving in the eighteenth century.

22. Small pieces of pith or paper can <u>be</u> attracted by amber if it has been rubbed with wool to accumulate a charge of static electricity.

23. The Second World War resulted in the devastation of cities and the <u>leaving</u> homeless of millions.

24. The evils of drunkenness have become increasingly <u>recognized</u> with the growing urbanization and mechanization of modern life.

25. The result of Chekhov's <u>qualifying</u> our sympathy for the victims is the dilution of the melodramatic pathos.

TEST 2

1. While gazing through his microscope at a drop of water, he saw many kinds of creatures with one or a few cells, which wriggled about and devoured food.
   BEGIN THE SENTENCE WITH
   Many kinds of creatures with one or a few cells wriggling about .....
   Somewhere in the part of the rewritten sentence indicated by dots is (are) the word(s)

   A. he saw
   B. and devoured
   C. which
   D. by him
   E. while gazing

2. The worship of ancestors in China must have arisen in prehistoric times, judging from the reference to it in the most ancient Chinese literature.
   SUBSTITUTE
   ....since the most ancient Chinese literature for judging ...
   The *NEXT* words in the rewritten sentence are

   A. the references
   B. is judged
   C. refers it
   D. refers to
   E. from the

3. She divided the bread among them, without considering a share for herself.
   BEGIN THE SENTENCE WITH
   She did not .....
   Somewhere in the part of the rewritten sentence indicated by dots is(are) the word(s)

   A. divided
   B. when she
   C. without
   D. considering
   E. dividing

4. Since Smith has been a resident here for twenty years, we should give serious consideration to his suggestions,
   SUBSTITUTE
   ... seriously for give serious
   THE *NEXT* WORD(S) IN THE REWRITTEN SENTENCE IS (ARE)

   A. to
   B. consideration
   C. consider
   D. give consideration
   E. would

5. In the fight for women's suffrage one judge's decision had little effect, for the most part, upon the ladies' determination.
   CHANGE
   ...effect to effected
   Somewhere in the part of the rewritten sentence indicated by dots is (are) the word(s)

   A. had
   B. upon
   C. part, upon
   D. had, for
   E. part, very little

6. His approach to the committee was certainly not conducive to a cordial reception of his proposals, which were, at best, of doubtful validity.
   BEGIN THE SENTENCE WITH
   He approached .....
   Somewhere in the part of the rewritten sentence Indicated by dots is(are) the word(s)

   A. was certainly
   B. which was
   C. to the
   D. his
   E. committee was

7. When the thirsty horse had drunk its fill, it trotted briskly down the road.   7._____
   BEGIN THE SENTENCE WITH
      The thirsty horse ......
   The *NEXT* word(s) in the rewritten sentence is (are)

   A. having   B. it trotted   C. when
   D. had   E. had trotted

8. This country must either set up flood controls or be prepared to lose billions of dollars annually.   8._____
   BEGIN THE SENTENCE WITH
      If......
   Somewhere in the part of the rewritten sentence indicated by dots is (are) the word(s)

   A. either   B. must set   C. does not
   D. or   E. country must

9. They are not in Boston now, but I think they're going to that city next week.   9._____
   BEGIN THE SENTENCE WITH
      I think .....
   Somewhere in the part of the rewritten sentence indicated by dots is (are) the word(s)

   A. but I   B. in Boston   C. to Boston
   D. to that   E. now, but

10. Mt.Kinley, in Alaska, is higher than any other mountain in North America.   10._____
    INSERT THE WORD
       the after is .....
    The *NEXT* word in the rewritten sentence is

    A. highest   B. other   C. any
    D. than   E. higher

11. As a result of the Industrial Revolution, cities grew very rapidly and the demand for food and raw materials increased.   11._____
    BEGIN THE SENTENCE WITH
       A result .....
    Somewhere in the part of the rewritten sentence indicated by dots is (are) the word(s)

    A. grew   B. rapidly   C. the demand
    D. materials increased   E. increased demand

12. Since the late eighteenth century, when the American and French revolutions took place, democracy has had a slow but persistent growth.   12._____
    SUBSTITUTE
       After for Since .....
    Somewhere in the part of the rewritten sentence indicated by dots is (are) the word(s)

    A. slow   B. has had   C. persistently
    D. growth   E. slow but persistent

13. The Treaty of Versailles placed the entire blame for World War I on Germany and her allies.   13._____
    BEGIN THE SENTENCE WITH
       Germany......
    Somewhere in the part of the rewritten sentence indicated by dots is the word

A. placed	B. on	C. blame
D. were	E. entire	

14. A few years after Harvey's death, other scientists began to study the blood vessels with the aid of microscopes.
   BEGIN THE SENTENCE WITH
      Blood vessels .....
   Somewhere in the part of the rewritten sentence indicated by dots is (are) the word(s)

   A. by   B. began   C. study
   D. to   E. the study

15. This pamphlet is in response to requests of various groups for a more permanent and usable form of this material.
   BEGIN THE SENTENCE WITH
      To provide .....
   Somewhere in the part of the rewritten sentence indicated by dots is (are) the word(s)

   A. responding to   B. as a response to   C. requested
   D. in response to   E. requesting

16. The space science events chosen for development illustrate types of experiences in which mathematics and science have a mutually enhancing effect on each other.
   SUBSTITUTE
      ...are illustrated by for illustrate...
   Somewhere in the part of the rewritten sentence indicated by dots is(are) the word(s)

   A. have had   B. have   C. had had
   D. may be shown to have   E. has

17. The criteria will be useful throughout the course in setting up specific objectives, providing learning experiences, and making periodic evaluations.
   SUBSTITUTE
      Use the criteria throughout the course for The criteria will be useful throughout the course ...
   The NEXT word in the rewritten sentence is

   A. in   B. for   C. to   D. with   E. by

18. The objectives of a training program are achieved by learning experiences designed to help the trainees develop those behaviors and abilities designated in the objectives.
   BEGIN THE SENTENCE WITH
      To achieve .....
   Somewhere in the part of the rewritten sentence indicated by dots is (are) the word(s)

   A. employ   B. to use   C. it will be useful
   D. create   E. to create

19. Because all of the suggested facilities will not be available in every community, it remains for the teacher to modify or supplement the following suggestions.
   BEGIN THE SENTENCE WITH
      The teacher .....
   The word that occurs IMMEDIATELY before the word modify, is

   A. could   B. might   C. would   D. must   E. should

20. Although teachers differ in their ways or organizing and coordinating important parts of their presentations, they agree that the purpose of a lesson is effective and meaningful classroom instruction.
BEGIN THE SENTENCE WITH
   Although teachers agree .....
The FIRST word of the main clause in the rewritten sentence is

   A. the   B. teachers   C. they   D. differing   E. it

21. Many common physical quantities such as temperature, the speed of a moving object, or the displacement of a ship can be expressed as a certain number of units.
BEGIN THE SENTENCE WITH
   One can express .....
The NEXT word(s) in the rewritten sentence is (are)

   A. as   B. many   C. in   D. a ship's   E. the

22. A parallel-tuned circuit, on the other hand, offers a very high impedance to currents of its natural, or resonant, frequency and a relatively low impedance to others.
BEGIN THE SENTENCE WITH
   A very high impedance .....
The NEXT words in the rewritten sentence are

   A. is offered to   B. offers to   C. is offered for
   D. is offered by   E. on the other hand

23. As the term implies, a voltage feedback amplifier transfers a voltage from the output of the amplifier back to its input.
CHANGE
   ... transfers to is transferred ...
The FIRST words of the rewritten sentence are

   A. A voltage
   B. Back to its input
   C. A voltage feedback amplifier
   D. In accordance with the term
   E. From the output

24. Unemployment among youth is a serious problem now, and unless the economy grows much more rapidly in the future than it has during the past decade, today's youngsters will feel the sharp pinch of declining ratios of new employment opportunities to persons seeking work.
BEGIN THE SENTENCE WITH
   Unless the economy grows, ...
The LAST CLAUSE in the rewritten sentence begins with

   A. today's   B. unemployment   C. and unless
   D. now   E. since

25. In a great society, talents are evoked and realized, creative minds probe the frontiers of knowledge, expectations of excellence are widely shared.
BEGIN THE SENTENCE WITH
   A great society .....
The NEXT words in the rewritten sentence are

A. evokes and realizes
B. talents, creative minds, and expectations of excellence
C. features
D. is characterized by
E. is one in which

KEYS (CORRECT ANSWERS)

1. D
2. D
3. B
4. C
5. E

6. B
7. A
8. C
9. C
10. A

11. E
12. C
13. D
14. A
15. D

16. B
17. C
18. A
19. E
20. C

21. A
22. E
23. A
24. E
25. E

ACCEPTABLY REWRITTEN

1. Many kinds of creatures with one or a few cells, wriggling about and devouring food, were seen <u>by him</u> while he was gazing through his microscope at a drop of water.

2. The worship of ancestors in China must have arisen in prehistoric times since the most ancient Chinese literature <u>refers to</u> it.

3. She did not consider a share for herself <u>when she</u> divided the bread among them.

4. Since Smith has been a resident here for twenty years, we should seriously <u>consider</u> his suggestions.

5. In the fight for women's suffrage one judge's decision affected the ladies' decision, for the most <u>part, very little.</u>

6. He approached the committee in a way which was certainly not conducive to a cordial reception of his proposals, which were, at best, of doubtful validity.

7. The thirsty horse, having drunk its fill, trotted briskly down the road.

8. If this country does not set up flood controls, it must be prepared to lose billions of dollars annually.

9. I think they're going to Boston next week, though they're not in that city now.

10. Mt.Kinley, in Alaska, is the highest mountain in North America.

11. A result of the Industrial Revolution was the very rapid growth of cities and the increased-demand for food and raw materials.

12. After the late eighteenth century, when the American and French revolutions took place, democracy grew slowly, but persistently.

13. Germany and her allies were blamed entirely for World War I by the Treaty of Versailles.

14. Blood vessels were studied by other scientists, with the aid of microscopes, a few years after Harvey's death.

15. To provide a more permanent and usable form of this material, in response to the requests of various groups, this pamphlet has been written.

16. The space science events chosen for development are illustrated by types of experiences in which mathematics and science have a mutually enhancing effect on each other.

17. Use the criteria throughout the course to set up specific objectives, provide learning experiences, and make periodic evaluations.

18. To achieve the objectives of a training program employ learning experiences designed to help the trainees develop those behaviors and abilities designated in the objectives.

19. The teacher should modify or supplement the following suggestions because all of the suggested facilities will not be available in every community.

20. Although teachers agree that the purpose of a lesson is effective and meaningful classroom instruction, they differ in their ways of organizing and coordinating important parts of their presentations.

21. One can express as a certain number of units many common physical quantities such as temperature, the speed of a moving object, or the displacement of a ship.

22. A very high impedance, on the other hand, is offered by a parallel-tuned circuit to currents of its natural, or resonant, frequency and a relatively low impedance to others.

23. A voltage is transferred from the output of the amplifier back to its input by a voltage feedback amplifier, as its name implies.

24. Unless the economy grows much more rapidly in the future than it has during the past decade, today's youngsters will feel the sharp pinch of declining ratios of new employment opportunities to persons seeking work <u>since</u> unemployment among youth is a serious problem now.

25. A great society <u>is one in which</u> talents are evoked and realized, creative minds probe the frontiers of knowledge, expectations of excellence are widely shared.

ENGLISH EXPRESSION
EXAMINATION SECTION
TEST 1

DIRECTIONS: Each question or incomplete statement is followed by several suggested answers or completions. Select the one that BEST answers the question or completes the statement. *PRINT THE LETTER OF THE CORRECT ANSWER IN THE SPACE AT THE RIGHT.*

Questions 1-9.

DIRECTIONS: The following sentences contain problems in grammar, usage diction (choice of words), and idiom. Some sentences are correct. No sentence contains more than one error. You will find that the error, if there is one, is underlined and lettered. Assume that all other elements of the sentence are correct and cannot be changed. In choosing answers, follow the requirements of standard written English. If there is an error, select the *one underlined* part that must be changed in order to make the sentence correct. If there is no error, mark E.

1. <u>In planning</u> your future, <u>one must be</u> as honest with yourself as possible, make careful 1._____
     A   B

   decisions about the best course <u>to follow to achieve</u> a particular purpose, and, above all,
                                             C

   have the courage <u>to stand by those</u> decisions. <u>No error</u>
                       D   E

2. <u>Even though</u> history does not actually repeat itself, knowledge <u>of</u> history <u>can give</u> 2._____
      A   B   C

   current problems a familiar, <u>less</u> formidable look. <u>No error</u>
                             D   E

3. The Curies <u>had almost exhausted</u> their resources, and <u>for a time it seemed</u> 3._____
                       A   B

   <u>unlikely that they ever</u> would find the <u>solvent to their financial problems</u>. <u>No error</u>
           C   D   E

4. <u>If the rumors are</u> correct, Deane <u>will not be convicted</u>, for each of the officers 4._____
         A   B

   on the court realizes that Colson and Holdman may be <u>the real culprit and</u> that
                                                               C

   <u>their</u> testimony is not completely trustworthy. <u>No error</u>
    D   E

5. The citizens of Washington, <u>like Los Angeles</u>, prefer to commute by automobile, 5.____
                                 A

   even though motor vehicles contribute <u>nearly as many</u> contaminants to the air
                                                        B

   <u>as do all other</u> sources <u>combined</u>. <u>No error</u>
        C   D   E

6. <u>By the time Robert Vasco completes</u> his testimony, every major executive of our 6.____
                         A

   company but Ray Ashurst <u>and I</u> <u>will have been</u> <u>accused of</u> complicity in the stock
                               B   C   D

   swindle. <u>No error</u>
             E

7. <u>Within six months</u> the store was operating <u>profitably and efficient</u>; shelves 7.____
        A   B

   <u>were well stocked</u>, goods were selling rapidly, and the cash register
         C

   <u>was ringing constantly</u>. <u>No error</u>
        D   E

8. Shakespeare's comedies have an advantage <u>over Shaw</u> in that <u>Shakespeare's</u> were 8.____
                                            A   B

   <u>written primarily</u> to entertain and <u>not to</u> argue for a cause. <u>No error</u>
       C   D   E

9. Any true insomniac <u>is well aware of</u> the futility of <u>such measures as</u> drinking 9.____
                        A   B

   hot milk, <u>regular hours, deep breathing</u>, counting sheep, and <u>concentrating on</u>
                         C   D

   black velvet. <u>No error</u>
                 E

Questions 10-15.

DIRECTIONS: In each of the following sentences, some part of the sentence or the entire sentence is underlined. Beneath each sentence you will find five ways of phrasing the underlined part. The first of these repeats the original; the other four are different. If you think the original is better than any of the alternatives, choose answer A; otherwise choose one of the others. In choosing answers, follow the requirements of standard written English; that is, pay attention to grammar, choice of words, sentence construction, and punctuation. Choose the answer that produces the most effective sentence—clear and exact, without awkwardness or ambiguity. Do not make a choice that changes the meaning of the original sentence.

10. The tribe of warriors believed that boys and girls should be <u>reared separate, and, as soon as he was weaned, the boys were taken from their mothers.</u> 10.____
    A. reared separate, and, as soon as he was weaned, the boys were taken from their mothers

B. reared separate, and, as soon as he was weaned, a boy was taken from his mother
C. reared separate, and, as soon as he was weaned, the boys were taken from their mothers
D. reared separately, and, as soon as a boy was weaned, they were taken from their mothers
E. reared separately, and, as soon as a boy was weaned, he was taken from his mother

11. Despite Vesta being only the third largest, it is by far the brightest of the known asteroids.
    A. Despite Vesta being only the third largest, it is by far the brightest of the known asteroids.
    B. Vesta, though only the third largest asteroid, is by far the brightest of the known ones.
    C. Being only the third largest, yet Vesta is by far the brightest of the known asteroids.
    D. Vesta, though only the third largest of the known asteroids, is by far the brightest.
    E. Vesta is only the third largest of the asteroids, it being, however, the brightest one.

11.____

12. As a result of the discovery of the Dead Sea Scrolls, our understanding of the roots of Christianity has had to be revised considerably.
    A. has had to be revised considerably
    B. have had to be revised considerably
    C. has had to undergo revision to a considerable degree
    D. have had to be subjected to considerable revision
    E. has had to be revised in a considerable way

12.____

13. Because it is imminently suitable to dry climates, adobe has been a traditional building material throughout the southwestern states.
    A. it is imminently suitable to   B. it is eminently suitable for
    C. It is eminently suitable when in   D. of its eminent suitability with
    E. of being imminently suitable in

13.____

14. Martell is more concerned with demonstrating that racial prejudice exists than preventing it from doing harm, which explains why his work is not always highly regarded.
    A. Martell is more concerned with demonstrating that racial prejudice exists than preventing it from doing harm, which explains
    B. Martell is more concerned with demonstrating that racial prejudice exists than with preventing it from doing harm, and this explains
    C. Martell is more concerned with demonstrating that racial prejudice exists than with preventing it from doing harm, an explanation of
    D. Martell's greater concern for demonstrating that racial prejudice exists than preventing it from doing harm—this explains
    E. Martell's greater concern for demonstrating that racial prejudice exists than for preventing it from doing harm explains

14.____

15. Throughout this history of the American West there runs a steady commentary on the deception and mistreatment of the Indians. 15.____
   A. Throughout this history of the American West there runs a steady commentary on the deception and mistreatment of the Indians.
   B. There is a steady commentary provided on the deception and mistreatment of the Indians and it runs throughout this history of the American West.
   C. The deception and mistreatment of the Indians provide a steady comment that runs throughout this history of the American West.
   D. Comment on the deception and mistreatment of the Indians is steadily provided and runs throughout this history of the American West.
   E. Running throughout this history of the American West is a steady commentary that is provided on the deception and mistreatment of the Indians.

Questions 16-20.

DIRECTIONS: In each of the following questions you are given a complete sentence to be rephrased according to the directions which follow it. You should rephrase the sentence mentally to save time, although you may make notes in your test book if you wish. Below each sentence and its directions are listed words or phrases that may occur in your revised sentence. When you have thought out a good sentence, look in the choices A through E for the word or entire phrase that is included in your revised sentence, and print the letter of the correct answer in the space at the right. The word or phrase you choose should be the most accurate and most nearly complete of all the choices given, and should be part of a sentence that meets the requirements of standard written English. Of course, a number of different sentences can be obtained if the sentence is revised according to directions, and not all of these possibilities can be included in only five choices. If you should find that you have thought of a sentence that contains none of the words or phrases listed in the choices, you should attempt to rephrase the sentence again so that it includes a word or phrase that is listed. Although the directions may at times require you to change the relationship between parts of the sentence or to make slight changes in meaning in other ways, make only those changes that the directions require; that is, keep the meaning the same, or as nearly the same as the directions permit. If you think that more than one good sentence can be made according to the directions, select the sentence that is most exact, effective, and natural in phrasing and construction.

EXAMPLES

I. Sentence: Coming to the city as a young man, he found a job as a newspaper reporter.
   Directions: Substitute He came for Coming.
   A. and so he found   B. and found
   C. and there he had found   D. and then finding
   E. and had found

5 (#1)

Your rephrased sentence will probably read: "He came to the city as a young man and found a job as a newspaper reporter." This sentence contains the correct answer: <u>B. and found</u>. A sentence which used one of the alternate phrases would <u>change the</u> meaning or <u>intention</u> of the original sentence, would be a <u>poorly written sentence</u>, or would be <u>less effective</u> than another possible revision.

II. <u>Sentence</u>: Owing to her wealth, Sarah had many suitors.
<u>Directions</u>: Begin with <u>Many men courted</u>.
   A. so   B. while   C. although   D. because E. and

Your rephrased sentence will probably read: "Many men courted Sarah because she was wealthy." This new sentence contains only choice D, which is the correct answer. None of the other choices will fit into an effective, correct sentence that retains the original meaning.

16. The archaeologists could only mark out the burial site, for then winter came.   16._____
    Begin with <u>Winter came before</u>.
     A. could do nothing more   B. could not do anything
     C. could only do   D. could do something
     E. could do anything more

17. The white reader often receives some insight into the reasons why black men   17._____
are angry from descriptions by a black writer of the injustice they encounter in a white society.
Begin with <u>A black writer often gives</u>.
     A. when describing   B. by describing
     C. he has described   D. in the descriptions
     E. because of describing

18. The agreement between the university officials and the dissident students   18._____
provides for student representation on every university committee and on the board of trustees.
Substitute <u>provides that</u> for <u>provides for</u>.
     A. be   B. are   C. would have
     D. would be   E. is to be

19. English Romanticism had its roots in German idealist philosophy, first   19._____
described in England by Samuel Coleridge.
Begin with <u>Samuel Coleridge was the first in</u>.
     A. in which English   B. and from it English
     C. where English   D. the source of English
     E. the birth of English

20. Four months have passed since his dismissal, during which time Alan has   20._____
looked for work daily.
Begin with <u>Each day</u>.
     A. will have passed   B. that have passed   C. that passed
     D. were to pass   E. <u>had passed</u>

KEY (CORRECT ANSWERS)

1.	B	11.	D
2.	E	12.	A
3.	D	13.	B
4.	C	14.	E
5.	A	15.	A
6.	B	16.	E
7.	B	17.	B
8.	A	18.	A
9.	C	19.	D
10.	E	20.	B

WRITTEN ENGLISH EXPRESSION
EXAMINATION SECTION
TEST 1

DIRECTIONS: In each of the sentences below, four portions are underlined and lettered. Read each sentence and decide whether any of the UNDERLINED parts contains an error in spelling, punctuation, or capitalization, or employs grammatical usage which would be inappropriate for carefully written English. If so, note the letter printed under the unacceptable form and indicate this choice in the space at the right. If all four of the underlined portions are acceptable as they stand, select the answer E. (No sentence contains more than ONE unacceptable form.)

1. The revised <u>procedure</u> was <u>quite</u> different <u>than</u> the one which <u>was</u> employed up
               A   B   C   D
   to that time. <u>No error</u>
                     E   1.____

2. <u>Blinded</u> by the storm that <u>surrounded</u> him, his plane <u>kept going</u> in <u>circles</u>.
     A   B   C   D
   <u>No error</u>
   E   2.____

3. They <u>should</u> give the book to <u>whoever</u> <u>they</u> think deserves <u>it</u>. <u>No error</u>
           A   B   C   D   E   3.____

4. The <u>government</u> will not consent to your <u>firm</u> <u>sending</u> that package as
          A   B C
   <u>second class</u> matter. <u>No error</u>
       D   E   4.____

5. She <u>would have</u> avoided all the trouble <u>that</u> followed if she <u>would have</u> waited
           A   B   C
   ten minutes <u>longer</u>. <u>No error</u>
             D   E   5.____

6. <u>His</u> poetry, <u>when</u> it was carefully examined, showed <u>characteristics</u> not unlike
   A   B   C
   <u>Wordsworth</u>. <u>No error</u>
      D   E   6.____

7. <u>In my opinion</u>, based upon long years of research, <u>I think</u> the plan offered by
        A   B
   my opponent is <u>unsound</u>, because it is not <u>founded</u> on true facts. <u>No error</u>
                   C   D   E   7.____

8. The soldiers of <u>Washington's</u> army at Valley Forge <u>were</u> men ragged in
                                   A   B
   <u>appearance</u> but <u>who were</u> noble in character. <u>No error</u>
       C   D   E

   8.____

9. Rabbits <u>have a distrust</u> of man <u>due to</u> the fact <u>that</u> they are <u>so often</u> shot.
                  A   B   C   D
   <u>No error</u>
      E

   9.____

10. <u>This</u> is the man <u>who</u> I believe <u>is</u> best <u>qualified</u> for the position. <u>No error</u>
       A   B   C   D   E

    10.____

11. Her voice was <u>not only good</u>, but <u>she</u> also very clearly <u>enunciated</u>.
                    A   B   C   D
    <u>No error</u>
       E

    11.____

12. <u>Today he</u> is wearing a <u>different</u> suit <u>than</u> the <u>one</u> he wore yesterday. <u>No error</u>
         A   B   C   D   E

    12.____

13. Our work <u>is</u> to improve the club; if anybody <u>must</u> resign, let it <u>not</u> be you or <u>I</u>.
              A   B   C   D
    <u>No error</u>
       E

    13.____

14. There was so much talking <u>in back of</u> me <u>as</u> I <u>could</u> not <u>enjoy</u> the music.
                                           A   B   C   D
    <u>No error</u>
       E

    14.____

15. <u>Being that</u> he is that <u>kind of boy</u>, he cannot be blamed <u>for</u> the mistake.
          A   B   C   D
    <u>No error</u>
       E

    15.____

16. <u>The king, having read</u> the speech, <u>he</u> and the <u>queen</u> <u>departed</u>. <u>No error</u>
                    A   B   C   D   E

    16.____

17. I <u>am</u> <u>so tired</u> I <u>can't</u> <u>scarcely</u> stand. <u>No error</u>
      A   B   C   D   E

    17.____

18. We are <u>mailing bills</u> to our customers <u>in Canada</u>, and, <u>being</u> eager to
                 A   B   C
    clear our books before the new season opens, it is <u>to be hoped</u> they will
                                                                                   D
    send their remittances promptly. <u>No error</u>
                                          E

    18.____

19. I reluctantly acquiesced to the proposal. No error   19.____
    A   B   C   D   E

20. It had lain out in the rain all night. No error   20.____
    A   B   C   D   E

21. If he would have gone there, he would have seen a marvelous sight.   21.____
            A   B   C   D
    No error
        E

22. The climate of Asia Minor is somewhat like Utah. No error   22.____
                  A   B   C   D   E

23. If everybody did unto others as they would wish others to do unto them, this   23.____
        A   B   C   D
    world would be a paradise. No error
                               E

24. This was the jockey whom I saw was most likely to win the race. No error   24.____
    A   B   C   D   E

25. The only food the general demanded was potatoes. No error   25.____
        A   B   C   D   E

KEY (CORRECT ANSWERS)

1.	C		11.	C
2.	A		12.	C
3.	B		13.	D
4.	B		14.	B
5.	C		15.	A
6.	D		16.	A
7.	B		17.	C
8.	D		18.	C
9.	B		19.	E
10.	E		20.	E

21. A
22. D
23. D
24. B
25. E

TEST 2

DIRECTIONS: In each of the sentences below, four portions are underlined and lettered. Read each sentence and decide whether any of the UNDERLINED parts contains an error in spelling, punctuation, or capitalization, or employs grammatical usage which would be inappropriate for carefully written English. If so, note the letter printed under the unacceptable form and indicate this choice in the space at the right. If all four of the underlined portions are acceptable as they stand, select the answer E. (No sentence contains more than ONE unacceptable form.)

1. A party <u>like</u> <u>that</u> <u>only</u> <u>comes</u> once a year. <u>No error</u>
         A   B   C   D   E   1.____

2. <u>Our's</u> <u>is</u> <u>a</u> <u>swift moving</u> age. <u>No error</u>
    A   B C   D   E   2.____

3. The <u>healthy</u> climate soon <u>restored</u> him <u>to</u> his <u>accustomed</u> vigor. <u>No error</u>
       A   B   C   D   E   3.____

4. <u>They</u> needed six typists and hoped that <u>only</u> that <u>many</u> <u>would</u> apply for the position. <u>No error</u>
   A   B   C   D   E   4.____

5. He <u>interviewed</u> people <u>whom</u> he thought had <u>something</u> <u>to impart</u>. <u>No error</u>   5.____
          A   B   C   D   E

6. <u>Neither</u> of his three sisters <u>is</u> older <u>than</u> <u>he</u>. <u>No error</u>   6.____
    A   B   C D   E

7. <u>Since</u> he is <u>that</u> <u>kind</u> of <u>a</u> boy, he cannot be expected to cooperate with us. <u>No error</u>   7.____
    A   B   C   D   E

8. <u>When passing</u> <u>through</u> the tunnel, the air pressure <u>affected</u> <u>our</u> years. <u>No error</u>   8.____
        A   B   C   D   E

9. <u>The story having</u> a sad ending, <u>it</u> never <u>achieved</u> popularity <u>among</u> the students. <u>No error</u>   9.____
      A   B   C   D   E

10. <u>Since</u> we are both hungry, <u>shall</u> we go <u>somewhere</u> for lunch? <u>No error</u>   10.____
     A   B   C   D E

11. Will you please bring this book down to the library and give it to my friend, 11.____
    A   B   C   D
    who is waiting for it? No error
                            E

12. You may have the book; I am finished with it. No error 12.____
        A   B   C   D   E

13. I don't know if I should mention it to her or not. No error 13.____
      A   B C   D   E

14. Philosophy is not a subject which has to do with philosophers and 14.____
                    A   B   C
    mathematics only. No error
                D   E

15. The thoughts of the scholar in his library are little different than the old woman 15.____
                                A   B
    who first said, "It's no use crying over spilt milk." No error
                    C   D   E

16. A complete system of philosophical ideas are implied in many simple 16.____
                A   B   C
    utterances. No error
        D   E

17. Even if one has never put them into words, his ideas compose a kind of a 17.____
         A   B   C   D
    philosophy. No error
                E

18. Perhaps it is well enough that most people do not attempt this formulation. 18.____
              A   B   C   D
    No error
        E

19. Leading their ordered lives, this confused body of ideas and feelings is 19.____
        A   B   C   D
    sufficient. No error
                E

20. Why should we insist upon them formulating it? No error 20.____
          A   B   C   D   E

21. Since it includes something of the wisdom of the ages, it is adequate for the 21.____
      A   B   C
    purposes of ordinary life. No error
        D   E

22. Therefore, I <u>have sought</u> to make a pattern <u>of mine,</u> <u>and so</u> there were, early
       　　　　　A　　　　　　　　　　　　　　　B　　　　C
    moments of <u>my trying</u> to find out what were the elements with which I had to
    　　　　　　　　D
    deal. <u>No error</u>
    　　　　　　E

23. I <u>wanted</u> <u>to get</u> <u>what</u> knowledge I <u>could</u> about the general structure of the
    　　A　　　　B　　　C　　　　　　　　　D
    universe. <u>No error</u>
    　　　　　　　E

24. I wanted to <u>know</u> <u>if</u> life <u>per se</u> had any meaning or <u>whether</u> I must strive to give
    　　　　　　　A　　B　　　　C　　　　　　　　　　　　　D
    it one. <u>No error</u>
    　　　　　E

25. <u>So,</u> in a <u>desultory</u> way, I <u>began</u> <u>to read</u>. <u>No error</u>
    　A　　　　B　　　　　　　C　　　D　　　E

KEY (CORRECT ANSWERS)

1. C
2. A
3. A
4. C
5. B

6. A
7. D
8. A
9. A
10. E

11. B
12. C
13. B
14. D
15. B

16. B
17. A
18. C
19. A
20. D

21. E
22. C
23. C
24. B
25. E

EXAMINATION SECTION
TEST 1

DIRECTIONS: In the following questions, you are given a complete sentence which you are to rewrite in your mind, starting with the words given just below it. Make whatever changes the new sentence plan requires, but no others; do not change the overall meaning of the sentence. (Note that you are not correcting a mistake in the original sentence; you are simply changing the construction. The revised sentence should be grammatically correct, but it need not necessarily be a better way of expressing the meaning. There may be more than one way of recasting the sentence but only one will enable you to answer the question.) Read the directions for each question carefully. They may specify that the missing word or expression appear somewhere in the rewritten sentence; they may ask for the next word in the rewritten sentence, the word following a specific word, etc. *PRINT THE LETTER OF THE CORRECT ANSWER IN THE SPACE AT THE RIGHT.*

1. *As a literary genre, the messianic drama falls into the category of myth or romance, for its central figure conforms to the definitions supplied by Northrup Frye, in THE ANATOMY OF CRITICISM, of the mythic hero.*
   REWRITTEN:
   Because its central figure conforms to the definitions of the mythic hero supplied by Northrup Frye, in THE ANATOMY OF CRITICISM, the messianic drama is....

   The NEXT WORD in the rewritten sentence is
   A. into   B. literary   C. categorized
   D. categorically   E. a

2. *In THE EMPEROR JULIAN, the second part of the drama, Ibsen reveals Julian to be a false Messiah.*
   REWRITTEN:
   Julian is....

   Somewhere in the part of the rewritten sentence indicated by dots is the word
   A. reveals   B. by   C. falsified
   D. in which   E. messianic

3. *More interesting, because more subtly hidden, is Chekhov's use of melodrama.*
   REWRITTEN:
   Because it is more....

   The NEXT WORD in the rewritten sentence is
   A. subtly   B. interesting   C. melodramatic
   D. used   E. hidden

4. *Shaw's response to this is to withdraw, partially, from his pubic concerns into a more personal, private, and poetic form of expression.*
   REWRITTEN:
   Shaw responded to this with a ....

   Somewhere in the part of the rewritten sentence indicated by dots is the word
   A. partially   B. is to   C. withdraws
   D. publicly   E. withdrawal

   4._____

5. *But life draws him back again, against his will, in the form of uncontrollable instinct.*
   REWRITTEN:
   He is....

   The NEXT WORD in the rewritten sentence is
   A. uncontrollable   B. instinctive   C. back
   D. drawn   E. willful

   5._____

6. *Such destructive criticism accounts, in part, for the unpopularity of this drama, for the modern world wants affirmations.*
   REWRITTEN:
   This drama is

   The NEXT WORD in the rewritten sentence is
   A. unpopular   B. accounted   C. criticized
   D. in part   E. destructive

   6._____

7. *Shaw is just as unable to accept the concept of a malevolent or determined man as to accept the concept of a determined and mindless universe.*
   REWRITTEN:
   It is equally difficult....

   Somewhere in the part of the rewritten sentence indicated by dots is(are) the word(s)
   A. unable   B. for him   C. just
   D. to conceive   E. to understand

   7._____

8. *We know from his descriptions that Leeuwenhoek saw both plant and animal microorganisms and that among them may have been some bacteria.*
   REWRITTEN:
   Among the plant and animal microorganisms which we....

   The nEXT WORD in the rewritten sentence is
   A. saw   B. described   C. know
   D. assume   E. discovered

   8._____

9. *The Japanese quickly overcame the Russian fleet and then landed troops on the mainland of Asia.*
   REWRITTEN:
   The Russian fleet....

   Somewhere in the part of the rewritten sentence indicated by dots is(are) the word(s)
   A. overcame   B. and then   C. defeated
   D. retreated   E. who

10. *Napoleon would not tolerate such an arrangement and sent an army of twenty thousand men to suppress the movement.*
    REWRITTEN:
    The movement....

    The NEXT WORD in the rewritten sentence is
    A. was   B. suppressed   C. would
    D. sent   E. of

11. *To have the program succeed, Marx realized he would need the united support of workingmen all over the world.*
    REWRITTEN:
    Marx realized that the success....

    Somewhere in the part of the rewritten sentence indicated by dots is the word
    A. he   B. would   C. have   D. required   E. to

12. *His beautiful descriptions of nature reflect the poet's deep belief in the closeness of nature to the human soul.*
    REWRITTEN:
    One reflection of....

    The NEXT WORD(S) in the rewritten sentence is(are)
    A. beauty   B. the poet's   C. poetry
    D. the descriptions E. closeness

13. *The extraordinary play is a chronicle of O'Neill's own spiritual metamorphosis from a messianic into an existential rebel.*
    REWRITTEN:
    O'Neill had undergone....

    The NEXT WORD in the rewritten sentence is
    A. extraordinary   B. existentialism   C. rebelliousness
    D. spirituality   E. a

14. *Considering its great influence, Europe is surprisingly small.*
    REWRITTEN:
    The smallness of Europe is surprising when one....

4 (#1)

The NEXT WORD in the rewritten sentence is
  A. influences   B. is   C. considers
  D. knows   E. consideration

15. *Until late in the 1800's we knew nothing of a remarkable civilization which was old when the Greeks arrived.*
REWRITTEN:
One remarkable civilization which was old when the Greeks arrived....

Somewhere in the part of the rewritten sentence indicated by dots if the word
  A. we   B. unknown   C. knew
  D. nothing   E. of

16. *Our knowledge of Aegean civilization comes largely from the work of two men.*
REWRITTEN:
The work of two men....

The NEXT WORD in the rewritten sentence is
  A. comes   B. teaches   C. acknowledges
  D. enhances   E. contributes

17. *Twelve of the most important deities formed a council, which was supposed to meet on snowcapped Mount Olympus, in northern Thessaly.*
REWRITTEN:
Mount Olympus, in northern Thessaly, was supposed to be the....

The NEXT WORD(S) in the rewritten sentence is(are)
  A. meeting place   B. council   C. most important
  D. epitome   E. deities'

18. *In the United States the states and local governments regulate the public schools and supply them with funds.*
REWRITTEN:
Public schools in the United States are....

Somewhere in the part of the rewritten sentence indicated by dots is the word
  A. them   B. regulate   C. subsidized
  D. governed   E. supplied

19. *The obstacle of distance was partly overcome by the invention of the steamship and the building of the Suez Canal.*
REWRITTEN:
The invention of the steamship and the building of the Suez Canal helped....

Somewhere in the part of the rewritten sentence indicated by dots is the word
  A. was   B. overcoming   C. overcome
  D. partly   E. shorten

20. *Although cotton has been used for cloth since ancient times, it was not known in England until the seventeenth century when the East India Company brought "calico" (named for Calicut) from India.*
REWRITTEN:
When the East India Company brought "calico" (named for Calicut) from India in the seventeenth century, it was England's first….

Somewhere in the part of the rewritten sentence indicated by dots is the word
  A. known   B. knowledge   C. was
  D. although   E. until

21. *In the eighteenth century weaving was still done on the hand loom.*
REWRITTEN:
The hand loom….

Somewhere in the part of the rewritten sentence indicated by dots is the word
  A. done   B. on   C. for
  D. remained   E. weaves

22. *When rubbed with wool, amber accumulates a charge of static electricity and will then attract small pieces of pith or paper.*
REWRITTEN:
Small pieces of pith or paper can….

The NEXT WORD in the rewritten sentence is
  A. accumulate B. be   C. attract
  D. charge   E. then

23. *As a result of the Second World War, cities were devastated and millions were left homeless.*
REWRITTEN:
The Second World War resulted….

Somewhere in the part of the rewritten sentence indicated by dots is(are) the word(s)
  A. leaving   B. devastating   C. were
  D. deprivation E. devastated

24. *With the growing urbanization and mechanization of modern life has come increasing recognition of the evils of drunkenness.*
REWRITTEN:
The evils of drunkenness have become….

Somewhere in the part of the rewritten sentence indicated by dots is the word
  A. recognition B. recognized   C. come
  D. increasing E. increased

25. *Chekhov dilutes the melodramatic pathos by qualifying our sympathy for the victims.*
    REWRITTEN:
    The result of Chekhov's....

    The NEXT WORD in the rewritten sentence is
    A. dilution
    B. diluting
    C. melodramatic
    D. qualification
    E. qualifying

    25.____

KEY (CORRECT ANSWERS)

1.	C		11.	D
2.	B		12.	B
3.	A		13.	E
4.	E		14.	C
5.	D		15.	B
6.	A		16.	E
7.	B		17.	A
8.	C		18.	E
9.	E		19.	C
10.	A		20.	D

21.	C
22.	B
23.	A
24.	B
25.	E

SOLUTIONS TO PROBLEMS

1. Because its central figure conforms to the definitions of the mythic hero supplied by Northrup Frye, in THE ANATOMY OF CRITICISM, the messianic drama is <u>categorized</u> in the literary genre of myth or romance.

2. Julian is revealed <u>by</u> Ibsen to be a false Messiah, in THE EMPEROR JULIAN, the second part of the drama.

3. Because it is more <u>subtly</u> hidden, Chekhov's use of melodrama is more interesting.

4. Shaw responded to this with a partial <u>withdrawal</u> from his public concerns into a more personal, private, and poetic form of expression.

5. He is <u>drawn</u> back again by life, against his will, in the form of uncontrollable instinct.

6. This drama is <u>unpopular</u> partly because it receives such destructive criticism when the modern world wants affirmations.

7. It is equally difficult for Shaw to accept the concept of a malevolent or determined man as it is <u>for him</u> to accept the concept of a determined and mindless universe.

8. Among the plant and animal microorganisms which we <u>know</u> that Leeuwenhoek saw because of his descriptions, there may have been some bacteria.

9. The Russian fleet was quickly overcome by the Japanese <u>who</u> then landed troops on the mainland of Asia.

10. The movement <u>was</u> suppressed by an army of twenty thousand men sent by Napoleon who would not tolerate such an arrangement.

11. Marx realized that the success of the program <u>required</u> the united support of workingmen all over the world

12. One reflection of <u>the poet's</u> deep belief in the closeness of nature to the human soul can be found in his beautiful descriptions of nature.

13. O'Neill had undergone <u>a</u> spiritual metamorphosis from a messianic into an existential rebel, of which this play is an extraordinary chronicle.

14. The smallness of Europe is surprising when one <u>considers</u> its great influence.

15. One remarkable civilization which was old when the Greeks arrived was <u>unknown</u> to us until late in the 1800's.

16. The work of two men <u>contributes</u> largely to our knowledge of Aegean civilization.

17. Snowcapped Mount Olympus, in northern Thessaly, was supposed to be the meeting place for a council formed by twelve of its most important deities.

18. Public schools in the United States are regulated and supplied with funds by the states and local government.

19. The invention of the steamship and the building of the Suez Canal helped to overcome the obstacle of distance.

20. When the East India Company brought "calico" (named for Calicut) from India in the seventeenth century, it was England's first introduction to cotton, although it has been used for cloth since ancient times.

21. The hand loom was still used for weaving in the eighteenth century.

22. Small pieces of pith or paper can be attracted by amber if it has been rubbed into wool to accumulate a charge of static electricity.

23. The Second World War resulted in the devastation of cities and the leaving homeless of millions.

24. The evils of drunkenness have become increasingly recognized with the growing urbanization and mechanization of modern life.

25. The result of Chekhov's qualifying our sympathy for the victims if the dilution of the melodramatic pathos.

TEST 2

DIRECTIONS: In the following questions, you are given a complete sentence which you are to rewrite in your mind, starting with the words given just below it. Make whatever changes the new sentence plan requires, but no others; do not change the overall meaning of the sentence. (Note that you are not correcting a mistake in the original sentence; you are simply changing the construction. The revised sentence should be grammatically correct, but it need not necessarily be a better way of expressing the meaning. There may be more than one way of recasting the sentence but only one will enable you to answer the question.) Read the directions for each question carefully. They may specify that the missing word or expression appear somewhere in the rewritten sentence; they may ask for the next word in the rewritten sentence, the word following a specific word, etc. *PRINT THE LETTER OF THE CORRECT ANSWER IN THE SPACE AT THE RIGHT.*

1. *While gazing through his microscope at a drop of water, he saw many kinds of of creatures with one or a few cells, which wriggled about and devoured food.*
   BEGIN THE SENTENCE WITH:
   Many kinds of creatures with one or a few cells wriggling about....

   Somewhere in the part of the rewritten sentence indicated by dots is(are) the word(s)
   A. he saw B. and devoured C. which
   D. by him E. while gazing

   1.____

2. *The worship of ancestors in China must have arisen in prehistoric times, judging from the references to it in the most ancient Chinese literature.*
   SUBSTITUTE:
   ...since the most ancient Chinese literature for judging

   The NEXT WORDS in the rewritten sentence are
   A. the references B. is judged C. refers it
   D. refers to E. from the

   2.____

3. *She divided the bread among them, without considering a share for herself.*
   BEGIN THE SENTENCE WITH:
   She did not....

   Somewhere in the part of the rewritten sentence indicated by dots is(are) the word(s)
   A. divided B. when she C. without
   D. considering E. dividing

   3.____

4. *Since Smith has been a resident here for twenty years, we should give serious consideration to his suggestions.*
   SUBSTITUTE:
   ...seriously for give serious

   4.____

175

The NEXT WORD(S) in the rewritten sentence is(are)
   A. to   B. consideration   C. consider
   D. give consideration   E. would

5. *In the fight for women's suffrage, one judge's decision had little effect, for the most part, upon the ladies' determination.*
CHANGE:
<u>effect</u> to <u>effected</u>

   Somewhere in the part of the rewritten sentence indicated by dots is(are) the word(s)
     A. had   B. upon   C. part, upon
     D. had, for   E. part, very little

5.____

6. *His approach to the committee was certainly not conducive to a cordial reception of his proposals, which were, at best, of doubtful validity.*
BEGIN THE SENTENCE WITH:
He approached....

   Somewhere in the part of the rewritten sentence indicated by dots is(are) the word(s)
     A. was certainly   B. which was   C. to the
     D. his   E. committee was

6.____

7. *When the thirsty horse had drunk its fill, it trotted briskly down the road.*
BEGIN THE SENTENCE WITH:
The thirsty horse....

   The NEXT WORD(S) in the rewritten sentence is(are)
     A. having   B. it trotted   C. when
     D. had   E. had trotted

7.____

8. *This country must either set up flood controls or be prepared to lose billions of dollars annually.*
BEGIN THE SENTENCE WITH:
If....

   Somewhere in the part of the rewritten sentence indicated by dots is(are) the word(s)
     A. either   B. must set   C. does not
     D. or   E. country must

8.____

9. *They are not in Boston now, but I think they're going to that city next week.*
BEGIN THE SENTENCE WITH:
I think....

9.____

Somewhere in the part of the rewritten sentence indicated by dots is(are) the word(s)
- A. but I
- B. in Boston
- C. to Boston
- D. to that
- E. now, but

10. *Mt. Kinley, in Alaska, is higher than any other mountain in North America.*
    INSERT THE WORD:
    the after is....

    The NEXT WORD in the rewritten sentence is
    - A. highest
    - B. other
    - C. any
    - D. than
    - E. higher

11. *As a result of the Industrial Revolution, cities grew very rapidly and the demand for food and raw materials increased.*
    BEGIN THE SENTENCE WITH:
    A result....

    Somewhere in the part of the rewritten sentence indicated by dots is(are) the word(s)
    - A. grew
    - B. rapidly
    - C. the demand
    - D. materials increased
    - E. increased demand

12. *Since the late eighteenth century, when the American and French revolutions took place, democracy has had a slow but persistent growth.*
    SUBSTITUTE:
    After for Since....

    Somewhere in the part of the rewritten sentence indicated by dots is(are) the word(s)
    - A. slow
    - B. has had
    - C. persistently
    - D. growth
    - E. slow but persistent

13. *The Treaty of Versailles placed the entire blame for World War I on Germany and her allies.*
    BEGIN THE SENTENCE WITH:
    Germany....

    Somewhere in the part of the rewritten sentence indicated by dots is the word
    - A. placed   B. on   C. blame   D. were   E. entire

14. *A few years after Harvey's death, other scientists began to study the blood vessels with the aid of microscopes.*
    BEGIN THE SENTENCE WITH:
    Blood vessels....

    Somewhere in the part of the rewritten sentence indicated by dots is(are) the word(s)
    - A. by   B. began   C. study   D. to   E. the study

15. *This pamphlet is in response to requests of various groups for a more permanent and usable form of this material.*
    BEGIN THE SENTENCE WITH:
    To provide....

    Somewhere in the part of the rewritten sentence indicated by dots is(are) the word(s)
    A. responding to
    B. as a response to
    C. requested
    D. in response to
    E. requesting

16. *The space science events chosen for development illustrate types of experiences in which mathematics and science have a mutually enhancing effect on each other.*
    SUBSTITUTE:
    ....are illustrated by for illustrate

    Somewhere in the part of the rewritten sentence indicated by dots is(are) the word(s)
    A. have had
    B. have
    C. had had
    D. may be shown to have
    E. has

17. *The criteria will be useful throughout the course in setting up specific objectives, providing learning experiences, and making periodic evaluations.*
    SUBSTITUTE:
    course....

    The NEXT WORD in the rewritten sentence is
    A. in   B. for   C. to   D. with   E. by

18. *The objectives of a training program are achieved by learning experiences designed to help the trainees develop those behaviors and abilities designated in the objectives.*
    BEGIN THE SENTENCE WITH:
    To achieve....

    Somewhere in the part of the rewritten sentence indicated by dots is(are) the word(s)
    A. employ
    B. to use
    C. it will be useful
    D. create
    E. to create

19. *Because all of the suggested facilities will not be available in every community, it remains for the teacher to modify or supplement the following suggestions.*
    BEGIN THE SENTENCE WITH:
    The teacher....

    The word that occurs immediately before the word *modify* is
    A. could   B. might   C. would   D. must   E. should

20. *Although teachers differ in their ways of organizing and coordinating important parts of their presentations, they agree that the purpose of a lesson is effective and meaningful classroom instruction.*
BEGIN THE SENTENCE WITH:
Although teachers agree....

    The FIRST WORD of the main clause in the rewritten sentence is
    A. the   B. teachers   C. they   D. differing   E. it

21. *Many common physical quantities such as temperature, the speed of a moving object, or the displacement of a ship can be expressed as a certain number of units.*
BEGIN THE SENTENCE WITH:
One can express....

    The NEXT WORD(S) in the rewritten sentence is(are)
    A. as   B. many   C. in   D. a ship's   E. the

22. *A parallel-tuned circuit, on the other hand, offers a very high impedance to currents of its natural, or resonant, frequency and a relatively low impedance to others.*
BEGIN THE SENTENCE WITH:
A very high impedance....

    The NEXT WORDS in the rewritten sentence are
    A. is offered to
    B. others to
    C. is offered for
    D. is offered by
    E. on the other hand

23. *As the term implies, a voltage feedback amplifier transfers a voltage from the output of the amplifier back to its input.*
CHANGE:
....transfers to is transferred

    The FIRST WORDS of the rewritten sentence are
    A. A voltage
    B. Back to its input
    C. A voltage feedback amplifier
    D. In accordance with the term
    E. From the output

24. *Unemployment among youth is a serious problem now, and unless the economy grows much more rapidly in the future than it has during the past decade, today's youngsters will feel the sharp pinch of declining ratios of new employment opportunities to persons seeking work.*
BEGIN THE SENTENCE WITH:
Unless the economy grows, ...

    The LAST CLAUSE in the rewritten sentence begins with
    A. today's   B. unemployment   C. and unless
    D. now   E. since

25. *In a great society, talents are evoked and realized, creative minds probe the frontiers of knowledge, expectations of excellence are widely shared.*
BEGIN THE SENTENCE WITH:
A great society....

The NEXT WORDS in the rewritten sentence are
   A. evokes and realizes
   B. talents, creative minds, and expectations of excellence
   C. features
   D. is characterized by
   E. in one in which

25.____

KEY (CORRECT ANSWERS)

1.	D		11.	E
2.	D		12.	C
3.	B		13.	D
4.	C		14.	A
5.	E		15.	D
6.	B		16.	B
7.	A		17.	C
8.	C		18.	A
9.	C		19.	E
10.	A		20.	C

21.	A
22.	E
23.	A
24.	E
25.	E

7 (#2)

SOLUTIONS TO PROBLEMS

1. Many kinds of creatures with one or a few cells, wriggling about and devouring food, were seen <u>by him</u> while he was gazing through his microscope at a drop of water.

2. The worship of ancestors in China must have arisen in prehistoric times since the most ancient Chinese literature <u>refers to</u> it.

3. She did not consider a share for herself <u>when she</u> divided the bread among them.

4. Since Smith has been a resident here for twenty years, we should seriously <u>consider</u> his suggestions.

5. In the fight for women's suffrage, one judge's decision affected the ladies' decision, for the most <u>part, very little</u>.

6. He approached the community in a way <u>which was</u> certainly not conducive to a cordial reception of his proposals, which were, at best, of doubtful validity.

7. The thirsty horse, having drunk its fill, trotted briskly down the road.

8. If this country <u>does not</u> set up flood controls, it must be prepared to lose billions of dollars annually.

9. I think they're going <u>to Boston</u> next week, though they're not in that city now.

10. Mr. Kinley, in Alaska, is the <u>highest</u> mountain in North America.

11. A result of the Industrial Revolution was the very rapid growth of cities and the <u>increased demand</u> for food and raw materials.

12. After the late eighteenth century, when the American and French revolutions took place, democracy grew slowly, but <u>persistently</u>.

13. Germany and her allies <u>were</u> blamed entirely for World War I by the Treaty of Versailles.

14. Blood vessels were studied <u>by</u> other scientists, with the aid of microscopes, a few years after Harvey's death.

15. To provide a more permanent and usable form of this material, <u>in response to</u> the requests of various groups, this pamphlet has been written.

16. The space scientist events chosen for development are illustrated by types of experiences in which mathematics and science <u>have</u> a mutually enhancing effect on each other.

17. Use the criteria throughout the course <u>to</u> set up specific objectives, provide learning experiences, and make periodic evaluations.

18. To achieve the objectives of a training program, <u>employ</u> learning experiences designed to help the trainees develop those behaviors and abilities designated in the objectives.

19. The teacher <u>should</u> modify or supplement the following suggestions because all of the suggested facilities will not be available in every community.

20. Although teachers agree that the purpose of a lesson is effective and meaningful classroom instruction, <u>they</u> differ in their ways of organizing and coordinating important parts of their presentations.]

21. One can express <u>as</u> a certain number of units many common physical quantities such as temperature, the speed of a moving object, or the displacement of a ship.

22. A very high impedance, <u>on the other hand</u>, is offered by a parallel-tuned circuit to currents of its natural, or resonant, frequency and a relatively low impedance to others.

23. <u>A voltage</u> is transferred from the output of the amplifier back to its input by a voltage feedback amplifier, as its name implies.

24. Unless the economy grows much more rapidly in the future than it has during the past decade, today's youngsters will feel the sharp pinch of declining ratios of new employment opportunities to persons seeking work <u>since</u> unemployment among youth is a serious problem now.

25. A great society <u>is one in which</u> talents are evoked and realized, creative minds probe the frontiers of knowledge, expectations of excellence are widely shared.

WRITTEN ENGLISH EXPRESSION
EXAMINATION SECTION
TEST 1

DIRECTIONS: The questions that follow the paragraph below are designed to test your appreciation of correctness and effectiveness of expression in English. The paragraph is presented first in full so that you may read it through for sense. Disregard the errors you find, as you will be asked to correct them in the questions that follow. The paragraph is then presented sentence by sentence with portions underlined and numbered. At the end of this material, you will find numbers corresponding to those below the underlined portions, each followed by five alternatives lettered A to E. In every case, the usage in the alternative lettered A is the same as that in the original paragraph and is followed by four possible usages. Choose the usage you consider BEST in each case. *PRINT THE LETTER OF THE CORRECT ANSWER IN THE SPACE AT THE RIGHT.*

    When this war is over, no nation will either be isolated in war or peace. Each will be within trading distance of all the others and will be able to strike them. Every nation will be most as dependent on the rest for the maintainance of peace as is any of our own American states on all the others. The world that we have known was a world made up of individual nations, each of which has the priviledge of doing about as they pleased without being embarassed by outside interference. The world has dissolved before the impact of an invention, the airplane has done to our world what gunpowder did to the feudal world. Whether the coming century will be a period of further tragedy or one of peace and progress depend very largely on the wisdom and skill with which the present generation adjusts their thinking to the problems immediately at hand. Examining the principal movements sweeping through the world, it can be seen that they are being accelerated by the war. There is undoubtedly many of these whose courses will be affected for good or ill by the settlement that will follow the war. The United States will share the responsibility of these settlements with Russia, England and China. The influence of the United States, however, will be great. This country is likely to emerge from the war stronger than any other nation. Having benefitted by the absence of actual hostilities on our own soil, we shall probably be less exhausted than our allies and better able to help restore the devastated areas. However many mistakes have been made in our past, the tradition of America, not only the champion of freedom but also fair play, still lives among millions who can see light and hope scarcely nowhere else.

1. When this war is over, no nation will <u>either be isolated in war or peace</u>.   1.____
   A. either be isolated in war or peace
   B. be either isolated in war or peace
   C. be isolated in neither war nor peace
   D. be isolated either in war or in peace
   E. be isolated neither in war or peace

2. <u>Each</u>   2.____
   A. Each   B. It   C. Some   D. They   E. A nation

3. within trading distance of all the others and will be able to strike them.
   A. within trading distance of all the others and will be able to strike them.
   B. near enough to trade with and strike all the others.
   C. trading and striking the others.
   D. within trading and striking distance of all the others.
   E. able to strike and trade with all the others,

4. Every nation will be most as dependent on
   A. most   B. wholly   C. much   D. mostly   E. almost

5. the rest for the maintainance of peace as is
   A. maintainance   B. maintainence   C. maintenence
   D. maintenance   E. maintanence

6. any of our own American states on all the others. The world that we have known was a world made up of individual nations, each
   A. nations, each   B. nations. Each   C. nations: each
   D. nations; each   E. nations each

7. of which had the priviledge of doing about as
   A. priviledge   B. priveledge   C. privelege
   D. privalege   E. privilege

8. they pleased without being
   A. they   B. it   C. they individually
   D. he   E. the nations

9. embarassed by outside interference. That
   A. embarassed   B. embarrassed   C. embaressed
   D. embarrased   E. embarressed

10. world has dissolved before the impact of an invention, the airplane has done to our world what gunpowder did to the feudal world. Whether the coming century will be a period of further tragedy or one of peace and
    A. invention, the   B. invention but the   C. invention: the
    D. invention. The   E. invention and the

11. progress depend very largely on the wisdom and skill with which the present generation
    A. depend   B. will have depended   C. depends
    D. depended   E. shall depend

12. adjusts their thinking to the problems immediately at hand.
    A. adjusts their   B. adjusts there   C. adjusts its
    D. adjust our   E. adjust it's

13. Examining the principal movements sweeping through the world, it can be seen
    A. Examining the principal movements sweeping through the world, it can be seen
    B. Having examined the principal movements sweeping through the world, it can be seen
    C. Examining the principal movements sweeping through the world can be seen
    D. Examining the principal movements sweeping through the world, we can see
    E. It can be seen examining the principal movements sweeping through the world

14. that they are being accelerated by the war.
    A. accelerated   B. acelerated   C. accelerated
    D. acellerated   E. acelerrated

15. There is undoubtedly many of these whose courses will be affected for good or ill by the settlements that will follow the war. The United States will share the responsibility of these settlements with Russia, England and China. The influence of the United
    A. is   B. were   C. was   D. are   E. might be

16. States, however, will be great. This country is likely to emerge from the war stronger than any other nation.
    A. , however,   B. however,   C. , however
    D. however   E. ; however

17. Having benefitted by the absence of actual hostilities on our own soil, we shall probably be less exhausted
    A. benefitted   B. benifitted   C. benefited
    D. benifited   E. benafitted

18. than our allies and better able than them to help restore the devastated areas. However many mistakes have been made in our past, the tradition of American,
    A. them   B. themselves   C. they
    D. the world   E. the nations

19. not only the champion of freedom but also fair play, still lives among millions who can
    A. not only the champion of freedom but also fair play,
    B. the champion of not only freedom but also of fair play,
    C. the champion not only of freedom but also of fair play,
    D. not only the champion but also freedom and fair play,
    E. not the champion of freedom only, but also fair play,

4 (#1)

20. see light and hope <u>scarcely nowhere else.</u> 20._____
    A. scarcely nowhere else
    B. elsewhere
    C. nowhere
    D. scarcely anywhere else
    E. anywhere

KEY (CORRECT ANSWERS)

1.	D	11.	C
2.	A	12.	C
3.	D	13.	D
4.	E	14.	A
5.	D	15.	D
6.	A	16.	A
7.	E	17.	C
8.	B	18.	C
9.	B	19.	C
10.	D	20.	D

TEST 2

DIRECTIONS: The questions that follow the paragraph below are designed to test your appreciation of correctness and effectiveness of expression in English. The paragraph is presented first in full so that you may read it through for sense. Disregard the errors you find, as you will be asked to correct them in the questions that follow. The paragraph is then presented sentence by sentence with portions underlined and numbered. At the end of this material, you will find numbers corresponding to those below the underlined portions, each followed by five alternatives lettered A to E. In every case, the usage in the alternative lettered A is the same as that in the original paragraph and is followed by four possible usages. Choose the usage you consider BEST in each case. *PRINT THE LETTER OF THE CORRECT ANSWER IN THE SPACE AT THE RIGHT.*

    The use of the machine produced up to the present time outstanding changes in our modern world. One of the most significant of these changes have been the marked decreases in the length of the working day and the working week. The fourteen-hour day not only has been reduced to one of ten hours but also, in some lines of work, to one of eight or even six. The trend toward a decrease is further evidenced in the longer weekend already given to employees in many business establishments. There seems also to be a trend toward shorter working weeks and longer summer vacations. An important feature of this development is that leisure is no longer the privilege of the wealthy few,—it has become the common right of most people. Using it wisely, leisure promotes health, efficiency, and happiness, for there is time for each individual to live their own "more abundant life" and having opportunities for needed recreation.
    Recreation, like the name implies, is a process of revitalization. In giving expression to the play instincts of the human race, new vigor and effectiveness are afforded by recreation to the body and to the mind. Of course not all forms of amusement, by no means, constitute recreation. Furthermore, an activity that provides recreation for one person may prove exhausting for another. Today, however, play among adults, as well as children, is regarded as a vital necessity of modern life. Play being recognized as an important factor in improving mental and physical health and thereby reducing human misery and poverty,
    Among the most important forms of amusement available at the present time are the automobile, the moving picture, the radio, television, and organized sports. The automobile, especially, has been a boon to the American people, since it has been the chief means of them getting out into the open. The motion picture, the radio and television have tremendous opportunities to supply wholesome recreation and to promote cultural advancement. A criticism often leveled against organized sports as a means of recreation is because they make passive spectators of too many people. It has been said "that the American public is afflicted with "spectatoritis," but there is some recreational advantages to be gained even from being a spectator at organized games. Such sports afford a release from the monotony of daily toil, get people outdoors and also provide an exhilaration that is tonic in its effect.
    The chief concern, of course, should be to eliminate those forms of amusement that are socially undesirable. There are, however, far too many people who, we know, do not use their leisure to the best advantage. Sometimes leisure leads to idleness, and idleness may lead to demoralization. The value of leisure both to the individual and to society will depend on the uses made of it.

2 (#2)

1. The use of the machine produced up to the
   A. produced B. produces C. has produced
   D. had produced E. will have produced

   1.____

2. present time many outstanding changes in our modern world. One of the most significant of these changes have been the marked
   A. have been B. was C. were
   D. has been E. will be

   2.____

3. decreases in the length of the working day and the working week. The fourteen-hour day not only has been reduced to one of ten hour but also, in some line of work, to one of eight or even six.
   A. The fourteen-hour day not only has been reduced
   B. Not only the fourteen-hour day has been reduced
   C. Not the fourteen-hour day only has been reduced
   D. The fourteen-hour day has not only been reduced
   E. The fourteen-hour day has been reduced not only

   3.____

4. The trend toward a decrease is further evidenced in the longer week end already given
   A. already B. all ready C. allready D. ready E. all in all

   4.____

5. to employees in many business establishments. There seems also to be a trend toward shorter working weeks and longer summer vacations. An important feature of this development is that leisure is no longer the privilege of the wealthy few,—it has become the common right of people.
   A. , —it B. : it C. ; it
   D. ...it E. omit punctuation

   5.____

6. Using it wisely, leisure promotes health, efficiency, and happiness, for there is time for
   A. Using it wisely B. If used wisely
   C. Having used it widely D. Because of its wise use
   E. Because of usefulness

   6.____

7. each individual to live their own "more abundant life"
   A. their B. his C. its D. our E. your

   7.____

8. and having opportunities for needed recreation.
   A. having B. having had C. to have
   D. to have had E. had

   8.____

9. Recreation, like the name implies, is a
   A. like B. since C. through D. for E. as

   9.____

10. process of revitalization. In giving expression to the play instincts of the human race, <u>new vigor and effectiveness are afforded by recreation to the body and to the mind.</u>
    A. new vigor and effectiveness are afforded by recreation to the body and to the mind.
    B. recreation affords new vigor and effectiveness to the body and to the mind.
    C. there are afforded new vigor and effectiveness to the body and to the mind.
    D. by recreation the body and mind are afforded new vigor and effectiveness.
    E. the body and the mind afford new vigor and effectiveness to themselves by recreation.

10._____

11. Of course not all forms of amusement, <u>by no means,</u> constitute recreation. Furthermore, an activity that provides recreation for one person may prove exhausting for another. Today, however, play among adults, as well as children, is regarded as a vital necessity of modern life.
    A. by no means   B. by those means   C. by some means
    D. by every means   E. by any means

11._____

12. <u>Play being recognized</u> as an important factor in improving mental and physical health and thereby reducing human misery and poverty.
    A. . Play being recognized as   B. . by their recognizing play as
    C. . They recognizing play as   D. . Recognition of it being
    E. , for play is recognized as

12._____

13. Among the most important forms of amusement available at the present time are the automobile, the moving picture, the radio, television, and organized sports. The automobile, especially, has been a boon to the American people, since it has been the chief means of <u>them</u> getting out into the open. The motion picture, the radio, and television have tremendous opportunities to supply wholesome recreation and to promote cultural advancement. A criticism often leveled against organized
    A. them   B. their   C. his   D. our   E. the people

13._____

14. sports as a means of recreation is <u>because</u> they make passive spectators of too many people
    A. because   B. since   C. as   D. that   E. why

14._____

15. It has been said "<u>that</u> the American public is afflicted with "spectatoritis,"
    A. "that   B. "that"   C. that"   D. 'that   E. that

15._____

16. but there <u>is</u> some recreational advantages to be gained even from being a spectator at organized games
    A. is   B. was   C. are   D. were   E. will be

16._____

17. Such sports afford a release from the monotony of daily toil, get people outdoors and also provide an exhilaration that is tonic in its effect. The chief concern, of course, should be to eliminate those forms of amusement that are socially undesirable. There are, however, far too many people who, we know, do not use their leisure to the best advantage. Sometimes leisure leads to idleness, and idleness may lead to demoralization. The value of leisure both to the individual and to society will depend on the uses made of it.
    A. who   B. whom   C. which   D. such as   E. that which

17.____

KEY (CORRECT ANSWERS)

1. C
2. D
3. E
4. A
5. C

6. B
7. B
8. C
9. E
10. B

11. E
12. E
13. B
14. D
15. E

16. C
17. A

TEST 3

DIRECTIONS: The questions that follow the paragraph below are designed to test your appreciation of correctness and effectiveness of expression in English. The paragraph is presented first in full so that you may read it through for sense. Disregard the errors you find, as you will be asked to correct them in the questions that follow. The paragraph is then presented sentence by sentence with portions underlined and numbered. At the end of this material, you will find numbers corresponding to those below the underlined portions, each followed by five alternatives lettered A to E. In every case, the usage in the alternative lettered A is the same as that in the original paragraph and is followed by four possible usages. Choose the usage you consider BEST in each case. *PRINT THE LETTER OF THE CORRECT ANSWER IN THE SPACE AT THE RIGHT.*

    The process by which the community influence the actions of its members is known as social control. Imitation which takes place when the action of one individual awakens the impulse in each other to attempt the same thing, is one of the means by which society gains this control. When the child acts as other members of his group acts, he receives their approval. There is also adults who seem almost equally imitative. Advertisers of luxuries are careful to convey the idea that important persons use and indorse the merchandise concerned, for most folk will do their utmost to follow the example of those whom they think are the best people.

    Akin to imitation as a means of social control is suggestion. The child is taught to think and feel as do the adults of his community. He is neither encouraged to be critical or to examine all the evidence for his opinion. To be sure, there would be scarcely no time left for other things if school children would have been expected to have considered all sides of every matter on which they hold opinions. It is possible, however and probably very desirable, for pupils of high school age to learn that the point of view accepted in their community is not the only one, and that many widely held opinions may be mistaken. The way in which suggestion operates is illustrated by advertising methods. Depending on skillful suggestion, argument is seldom used in advertising. The words accompanying the picture do not seek to convince the reason but only to intensify the suggestion.

    Some persons are more susceptible to suggestion than others. The ignorant person is more easily moved to action by suggestion than he who is well educated, education developing the habit of criticizing what is read and heard. Whoever would think clearly, freeing himself from emotion and prejudice, must beware of the influence of the crowd or mob. A crowd is a group of people in a highly suggestible condition, each stimulating the feelings of the others until an intense uniform emotion has control of the group. Such a crowd may become irresponsible and anonymous, and whose activity may lead in any direction. The educated person ought to be beyond reach of this kind of appeal, no one may be said to have a real individuality who, at the mercy of the suggestions of others, allow themselves to succumb to "crowd-mindedness."

1. The process by which the community <u>influence the action of its members</u> is known as social control.
    A. influence the actions of its members
    B. influences the actions of its members
    C. had influenced the actions of its members
    D. influences the actions of their members
    E. will influence the actions of its members

1.____

191

2. Imitation which takes place when the action
    A. which B. , which C. —which D. that E. what

3. of one individual awakens the impulse in each other to attempt the same thing, is one of the means by which society gains this control.
    A. each other   B. some other   C. one other
    D. another   E. one another

4. When the child acts as other members of his group acts, he receives their approval
    A. acts   B. act   C. has acted
    D. will act   E. will have acted

5. There is also adults who seem almost equally imitative.
    A. is B. are C. was D. were E. will be

6. Advertisers of luxuries are careful to convey the idea that important persons use and indorse the merchandise concerned, for most folk will do their utmost to follow the example of those whom they think are the best people.
    A. whom   B. what   C. which
    D. who   E. that which

7. Akin to imitation as a means of social control is suggestion. The child is taught to think and feel as do the adults of his community.
    A. do B. does C. had D. may E. might

8. He is neither encouraged to be critical or to examine all the evidence for his opinions.
    A. neither encouraged to be critical or to examine
    B. neither encouraged to be critical nor to examine
    C. either encouraged to be critical or to examine
    D. encouraged either to be critical nor to examine
    E. not encouraged either to be critical or to examine

9. To be sure, there would be scarcely no time left for other things.
    A. scarcely no   B. hardly no   C. scarcely any
    D. enough   E. but only

10. if school children would have been expected
    A. would have been   B. should have been   C. would have
    D. were   E. will be

11. to have considered all sides of every matter on which they hold opinions
    A. to have considered   B. to be considered
    C. to consider   D. to have been considered
    E. and have considered

3 (#3)

12. It is possible, however and probably very desirable, for pupils of high school age to learn that the point of view accepted in their community is not the only one, and that many widely held opinions may be mistaken. The way in which suggestion operates is illustrated by advertising methods.
    A. , however
    B. however,
    C. ; however,
    D. however
    E. , however,

    12._____

13. Depending on skillful suggestion, argument is seldom used in advertising. The words accompanying the picture do not seek to convince the reason but only to intensify the suggestion.
    A. Depending on skillful suggestion, argument is seldom used in advertising.
    B. Argument is seldom used by advertisers, who depend instead on skillful suggestion.
    C. Skillful suggestion is depended on by advertisers instead of argument.
    D. Suggestion, which is more skillful, is used in place of argument by advertisers.
    E. Instead of suggestion, depending on argument is used by skillful advertisers.

    13._____

14. Some persons are more susceptible to suggestion than others. The ignorant person is more easily moved to action by suggestion than he who is well educated, education developing the habit of criticizing what is read and heard. Whoever would think clearly, freeing himself from emotion and prejudice, must beware of the influence of the crowd or mob.
    A. , education developing
    B. , education developed by
    C. , for education develops
    D. . Education will develop
    E. . Education developing

    14._____

15. A crowd is a group of people in a highly suggestible condition, each stimulating the feelings of the others until an intense uniform emotion has control of the group. Such a crowd may become irresponsible and anonymous, and whose activity may lead in any direction. The educated person ought to be beyond reach of this kind of appeal,
    A. and whose
    B. whose
    C. and its
    D. and the
    E. and the crowd's

    15._____

16. no one may be said to have a real individuality who,
    A. , no
    B. : no
    C. —no
    D. . No
    E. omit punctuation

    16._____

17. at the mercy of the suggestions of others, allow themselves to succumb to "crowd-mindedness."
    A. allow themselves
    B. allows themselves
    C. allow himself
    D. allows himself
    E. allow ourselves

    17._____

KEY (CORRECT ANSWERS)

1.	B	11.	C
2.	B	12.	E
3.	D	13.	B
4.	B	14.	C
5.	B	15.	C
6.	D	16.	D
7.	A	17.	D
8.	E		
9.	C		
10.	D		

TEST 4

DIRECTIONS: The questions that follow are designed to test your appreciation of correctness and effectiveness of expression in English. In each statement, you will find underlined portions. In some cases, the usage in the underlined portion is correct. In other cases, it requires correction. Five (5) alternatives lettered A to E are presented. In every case, the usage in the alternative lettered A (No Change) is the same as that in the original statement and is followed by four (4) other possible usages. Choose the usage you consider BEST in each case. *PRINT THE LETTER OF THE CORRECT ANSWER IN THE SPACE AT THE RIGHT.*

Sample Questions and Answers

Questions
1. John ran home.
   A. No change
   B. run
   C. runned
   D. runed
   E. None right

2. John aint here.
   A. No change
   B. ain't
   C. am not
   D. arre'nt
   E. None right

Answers
1. A
   (The sentence is obviously correctly written. Therefore, the correct answer is A. No change.)

2. E
   (word aint is unacceptable in usage today. The correct answer should be is not or isn't. Since the alternatives offered in A, B, C, and D are all incorrect, the correct answer is, therefore, E. None right.)

1. It takes study to become a lawyer.
   A. No change
   B. before you can become
   C. in becoming
   D. for becoming
   E. None right

   1._____

2. His novels never concern old people who wished to be young.
   A. No change
   B. concerned old people who wish
   C. concerned old people who had wished
   D. concern old people who wish
   E. None right

   2._____

3. You people like we boys as much as we. boys like you.
   A. No change
   B. we boys as much as us
   C. us boys as much as us
   D. us boys as much as we
   E. None right

   3._____

195

4. Jane and Mary are <u>more poised than he, but Bill is the brighter</u> of all three.   4._____
   A. No change
   B. more poised than he, but Bill is the brightest
   C. more poised than him, but Bill is the brightest
   D. more poised than him, but Bill is the brighter
   E. None right

5. It is a thing of joy, beauty, <u>and containing</u> terror.   5._____
   A. No change   B. and abounding in   C. and of
   D. and contains   E. None right

6. If he <u>was able, he would demand that she return</u> home.   6._____
   A. No change
   B. were able, he would demand that she return
   C. was able, he would demand that she returns
   D. were able, he would demand that she returns
   E. None right

7. He <u>use to visit when he was supposed to.</u>   7._____
   A. No change
   B. use to visit when he was suppose to.
   C. used to visit when he was suppose to.
   D. used to visit when he was supposed to.
   E. None right

8. I saw the <u>seamstress and asked her for a needle, hook and eye,</u> and thimble.   8._____
   A. No change
   B. seamstress, and asked her for a needle, hook and eye
   C. seamstress and asked her for a needle, hook and eye
   D. seamstress, and asked her for a needle, hook and eye
   E. None right

9. A tall, young<u>, man threw the heavy, soggy,</u> ball.   9._____
   A. No change
   B. , young man threw the heavy, soggy
   C. young man threw the heavy, soggy
   D. , young man threw the heavy soggy
   E. None right

10. The week <u>before my sister, thinking of other matters,</u> thrust her hand into the fire.   10._____
    A. No change
    B. before, my sister thinking of other matters
    C. before my sister thinking of other matters
    D. before my sister, thinking of other matters
    E. None right

11. We seldom eat a roast at our house. <u>My</u> wife being a vegetarian.   11._____
    A. No change   B. my   C. , my
    D. ; my   E. None right

3 (#4)

12. I have only one request. That you leave at once.
    A. No change B. that C. ; that
    D. : that E. None right

13. I admire stimulating conversation and appreciative listening, therefore I talk to myself.
    A. No change B. , therefore, C. therefore
    D. therefore, E. None right

14. The battle-scarred veteran was as bald as a newlaid egg.
    A. No change
    B. battlescarred veteran was as bald as a new-laid egg.
    C. battle-scarred veteran was as bald as a new-laid egg.
    D. battle scarred veteran was as bald as a new laid egg.
    E. None right

15. The President's proclamation opened with the following statement: "The intention of the government is, to make the people aware of one of the greatest dangers to the safety of the country."
    A. No change
    B. , "The intention of the government is
    C. : "The intention of the government is:
    D. : "The intention of the government is
    E. None right

16. I get only a week vacation after two years work.
    A. No change
    B. week's vacation after two years work.
    C. week's vacation after two years' work.
    D. weeks vacation after two years work.
    E. None right

17. You first wash your brush in turpentine. Then hang it up to dry.
    A. No change B. First you C. First you should
    D. First E. None right

18. The teacher insisted that you and he were responsible for the mistakes of Joe and me.
    A. No change
    B. him were responsible for the mistakes of Joe and me.
    C. he were responsible for the mistakes of Joe and I.
    D. him were responsible for the mistakes of Joe and I.
    E. None right

19. He sometimes in a generous mood gave the flowers to others that he had grown in his garden.
    A. No change
    B. He in a generous mood sometimes gave to others the flowers
    C. In a generous mood he sometimes gave the flowers to others

4 (#4)

D. Sometimes in a generous mood he gave to others the flowers
E. None right

20. He is attending college since September.
    A. No change
    B. has attended
    C. was attending
    D. attended
    E. None right

21. He enjoys me hearing him singing.
    A. No change
    B. my hearing him sing
    C. me hearing him sing
    D. me hearing his singing
    E. None right

22. Even patients of anxious temperament occasionally feel an element of primitive pleasure.
    A. No change
    B. temperament occasionally feel an element of primitive
    C. temperment occasionally feel an element of primitive
    D. temperament occasionally feel an element of primitive
    E. None right

23. Undoubtedly even the loneliest patient feels tranquill.
    A. No change
    B. Undoubtably even the loneliest patient feels tranquill.
    C. Undoubtedly even the loneliest patient feels tranquil.
    D. Undouvtably even the loneliest patient feels tranquil.
    E. None right

24. Sophmores taking behavioral psychology must pay a labratory fee.
    A. No change
    B. Sophmores taking behavioral psychology must pay a laboratory
    C. Sophmores taking behavioral psychology must pay a laboratory
    D. Sophomores taking behavioral psychology must pay a labratory
    E. None right

25. Atheletic heroes often find their studies an unnecessary hinderance.
    A. No change
    B. Athletic heroes often find their studies an unnecessary hinderance.
    C. Athletic heros often find their studies an unnecessary hindrance.
    D. Athletic heroes often find their studies an unnecessary hindrance.
    E. None right

KEY (CORRECT ANSWERS)

1.	A	11.	C
2.	D	12.	D
3.	D	13.	E
4.	B	14.	C
5.	E	15.	D
6.	B	16.	C
7.	D	17.	D
8.	D	18.	A
9.	C	19.	D
10.	E	20.	B

21. B
22. A
23. E
24. C
25. D

TEST 5

DIRECTIONS: The questions that follow are designed to test your appreciation of correctness and effectiveness of expression in English. In each statement, you will find underlined portions. In some cases, the usage in the underlined portion is correct. In other cases, it requires correction. Five (5) alternatives lettered A to E are presented. In every case, the usage in the alternative lettered A (No Change) is the same as that in the original statement and is followed by four (4) other possible usages. Choose the usage you consider BEST in each case. *PRINT THE LETTER OF THE CORRECT ANSWER IN THE SPACE AT THE RIGHT.*

1. Many of the <u>childrens' games were supervised by students who's</u> interests lay in teaching.   1.____
   A. No change
   B. children's games were supervised by students who's
   C. childrens' games were supervised by students whose
   D. children's games were supervised by students whose
   E. None right

2. I told <u>father that a college president</u> was invited to speak.   2.____
   A. No change
   B. Father that a college president
   C. father that a College President
   D. Father that a College president
   E. None right

3. One should either <u>be able to read</u> German or French.   3.____
   A. No change
   B. be able either to read
   C. be able to either read
   D. be able to read either
   E. None right

4. <u>Twirling around on my piano stool, my head begins to swim.</u>   4.____
   A. No change
   B. My head begins to swim, twirling around on my piano stool.
   C. Twirling around on my piano stool, a dizzy spell ensues.
   D. Twirling around on my piano stool, I begin to feel dizzy.
   E. None right

5. As the reverberations of my deep bass voice <u>increase, one of my dogs starts</u> to howl.   5.____
   A. No change
   B. increase, one of my dogs start
   C. increases, one of my dogs start
   D. increases, one of my dogs starts
   E. None right

6. Roy bellows at Eve that it is <u>her, not he</u> who shouts.   6.____
   A. No change
   B. her, not him
   C. she, not him
   D. she, not he
   E. None right

200

7. The only man <u>who I think will knock out whoever</u> he fights is Roy.
   A. No change
   B. who I think will knock out whomever
   C. whom I think will knock out whomever
   D. whom I think will knock out whoever
   E. None right

8. The <u>more prettier</u> of my eyes is the glass one.
   A. No change   B. most pretty   C. prettier
   D. prettiest   E. None right

9. When a good actress cries, she <u>feels real sad.</u>
   A. No change   B. feels real sadly
   C. feels really sadly   D. really feels sad
   E. None right

10. I asked the instructor what I should do with this examina-paper. <u>Can you imagine what he said?</u>
    A. No change   B. ? Can you imagine what he said.
    C. ? Can you imagine what he said?   D. . Can you imagine what he said.
    E. None right

11. Not wishing to hurt my friend's feeling, <u>I tell him that I am leaving,</u> because I have a previous engagement.
    A. No change   B. I tell him that I am leaving
    C. , I tell him that I am leaving D. I tell him that I am leaving,
    E. None right

12. I remember Utopia <u>College where I studied, while I lived abroad,</u> when the world was at peace.
    A. No change
    B. College where I studied, while I lived abroad
    C. College, where I studied while I lived abroad
    D. College, where I studied, while I lived abroad
    E. None right

13. Would Robinson Crusoe have survived if he <u>was</u> less unimaginative?
    A. No change   B. were   C. had been
    D. would have been E. None right

14. Neither time nor tide <u>delay either the traveler or the stay-at-home from his</u> pastime.
    A. No change
    B. delays either the traveler or the stay-at-home from his
    C. delay either the traveler or the stay-at-home from their
    D. delays either the traveler or the stay-at-home from their
    E. None right

15. When the committee reports <u>its findings somebody will lose their</u> composure.   15.____
    A. No change
    B. their findings somebody will lose their
    C. their findings somebody will lose his
    D. its findings somebody will lose his
    E. None right

16. The worst one of the problems which <u>is confronting me concern</u> money.   16.____
    A. No change
    B. are confronting me concern
    C. is confronting me concerns
    D. are confronting me concerns
    E. None right

17. Far in the distance <u>rumble the motors of the convoy, but there's</u> no signs of it yet.   17.____
    A. No change
    B. rumbles the motors of the convoy, but there is
    C. rumbles the motors of the convoy, but there are
    D. rumble the motors of the convoy, but there are
    E. None right

18. Neither of the patients <u>believe that Hansel or Gretel are</u> alive.   18.____
    A. No change
    B. believes that Hansel or Gretel are
    C. believe that Hansel or Gretel is
    D. believes that Hansel or Gretel is
    E. None right

19. <u>Its in untried emergencies that a man's native metal receives its</u> ultimate test.   19.____
    A. No change
    B. It's in untried emergencies that a man's native metal receives its
    C. It's in untried emergencies that a man's native metal receives its
    D. It's in untried emergencies that a man's native metal receives its'
    E. None right

20. Expecting my friends to be on time, <u>their tardiness seemed almost an insult.</u>   20.____
    A. No change
    B. it seemed that their tardiness was almost an insult.
    C. resentment at their tardiness grew in my mind.
    D. only an accident on the way could account for their tardiness.
    E. None right

21. <u>On first reading "The Wasteland" seems obscure.</u>   21.____
    A. No change
    B. On first reading it, "The Wasteland" seems obscure.
    C. "The Wasteland" seems an obscure poem on first reading it.
    D. On first reading "The Wasteland," it seems an obscure poem.
    E. None right

22. A special light will be required to inspect the engine. 22.____
    A. No change
    B. To inspect the engine, a special light will be required.
    C. To inspect the engine, you will require a special light.
    D. To inspect the engine, your light must be special.
    E. None right

23. When mixing it, the cake batter must be thoroughly beaten. 23.____
    A. No change   B. mixing   C. being mixed
    D. being mix   E. None right

24. What you say may be different from me. 24.____
    A. No change   B. from what I say   C. than me
    D. than mine   E. None right

25. Trumping is playing a trump when another suit has been led. 25.____
    A. No change   B. to play   C. if you play
    D. where one plays   E. None right

KEY (CORRECT ANSWERS)

1. D   11. C
2. A   12. C
3. D   13. C
4. D   14. B
5. A   15. D

6. D   16. D
7. B   17. D
8. C   18. D
9. D   19. B
10. A   20. E

21. B
22. B
23. C
24. B
25. A

WRITTEN ENGLISH EXPRESSION
EXAMINATION SECTION
TEST 1

DIRECTIONS: In each of the sentences below, four portions are underlined and lettered. Read each sentence and decide whether any of the underlined parts contains an error in spelling, punctuation, or capitalization, or employs grammatical usage which would be inappropriate for carefully written English. If so, note the letter printed under the unacceptable form and print it in the space at the right. If all four of the underlined portions are acceptable as they stand, print the letter E. No sentences contains more than one unacceptable form.

1. A low ceiling <u>is</u> <u>when</u> the atmospheric conditions <u>make</u> <u>flying</u> inadvisable.   1.____
              A B   C D

2. <u>They</u> couldn't <u>tell</u> <u>who</u> the card was <u>from</u>.   2.____
    A   B C   D

3. No one <u>but</u> you and <u>I</u> <u>are</u> <u>to help</u> them.   3.____
         A   B C D

4. To <u>him</u> <u>fall</u> the <u>duties</u> of <u>foster parent</u>.   4.____
      A.   B.   C   D

5. If the word <u>should</u> somehow find peace <u>within itself</u>, so that all <u>her</u> people   5.____
                A   B   C
<u>would</u> stop fighting everlastingly…that would be the day!
 D

6. <u>Everyone</u> of the <u>teachers</u> prepared <u>his</u> lesson in a <u>consummate</u> manner.   6.____
      A   B   C   D

7. <u>Didn't</u> <u>they</u> <u>used</u> to <u>pay</u> promptly?   7.____
    A   B   C   D

8. The services <u>rendered</u> by these people and <u>their</u> share <u>in making</u> the work a   8.____
                      A   B   C
success <u>is</u> to be commended.
      D

9. <u>They</u> <u>couldn't</u> tell <u>whom</u> the cable was <u>recieved</u> from…   9.____
   A   B   C   D

10. We like <u>these</u> <u>better</u> than <u>those</u> <u>kind</u>.   10.____
         A   B   C   D

11. It is a test of you more than I.
    A   B   C   D

12. The person in charge being him there can be no change in policy.
        A   B   C   D

13. A large amount of information and news are to be found there.
      A   B   C   D

14. I should have liked to have seen it again.
       A   B   C D

15. The desire to travel made him restless.
               A   B   C   D

16. Should that effect their decision?
      A   B   C   D

17. Do as we do for the celebration of the childrens' event.
    A B   C   D

18. Do either of you care to join us?
    A B   C   D

19. A child's food requirements differ from the adult.
      A   B   C   D

20. A large family, including two uncles and four grandparents live at the
            A   B   C   D
    hotel.

21. If they would have done that, they might have succeeded.
                A   B   C   D

22. Neither the hot days or the humid nights annoy our Southern visitor.
      A   B   C   D

23. Some people do not gain favor because they are kind of tactless.
      A   B   C   D

24. No sooner had the turning point come than a new embarassing issue arose.
          A   B   C   D

25. An usher seldom rises above a theatre manager.
             A   B   C   D

KEY (CORRECT ANSWERS)

1.	B	11.	D
2.	C	12.	C
3.	B	13.	C
4.	E	14.	B
5.	C	15.	E
6.	D	16.	B
7.	C	17.	D
8.	D	18.	A
9.	D	19.	D
10.	C	20.	C

21. A
22. B
23. D
24. D
25. C

TEST 2

DIRECTIONS: In each of the sentences below, four portions are underlined and lettered. Read each sentence and decide whether any of the underlined parts contains an error in spelling, punctuation, or capitalization, or employs grammatical usage which would be inappropriate for carefully written English. If so, note the letter printed under the unacceptable form and print it in the space at the right. If all four of the underlined portions are acceptable as they stand, print the letter E. No sentences contains more than one unacceptable form.

1. The <u>epic,</u> "Gone With the Wind<u>,"</u> deals with events that <u>ocurred</u> during the
     A   B   C
Civil War <u>era</u>.
          D

    1.____

2. <u>Shall</u> you <u>be</u> at home, <u>let us say</u>, on Sunday at two o'clock?
     A   B   C   D

    2.____

3. We <u>see</u> Mr. <u>Lewis'</u> <u>take</u> his car <u>out of the garage</u> daily.
       A   B   C   D

    3.____

4. We <u>have</u> <u>no</u> place <u>to keep</u> our rubbers, <u>only</u> in the hall closet.
     A B   C   D

    4.____

5. <u>Isn't it</u> true <u>what</u> <u>you</u> <u>told</u> me about the best way to prepare for an examination?
    A   B   C D

    5.____

6. "<u>Who</u> <u>shall</u> I say called," the butler <u>asked</u> <u>?</u>
    A   B   C D

    6.____

7. The museum <u>is</u> often visited by students who <u>are</u> fond of <u>Primitive</u> paintings,
               A   B   C
and by <u>patent</u> attorneys.
       D

    7.____

8. I <u>rose to nominate</u> the <u>superintendant,</u> the man <u>who</u> most of us felt was the
      A   B   C   D
best.

    8.____

9. The child <u>was</u> sent to the store to <u>purchase</u> a bottle of milk and <u>brought</u>
            A   B   C
home fresh rolls, <u>too</u>.
                D

    9.____

10. The garden tool <u>was sent</u> <u>to be sharpened</u> and a new handle <u>to be</u> <u>put on</u>.
                     A   B   C   D

    10.____

2 (#2)

11. At the end of her vacation, Joan came home with little money, nevertheless, it was a joyous occasion.
    A   B   C   D

11.____

12. We people have opportunities to show the rest of the world how real democracy functions and leads to the perfectability of man.
    A   B   C   D

12.____

13. The guide paddled along and then fell into a reverie where he related the history of the region.
    A   B   C   D

13.____

14. We should have investigated the cause of the noise in the Hotel by bringing the car to a halt.
    A   B   C   D

14.____

15. The first few strokes of the brush were enough to convince me that Tom could paint much better than me.
    A   B   C   D

15.____

16. We inquired whether we could see the owner of the store, after we waited for one hour.
    A   B   C   D

16.____

17. The irratation of the high-strung parent was aggravated by the slightest noise that the baby made.
    A   B   C   D

17.____

18. There is a large demand for men interested in the field of Information Retrieval.
    A   B   C   D

18.____

19. Snow after the rains delay the coming crops.
    A   B   C   D

19.____

20. They intend to partially do away with ceremonies.
    A   B   C   D

20.____

21. If that be done and turns out badly we shall see horror.
    A   B   C   D

21.____

22. The new plant is to be electrically lighted; increasing brightness by 50%.
    A   B   C   D

22.____

23. The reason the speaker was offended was that the audience was inattentive. 23.____
　　　　A　　　　　　　　　　　　　B　C　　　　　　　D

24. There appear to be conditions that govern the behavioral Sciences. 24.____
　　　　　A　　B　　　　　　　　C　　　　　　　　　　　D

25. Either of the men are influential enough to control the situation. 25.____
　　　A　　　　　　　B　　　　　　　C　　　D

KEY (CORRECT ANSWERS)

1.	C	11.	A
2.	E	12.	D
3.	B	13.	C
4.	D	14.	C
5.	B	15.	D
6.	D	16.	C
7.	C	17.	A
8.	C	18.	D
9.	C	19.	C
10.	C	20.	E

21. C
22. C
23. E
24. D
25. B

TEST 3

DIRECTIONS: In each of the sentences below, four portions are underlined and lettered. Read each sentence and decide whether any of the underlined parts contains an error in spelling, punctuation, or capitalization, or employs grammatical usage which would be inappropriate for carefully written English. If so, note the letter printed under the unacceptable form and print it in the space at the right. If all four of the underlined portions are acceptable as they stand, print the letter E. No sentences contains more than one unacceptable form.

1. <u>Who</u> <u>did</u> you predict <u>would win</u> the election <u>this</u> year?
     A   B   C   D

   1.____

2. <u>It</u> takes a <u>lot</u> <u>more</u> effort <u>to sell</u> houses this year than last year.
   A   B C   D

   2.____

3. <u>Having pranced</u> into the arena <u>with little grace and unsteady hoof</u>
          A   B

   <u>for the jumps ahead,</u> <u>the driver reined his horse</u>.
           C   D

   3.____

4. Once the dog wagged <u>it's</u> tail, <u>you</u> knew <u>it</u> <u>was</u> a friendly animal.
                               A   B   C D

   4.____

5. The record of the winning team was <u>among</u> the <u>most</u> <u>noteworthy</u>
                                                  A   B   C

   <u>of the season</u>.
       D

   5.____

6. <u>When</u> <u>asked</u> to choose corn, cabbage, <u>or</u> potatoes, the diner selected the
     A   B   C

   <u>latter.</u>
    D

   6.____

7. The maid <u>wasn't</u> <u>so</u> small <u>that</u> she <u>couldn't</u> reach the top window for cleaning.
                A   B   C   D

   7.____

8. Many people <u>feel</u> that powdered coffee <u>produces</u> a <u>really</u> <u>abhorent</u> flavor.
               A   B   C   D

   8.____

9. <u>Would you mind</u> <u>me</u> <u>trying</u> that coat on for <u>size?</u>
         A   B C   D

   9.____

10. This chair <u>looks</u> <u>much</u> <u>different</u> <u>than</u> the chair we selected in the store.
               A   B   C   D

    10.____

11. After <u>trying</u> unsuccessfully <u>to land</u> a <u>job</u> in the city, Will <u>settled</u> in the
         A   B   C   D

    country on a farm.

    11.____

12. On the last attempt, the pole-vaulter came nearly to getting hurt.
                                                     A   B   C   D

13. The observance of armistice day throughout the world offers an opportunity
               A   B   C
    to reflect on the horrors of war.
       D

14. Outside of the mistakes in spelling, the child's letter was a very good one.
         A   B   C   D

15. Scisors are always dangerous for a child to handle.
      A   B   C   D

16. I assure you that I will not yield to pressure to sell my interest.
             A   B   C   D

17. Ask him if he recalls the incident which took place at our first meeting.
        A B   C   D

18. The manager felt like as not to order his usher-captain to surrender his
                       A   B   C   D
    uniform.

19. The mother of the bride climaxed the occasion by exclaiming, "I want my
                               A   B   C
    children should be happy forever."
             D

20. We read in the papers where the prospects for peace are improving.
        A   B   C   D

21. "Can I share the cab with you?" was frequently heard during the period of
      A   B   C   D
    gas rationing.

22. Had the police suspected the ruse, they would have taken relevant
     A   B   C   D
    precautions.

23. The teacher admonished the other students neither to speak to John, nor
                            A   B   C
    should they annoy him.
       D

24. Fortunately, we had been told that there was but one availible service
                  A   B   C   D
    station in that area.

25. We haven't hardly enough time to make it.   25.____
    　　 A　　 B　　　 C　　　　 D

KEY (CORRECT ANSWERS)

1. E   11. B
2. B   12. B
3. D   13. B
4. A   14. A
5. E   15. A

6. D   16. E
7. B   17. B
8. D   18. B
9. B   19. D
10. A   20. C

21. A
22. D
23. D
24. D
25. A

TEST 4

DIRECTIONS: In each of the sentences below, four portions are underlined and lettered. Read each sentence and decide whether any of the underlined parts contains an error in spelling, punctuation, or capitalization, or employs grammatical usage which would be inappropriate for carefully written English. If so, note the letter printed under the unacceptable form and print it in the space at the right. If all four of the underlined portions are acceptable as they stand, print the letter E. No sentences contains more than one unacceptable form.

1. He <u>either</u> <u>will fail</u> in his attempt <u>or</u> will seek other <u>Government</u> employment. 1._____
      A   B   C   D

2. <u>After</u> each side <u>gave</u> <u>their</u> version, the case <u>was</u> closed. 2._____
    A   B C   D

3. <u>Every</u> <u>one</u> of the cars <u>were</u> <u>tagged</u> by the police. 3._____
    A   B   C   D

4. They <u>can't</u> <u>seem</u> <u>to see</u> <u>it</u> when I explain the theory. 4._____
          A   B   C D

5. <u>It</u> is difficult <u>to find</u> the genuine signature <u>between</u> all <u>those</u> submitted. 5._____
    A   B   C   D

6. She can't understand why <u>they</u> <u>don't remember</u> <u>who</u> to give the letter <u>to</u>. 6._____
                                  A   B   C   D

7. <u>Every</u> <u>man and woman</u> in America <u>is</u> interested in <u>his</u> tax bill. 7._____
    A   B   C   D

8. A guard <u>was called</u> <u>to prevent</u> <u>them</u> <u>carrying away</u> souvenirs. 8._____
             A   B   C   D

9. <u>Neither</u> you <u>nor</u> <u>I</u> <u>am</u> to blame for the sudden slump in business. 9._____
    A   B C D

10. To <u>you</u> and <u>him</u> <u>belong</u> the <u>credit.</u> 10._____
       A   B   C   D

11. The auctioneer had <u>less</u> items to <u>sell</u> this year <u>than</u> last <u>year.</u> 11._____
                        A   B   C   D

12. <u>Theirs</u> <u>instead of</u> <u>his</u> instructions <u>will be followed</u>. 12._____
      A   B   C   D

13. <u>It</u> is the <u>same</u> at his local <u>broker's</u> Frank <u>Smith</u>. 13._____
     A   B   C   D

14. The teacher <u>politely</u> <u>requested</u> <u>each</u> pupil to <u>step in</u> the room.   14.____
             A   B   C   D

15. <u>Too</u> many parents <u>leave</u> <u>their</u> children do as <u>they</u> please.   15.____
   A   B   C   D

16. <u>He</u> arrived <u>safe,</u> his papers <u>untouched,</u> his composure <u>unrufled.</u>   16.____
   A   B   C   D

17. I <u>do not</u> have <u>any</u> faith in <u>John</u> <u>running</u> for office.   17.____
     A   B   C   D

18. The musicians began to play <u>tunefully</u> ; <u>keeping</u> the proper tempo <u>indicated</u>   18.____
                                   A   B   C   D
for the selection.

19. <u>Mary's</u> maid of honor bought the <u>kind of an</u> <u>outfit</u> suitable for an afternoon   19.____
    A   B   C D
wedding.

20. After the debate, <u>every one</u> of the <u>Speakers</u> realized that, <u>given</u> another   20.____
                    A   B   C
chance, he <u>could have done</u> better.
               D

21. The reason <u>given</u> by the physician for the patient's trouble <u>was</u> <u>because</u> of   21.____
             A   B   C
his poor eating <u>habits</u>.
                    D

22. The fog was so <u>thick</u> that the driver <u>couldn't</u> <u>hardly</u> see more than ten feet   22.____
                 A   B   C
<u>ahead.</u>
 D

23. I suggest that you <u>present</u> the medal to <u>who</u> you <u>deem</u> <u>best</u>.   23.____
                  A   B   C   D

24. A decision made by a man <u>without much deliberation</u> is sometimes <u>no</u>   24.____
                                    A   B
different <u>than</u> a <u>slow one</u>.
      C   D

25. <u>By the time</u> Jones <u>graduates</u> from <u>Dental School,</u> he <u>will be</u> twenty-six years   25.____
    A   B   C   D
of age.

KEY (CORRECT ANSWERS)

1.	D	11.	A
2.	C	12.	A
3.	C	13.	D
4.	C	14.	D
5.	C	15.	B
6.	C	16.	D
7.	E	17.	C
8.	C	18.	B
9.	E	19.	C
10.	C	20.	B

21. C
22. B
23. B
24. D
25. C

TEST 5

Questions 1-18.

DIRECTIONS: Each of the sentences numbered 1 through 18 may be classified most appropriately under one of the following three categories:
    A. faulty because of incorrect grammar
    B. faulty because of incorrect punctuation
    C. correct
Examine each sentence carefully. Then, in the space at the right, print the letter preceding the option which is BEST of those suggested above. All incorrect sentences contain but one type of error. Consider a sentence correct if it contains none of the types of errors mentioned, even though there may be other correct ways of expressing the same thought.

1. He sent the notice to the clerk who you hired yesterday.   1.____

2. It must be admitted, however that you were not informed of this change.   2.____

3. Only the employees who have served in this grade for at least two years are eligible for promotion.   3.____

4. The work was divided equally between she and Mary.   4.____

5. He thought that you were not available at that time.   5.____

6. When the messenger returns; please give him this package.   6.____

7. The new secretary prepared, typed, addressed, and delivered, the notices.   7.____

8. Walking into the room, his desk can be seen at the rear.   8.____

9. Although John has worked here longer than she, he produces a smaller amount of work.   9.____

10. She said she could of typed this report yesterday.   10.____

11. Neither one of these procedures are adequate for the efficient performance of this task.   11.____

12. The typewriter is the tool of the typist; the cash register, the tool of the cashier.   12.____

13. "The assignment must be completed as soon as possible" said the supervisor.   13.____

14. As you know, office handbooks are issued to all new employees.   14.____

15. Writing a speech is sometimes easier than to deliver it before an audience.   15.____

16. Mr. Brown our accountant, will audit the accounts next week. 16._____

17. Give the assignment to whomever is able to do it most efficiently. 17._____

18. The supervisor expected either your or I to file these reports. 18._____

Questions 19-28.

DIRECTIONS: Each of the following sentences may be classified most appropriately under one of the following four categories:
    A. faulty because of incorrect grammar
    B. faulty because of incorrect punctuation
    C. faulty because of incorrect spelling
    D. correct

Examine each sentence carefully. Then, in the space at the right, print the letter preceding the option which is BEST of those suggested above. All incorrect sentences contain but one type of error. Consider a sentence correct if it contains none of the types of errors mentioned, even though there may be other correct ways of expressing the same thought.

19. The fire apparently started in the storeroom, which is usually locked. 19._____

20. On approaching the victim two bruises were noticed by the officer. 20._____

21. The officer, who was there examined the report with great care. 21._____

22. Each employee in the office had a separate desk. 22._____

23. All employees including members of the clerical staff, were invited to the lecture. 23._____

24. The suggested procedure is similar to the one now in use. 24._____

25. No one was more pleased with the new procedure than the chauffeur. 25._____

26. He tried to pursuade her to change the procedure. 26._____

27. The total of the expenses charged to petty cash were high. 27._____

28. An understanding between him and I was finally reached. 28._____

KEY (CORRECT ANSWERS)

1.	A	11.	A	21.	B
2.	B	12.	C	22.	C
3.	C	13.	B	23.	B
4.	A	14.	C	24.	D
5.	C	15.	A	25.	D
6.	B	16.	B	26.	C
7.	B	17.	A	27.	A
8.	A	18.	A	28.	A
9.	C	19.	D		
10.	A	20.	A